"Energy Tapping is the instant way out of the negative and getting way into the positive. You'll love it."

—Mark Victor Hansen
Co-creator, #1 New York Times Best-selling series *Chicken Soup for the Soul®*.

"The understanding of how psychological problems can get locked into your energy systems is a major breakthrough. Fred Gallo and Harry Vincenzi are pioneers in this important energy discipline."

—Donna Eden, *Energy Medicine*

ENERGY TAPPING

Fred P. Gallo, Ph.D., and Harry Vincenzi, Ed.D.

New Harbinger Publications, Inc.

Distributed in Canada by Raincoast Books.

Copyright © 2000 by Fred P. Gallo & Harry Vincenzi
New Harbinger Publications, Inc.
5674 Shattuck Avenue
Oakland, CA 94609

Cover design © 2000 by Lightbourne Images
Edited by Jueli Gastwirth
Text design by Michele Waters

Library of Congress Catalog Card Number: 99-75290
ISBN 1-57224-195-0 Paperback

All Rights Reserved

Printed in the United States of America

New Harbinger Publications' Web site address: www.newharbinger.com

07   06

15   14   13   12

To my sister, Kathy, and my brothers, Philip, David, and Michael.

—FPG

To my parents.

—HV

Contents

Acknowledgments

Just as no person is an island, a book comes into being as a result of a host of influences. Sir Isaac Newton, great discoverer of physical laws, bowed to such a truth in acknowledging, "If I have seen further than others, it is by standing upon the shoulders of giants." And Harry S. Truman, in his own down-to-earth manner, said, "There is nothing new in the world except the history you do not know." Therefore we would like to acknowledge everyone who contributed to the creation of this work, even those whom we personally have not met.

We are deeply indebted to the contributions of Huang Ti, who catalogued meridian theory approximately 4,500 years ago; George J. Goodheart, founder of applied kinesiology; and John Diamond and Roger J. Callahan, for their contributions to the application of meridian theory in the treatment of emotional problems.

We would like to thank our family, friends, and colleagues for their support and encouragement throughout the writing of this book. We would also like to acknowledge David and Justin Lee for helping us create the diagrams used in *Energy Tapping*.

Finally, thank you to all the talented people at New Harbinger Publications, including Matt McKay, editor-in-chief, and Kristin Beck and Catharine Sutker, in acquisitions, for contacting us and supporting this project. Special appreciation and acknowledgment go to Jueli Gastwirth, our editor, for her patience, warmth, and energetic attention throughout the writing of *Energy Tapping*.

PART I

Understanding and Using Energy Psychology

Introduction

Your body has the ability to heal itself.

—Andrew Weil, M.D.

Energy Tapping is a unique book that will help you to learn how to use your body's energy system to better manage your life. Although several different names can be used to identify this process, the term we use is *energy psychology*. This healing technique is based on the ancient Chinese art of acupuncture, although instead of using needles to stimulate a change in the way you think and feel, energy psychology uses a simple tapping method of two fingers on specific points of your body. Once you understand this process and the location of the meridian points (provided via the diagrams throughout this book), you will learn how you can cope with or eliminate problems that you have struggled with for years. As psychologists who have been trained in numerous techniques and strategies, we have found energy psychology to be the most effective and efficient process for creating rapid change and effectively treating emotional and/or psychological issues.

The Genesis of Energy Work

It is not clear when the development and use of energy work began, but legend has it that it was first discovered five thousand years ago in China. At that time, when wars were fought with knives and bows and arrows, a strange phenomenon occurred: Soldiers who received minor wounds in just the right places found that the physical pains and ailments that they had suffered with for years suddenly disappeared. It has been said that incidents such as these led the Chinese to discover the existence of an energy system that communicates energetic information throughout the human body. This energy system has been called chi (pronounced chee), and is also known as life force, ki, prana, and life energy.

Acupuncture

The discovery of the human energy system eventually led to the development of acupuncture, a procedure by which the body's energy is altered by stimulating, with needles, specific points along twelve major pathways that are known as *meridians*. Each of the meridians passes through a specific organ of the body, such as the lungs, heart, or stomach. The entire system is interconnected so that the chi, or life energy, travels from one meridian to the next, circulating throughout the body. These meridians interact with a number of more concentrated energy fields called *chakras*.

In acupuncture treatments, needles are inserted into the body at selected tonification or stimulation points (to increase energy), or at selected sedation points (to decrease energy). Through trial and error, acupuncture has been developed and used by Chinese physicians to eliminate pain and to treat a wide variety of illnesses. Interestingly, several countries now use acupuncture as an alternative anesthesia during surgery.

Increasingly, more people in the United States are accepting acupuncture as a viable alternative health care treatment (although we think people hesitate because they don't like needles). The World Health Organization cited 104 conditions that can be treated by acupuncture, including gastrointestinal disorders and sciatica problems (Burton Goldberg Group 1993).

Scientific Research

From a scientific viewpoint, one problem with energy psychology is the challenge of creating the concrete proof that it exists. Trying to prove that there is an energy system with meridian points, for example, is much like trying to prove that gravity or energy in general exists. You can't see it, but intuitively you know that it's there and you can create tests that will verify its existence.

One of the early findings that support the belief that an energy field or *aura* surrounds each person was conducted in the 1970s. A researcher at Yale, Harold Saxon Burr (1972), took measurements of the electromagnetic fields around trees, animals, and human beings. He called these energy fields *Life Fields* or *L-Fields*. His work suggests that the body grows into an already existent energy field that serves as a blueprint of its physical form. For example, even after a section of a leaf is severed, the energy form of the severed section continues to be detectable. Other studies (Burr 1972) have demonstrated that a baby animal has a detectable energy field that approximates its size as an adult.

Richard Gerber (1988), author of *Vibrational Medicine*, suggests that physical disease may begin at the energy level and then eventually migrate into or show up in the physical body. Therefore, if disturbances can be detected at the energy field level before physical problems develop, treatment methods in time will emerge that can alleviate the energy disturbance and thus prevent the physical disease from ever occurring. This is not so far-fetched when we consider the fact that human bodies completely regenerate approximately every four years. That is, not one single atom of your body today existed four years ago. And some parts of our bodies are recycled even more frequently. For example, we get a new liver every six weeks. This all points to the existence of energy fields as the basis of all physical form. The energy field is what holds the body together and provides the mold into which the body and its parts can be created anew.

Louis Langman (1972) conducted another study that examines the relationship between energy and disease. He found that in a sample of 123 women with malignant cervical conditions, 5 had a positive energy charge in the cervix, and 118 had a negative electrical charge. The numbers were reversed in a sample of women with no cancerous conditions. This study does not prove that negative polarity causes cancer, because it is possible that the cancer itself leads to the negative charge. However, this research does demonstrate that an energy difference exists between those who are healthy and those with a disease.

There have been several attempts to document the existence of meridian points. Robert Becker is an orthopedic surgeon who wrote *Cross Currents* (1990) and co-authored *The Body Electric* (1985). He was encouraged to further explore acupuncture when it became of interest in the 1970s after President Nixon's trip to China and journalist James Reston's remarkable acupuncture treatment for postoperative pain and healing. Much of the early research has disproved the theory that acupuncture works as a result of a placebo effect. That is, when a person simply believes in a treatment so much so that it proves to be effective (Becker and Seldon 1985).

Becker examined the theory that meridian *acupoints* are electrical conductors and that meridians are used to send messages back and forth from the brain and the injury site to promote healing and create the conscious perception of pain. He developed an interesting and pertinent research approach. He proposed that the meridians were the electrical conductors that relay information from the site of an injury to the central nervous system. He thought that perhaps acupuncture needles served to block the pain message from getting to the brain by short-circuiting the electromagnetic current in the meridian. Becker theorized that the acupoints functioned similarly to booster amplifiers that are positioned along power lines. He noted that because the electric current of the meridians would have to be of a very low intensity, the booster amplifiers would have to be placed very close to each other (within inches). This is the case with the acupoints.

Maria Reichmanas, a biophysicist associate of Becker's, developed a pizza-cutter-like device that could be rolled along the meridians to detect differences in electrical skin resistance. They theorized that if an electrical charge truly existed at the location of the acupoint, then there would be a difference in skin resistance at that point as compared to the surrounding skin. Their findings were consistent enough across subjects to strongly suggest that acupoints and meridians exist. In fact, all of these studies imply that meridian pathways exist and that they are used to transmit information.

The Development of Energy Psychology

The development of energy psychology began in the early 1960s, as George Goodheart, a chiropractor from Detroit, Michigan, experimented with tapping on various meridian acupoints to relieve pain while treating patients holistically. In the 1980s, psychiatrist John Diamond (1985) and psychologist Roger Callahan (1985) each experimented with the treatment of mental health problems. They found that tapping on acupoints helped eliminate negative emotions, such as anxieties, phobias, and painful memories. Callahan, whose system is one of the power therapies known as Thought Field Therapy, provided the majority of the clinical work. In the 1990s, Fred Gallo (1998) and Gary Craig (Craig and Fowlie 1995) developed their own accessible approach to energy psychology and helped mental health clinicians throughout the world learn its procedures.

These studies show that the same concepts used in acupuncture can effectively be used to treat psychological problems. The discovery that psychological change can occur in such a simple way is a breakthrough in mental health. It's a radical departure from talk therapy, which dominated psychology in the twentieth century.

Many people still believe that the most effective and healthy method of emotional change occurs through talk therapy, in which new knowledge is learned or new life skills are developed through verbal communication. Although it may not seem realistic that tapping on meridian points located on your face or hands can change how you think or feel, we have not found another treatment that is as fast or effective as energy psychology. Many people, however, remain skeptical until they use this method to eliminate one of their own problems.

Although the concepts of energy psychology will be explored further, the basis of the technique is that you eliminate psychological issues by simply thinking about a painful issue or memory while tapping on specific meridian points. Additionally, we will examine a related treatment that helps to eliminate self-sabotaging thoughts and beliefs that often occur after someone has been traumatized or is in the middle of a stressful situation.

> *Energy Psychology* provides you with the keys to unlock psychological issues by helping you to understand and use the power of your own energy system.

A Step-By-Step Process for Changing Your Life

The book is divided into two parts: Part I addresses the basic concepts required to help you understand and utilize the methods of energy psychology. Part II provides specific treatment methods for a variety of psychological issues, including self-sabotaging behaviors, trauma, and emotions (such as shame, fear, and depression). The book concludes by examining more complex issues, such as weight loss, addictive behavior, and relationships. A chapter on improving your sports performance also is included.

It is important that you first learn how to treat common problems before attempting to heal the more complex ones. Often complex issues consist of several smaller problems that must first be treated before complete healing can occur. Once you have learned the basics of energy psychology, which are presented in this book, you will have a new set of skills that will help you to eliminate self-sabotaging behaviors and to better manage your life.

Many of the chapters guide you through specific treatment methods. Because an experienced energy psychology therapist will not be present to help you determine where your energy imbalances exist, we have developed treatment sequences (patterns of places to tap) for each of the problems explored in this book. We also pose questions that may help you to determine which of your feelings and/or behaviors are disruptive and need to be treated. A brief outline of each chapter follows:

Chapter 1 further explores energy psychology and helps you to understand how different levels of energy affect your behavior.

Chapter 2 provides figures and diagrams of locations for each of the meridian points that you will be tapping for particular problems. These diagrams also appear in the chapters that deal with the specific psychological challenges we will be addressing. You will learn in chapter 2 which emotional areas are affected by each meridian, and how to do a simple treatment sequence.

Chapter 3 addresses how potential toxins, such as food, tobacco, or alcohol, can negatively affect your energy system. It has been found that these substances produce symptoms that weaken your energy. Various solutions, such as detoxification, are examined.

Chapter 4 explores the beliefs and habits that are negatively affecting your life. It also addresses several approaches that will help you to change habits that are no longer productive.

Chapter 5 provides a format that will help you develop a personal profile of the problems that you want to resolve.

Chapter 6 reveals ways to identify and treat psychological reversals. Reversals are the primary cause of self-sabotage in your life. Your energy can be disrupted in a way that causes you to act in opposition to something that you consciously are trying to attain. For example, you may tell yourself, "I'm tired of fighting with my mate; tonight we are going to relax." Yet, for some reason, after your mate comes home and you begin to interact, a fight still occurs. It's not a lack of willpower; it is a reversal in your energy system.

Chapter 7 addresses your fears and phobias, which often can lower your self-confidence and limit your life experiences. Several specific fears and phobias are explored, including fears of heights, insects, animals, public speaking, elevators, test taking, flying, intimidating situations, and panic attacks.

Chapter 8 helps you learn to better manage those powerful but common feelings of anger, rage, embarrassment, guilt, jealousy, shame, loneliness, and rejection.

Chapter 9 offers a drug-free approach to effectively deal with depression, which is a prevalent problem in the United States.

Chapter 10 focuses on trauma, which occurs in everyone's life at some time. Trauma includes everything from the loss of a job or a home to more difficult experiences, such as losing a loved one, suffering child abuse, or being in a severe accident. Painful memories affect many people and prevent them from moving forward with their lives. The ability to learn how to cope with a past event and move on can be attained through energy psychology. This chapter focuses on these issues and how to treat them. In many cases, a painful memory can be addressed with a single treatment.

Chapter 11 provides strategies to eliminate sports anxiety and other self-sabotaging beliefs that create mental errors during sporting activities.

Chapter 12 is the first chapter to deal with the more complex issues. This chapter addresses weight loss, which is complex because many related issues often sabotage your efforts to lose weight. Although many people have trouble losing weight, there actually is a relatively simple solution: diet and exercise. It is an energy imbalance and most likely a psychological reversal that prevents the obese or overweight person from losing weight. In this chapter, you will identify the beliefs that sabotage your ability to stay on a diet. By learning to balance the energy in your meridians, you will be able to pick a diet of your choice, have the control to stick to it, and achieve the elusive goal of having a slimmer, healthier body.

Chapter 13 addresses addictive behavior, which by itself is a form of self-sabotage. This chapter also helps you to identify possible avoidance behaviors you may have. The chapter has a very strong focus on exploring belief systems and psychological reversals. Because addictions are very hard to break and often exist for a reason, emphasis is placed on daily treatment methods as well as identifying replacement activities or behaviors.

Chapter 14 focuses on relationships, a complex issue that has no easy answers. Energy psychology provides an approach to help people understand how they sabotage their relationships by the partners they chose or by their own behaviors. This information is used to determine which problems must be addressed and which energy psychology treatments will be most helpful.

Chapter 15 addresses what we believe will be future directions in the use of energy psychology and concludes by summarizing the current uses of this unique tool. It is an approach that anyone can use to help hurdle old problems and cope with new ones. Energy psychology provides the tools that allow you to create the balance and control that have been missing from your life.

Frequently Asked Questions

In this section, we hope to answer many of the questions that you may have about energy psychology.

Q: *What types of issues or problems does energy psychology address?*

A: Energy psychology addresses two types of problems: the events in your life that cause energy imbalances and psychological reversals. The first type often occurs when an event affects specific meridian points in your energy system. The result is an energy imbalance that creates consequences that you interpret as painful memories or feelings of inadequacy. There are a number of ways to think about your energy system. When a term like *balance* is used, it means that your energy flows freely through your body and each meridian has the same amount of energy. When one of your meridians is impacted by a trauma, some of the energy in that meridian may become depleted, creating an imbalance. Tapping on the acupoints stimulates the meridian and increases the energy, which in turn creates balance. Although most of this book addresses specific problems, it also is possible to stimulate meridians to move to a higher energy level and increase your ability to deal with life issues in general.

The second type of problem energy psychology addresses is *psychological reversals*, i.e., when your energy system is reversed. For example, once you have experienced a trauma, each time you encounter or think about that trauma or similar situations your energy responds as if it were reexperiencing it. Psychological reversals create negative or false beliefs, which is why people behave in ways that sabotage their lives. Although this may sound strange, it explains why people do things that they know will be bad for them. They can't stop themselves, because their behavior seems like the right thing to do. Psychological reversals also prevent the energy balance in your meridians from being restored.

Q: *How is an energy system disrupted?*

A: The simplest explanation is that an energy disruption is caused by a traumatic situation. The resulting imbalance in your energy system leaves you unable to resolve that problem and vulnerable to similar problems. Every situation you encounter is embedded in your nervous system, and although your mind may have forgotten particular events, your body remembers them. When you experience a trauma, for example, you respond in a normal manner, feeling the appropriate emotion. If you were beaten and robbed, for instance, fearfulness would be natural at the time. The problems, however, arise when this trauma creates an energy imbalance that perpetuates the fearful experience indefinitely. The result can be that you develop a phobic reaction that limits your lifestyle and the manner in which you interact with other people.

> It takes an external experience to disrupt your energy system. Another external experience (energy treatment) is required to balance it.

There are numerous social reasons why energy imbalances occur in people. For example, for at least two generations there have been more than one million divorces each year in the United States. Divorce is one example of a type of trauma that can affect you, resulting in feelings of anger, sadness, or a loss of trust. Another is the changing dynamics of communities. As communities continue to be more transient and family members choose to live in different cities, the sense of belonging to and the safety of living in a caring community are undermined. If you feel that no one cares about you, this easily can lead to other problems.

It also is possible that energy imbalances can be passed on from one generation to another. Rupert Sheldrake's (1988) research examines how instinctual information is passed on to new generations. As there is no evidence that emotional feelings are passed through one's DNA, Sheldrake believes that emotional feelings and learned behaviors can be passed on from one generation to another via energy fields. Under this theory, a trauma suffered by your grandmother could be passed on to you in the form of an energy imbalance. This may explain why babies respond to situations with distinct patterns of behavior. For example, a baby's ability to cope with frustrating situations is very observable within a few months of birth. Of course, once children are born, their energy system is affected by their parents and their surrounding environment. If any of these situations creates an energy imbalance, it will affect what someone thinks as well as their sense of self. It could be argued that energy disruptions at birth lead to certain emotional feelings and thoughts that make you more vulnerable or likely to have certain negative experiences.

Although knowing the actual cause of the energy disruption is not crucial to resolving the problem, it can help explain many of your problems as well as your behavior. Energy disruptions can have a major impact on your life and if they are not treated, it is unlikely that the problems will be resolved.

Q: *How can an energy imbalance affect your thinking?*

A: It is well known by scientists that when a person has a thought, a chemical presence or reaction occurs, and neuropeptides, the chemical correlates of thought, become detectable. Neuropeptides not only are present in the brain, but also can be found throughout the body, including in the stomach, kidneys, and liver. Thus, a thought has a real embodied, physical presence. At the same time, an electromagnetic-like field also can be detected when a person has a thought. This is the energetic presence or manifestation of the thought, which Roger Callahan (Callahan and Callahan 1996) termed a *thought field*.

Negative emotions are created by a disturbance in the thought field, which can be caused by a physical or emotional trauma. The theory is that the disturbance affects a specific energy point that, in turn, sets off hormonal, physiological, neurological, chemical, and cognitive events that result in the experience of a negative emotion. The disturbances cause energy imbalances that can be experienced as depression, fears, or addictive behaviors.

When a disturbance occurs within a thought field, it always corresponds to a specific energy point on the body. This is why energy psychologists have been able to correlate meridian points with specific problems and develop treatments.

Q: *What is a psychological reversal?*

A: It's not really clear what happens to your energy system when you experience a psychological reversal. One theory is that when a traumatic event depletes your energy to a low level, your energy can become negative. This, in turn, elicits self-sabotaging beliefs or behaviors and you end up creating a situation that is the opposite—or reverse—of what you would prefer. Hence, the term *reversal*.

Most often reversals are situation-specific, meaning that they only affect specific areas of your life, such as your ability to achieve a particular goal, overcome a phobia, or get along better with another person. If there was an event in your life that created strong feelings of shame or guilt, for instance, it's possible that this event created a reversal, which partly accounts for why you may not be coping well with similar situations in your life today. Another feature of a psychological reversal is a lack of self-acceptance. For example, when you don't accept a part of who you are, what you did, or what you are doing, there can be a reversal in your energy system. The outcome is an unconscious act of sabotage against your consciously expressed goals.

For example, you might be reversed about being successful. That is, you may unconsciously think, "I don't deserve to have success in my life." Or, "I am not worthy of having a successful situation in my life." The impact of the reversal is clear when you have the potential to be successful in a particular part of your life, but you aren't. Psychological reversal creates the feelings and thoughts that sabotage the parts of your life that you do not accept or feel that you deserve.

Psychological reversals create situations that we've all experienced. In certain circumstances you know what you have to do—or not do—and yet you are unable to act the way in which you know you should. For instance, consider a situation in which it would be best to avoid saying anything. When you have a reversal, what happens is that you voice words that make a situation even worse. Further, if you don't accept yourself and believe that you deserve—or are good enough to have—a specific situation in your life, you will sabotage it.

For example, a woman who doesn't think she deserves to be married will continually pick the wrong man as a potential partner. Although other issues are most likely also involved, this type of behavior is a perfect form of self-sabotage. The woman appears to be actively seeking marriage, but really she is only reinforcing her belief that she doesn't deserve to be married. Although this example is specific, self-sabotage can occur and affect any life event that you feel you don't deserve.

Self-sabotaging behavior can ruin years of hard work. Energy psychologists believe that sabotaging beliefs are a primary reason why many people experience difficulty in their lives even though they have the skill and ability to achieve their goals. When you have finished reading this book, you will know how to correct the reversals that sabotage your actions. You also may be able to give helpful advice to your friends and to your children about how to overcome self-sabotage.

Q: *How do you correct an energy imbalance?*

A: The process of correcting an energy imbalance usually involves working with an energy therapist who has been extensively trained in the field. The techniques in this book will teach you how to do this without the assistance of a trained therapist.

Typically, once a client has described their problem to a therapist, the client is asked to think about that problem and become aware of its associated feelings. For example, if a fear of heights were being treated, the client would be asked to remember the last time they were on a balcony or in a similar location where the problem occurred.

When you focus your awareness on a problem, all you are doing is thinking about a problem or situation that is distressing to you. There is nothing magical or difficult that you have to do other than think about the situation. You don't even have to visualize it (although that may be one way of getting in touch with the problem). Once you focus your attention on the problem at hand, your body-mind will respond in a small way as if you were actually in that situation.

If there are meridian points that need to be treated, you once again bring your energy into that problem pattern or thought field by focusing your attention on the problem you are trying to overcome. Once you have done this, you are ready for the energy psychology treatment techniques to help you overcome your obstacles. Remember that the emotional problems that you perceive are mere disturbances in your energy system.

To treat a problem, specific meridian points—which are different for each problem—need to be stimulated. We use the word "algorithm" to mean treatment sequences or patterns of places to tap on your face, hands, and upper torso that address specific issues. Through years of experience and testing, these patterns have been found to be effective. After you learn the locations of specific meridian points, you will find it easy to use the treatment sequences that are provided.

Q: *What is applied kinesiology and how is it related to energy psychology?*

A: One of the procedures used in energy psychology is called applied kinesiology, which is an unique method of evaluating bodily functions by means of manual muscle testing. Most often, testing is done on an isolated muscle, such as the deltoid, a large, strong muscle in the shoulder area. During the procedure, clients are asked to think about a problem while extending an arm parallel to the floor, thus tensing the deltoid muscle. What applied kinesiologists found is that when clients mentally tune in to their issue, there is a momentary weakening of the muscles. This is the result of an energy imbalance. The application of this highly specified procedure pivots on this essential muscle-weakening phenomenon, which allows the energetic aspects of the psychological problem to be diagnosed.

Although the process of energy psychology was developed using applied kinesiology, muscle testing is not required to do the techniques in this book. We have analyzed various types of problems and through extensive clinical experience have provided you with treatment sequences for every issue examined in this book. As you will learn, tapping with your fingers on different meridian points will, in most cases, successfully treat each condition or problem.

Q: *Does energy psychology really work?*

A: Some of the best testimonials that energy psychology is effective come from the growing number of therapists who are using these treatments in their private practice. The president of the Canadian Society of Clinical Hypnosis, Lee Pulos (1999), says, "I find energy psychology to be among the most powerful and effective tools in the treatment of all varieties of psychological problems."

Research on energy psychology often uses Subjective Units of Distress (SUD) to evaluate its success. The term SUD was first used to evaluate a therapeutic technique called systematic desensitization, developed by Joseph Wolpe (1958). As the term implies, SUD is a subjective evaluation by the person as to the impact of a problem. When doing the treatment sequences in this book, you will be asked to think about a problem and then rate it as to how much it affects you. For example, if you have a fear of elevators, you would imagine being in an elevator and then rate the SUD from 0 to 10, with 0 indicating no impact or distressing feeling and 10 indicating the highest level of distress. As you will notice in Part II of this book, energy psychology uses a rating scale similar to the SUD to determine the magnitude of the emotional problem or challenge that you are addressing.

In 1995, two researchers at the University of Florida, Figley and Carbonell, conducted clinical studies with several *power therapies*, one of which was an energy therapy. Power therapies are those that can rapidly eliminate trauma. The treatments were used to help patients who suffered from post-traumatic stress disorder. The results found that the energy therapy was not only a very effective approach, it worked the fastest.

Additional surveys involved two therapists who treated individuals who called in on radio talk shows. In 1986, Roger Callahan (Callahan and Callahan 1996) treated sixty-eight people on radio shows and had a 97 percent success rate. On average, problems that were presented by callers had an average SUD rating of 8.3; after callers did the treatment prescribed by Callahan, their average SUD rating was reduced to 2.1. Ten years later, Glenn Leonoff replicated Callahan's radio show study (Callahan and Callahan 1996). He also worked with sixty-eight callers and also had a success rate of 97 percent. The average SUD rating was 8.1 before the treatment and 1.5 after the treatment.

Our experience has shown that a problem that has an SUD rating of 8 to 10 has a very powerful impact on an individual's life. Conversely, a problem that has an SUD rating of one or two, most often is being well managed by the individual and has minimal impact on their life.

Q: *Will you give an example of someone who has been helped by energy psychology?*

A: Our clinical experiences with energy psychology have resulted in many successes. For instance, one bright, yet depressed, teenage girl who was ready to repeat her senior year in high school was greatly helped by energy psychology. She was unmotivated and would not complete the minimal amount of work required for her to graduate. Once she agreed to treatment, there was a smile on her face in less than thirty minutes and a newfound belief that she could succeed. She not only completed her course work for graduation, she was motivated to apply to colleges as well.

Another example is a thirty-two-year-old woman who was raped when she was thirteen and was still tormented by memories of the event. Her self-image was so poor that she perpetually sabotaged her life. After one energy treatment, she was no longer bothered by the event. She readily changed her view of herself in such a positive direction that she later went on to complete college and graduate school and eventually became a licensed psychotherapist.

Weight loss is another area in which energy psychology is effective. For example, one middle-aged man was unable to lose weight, despite trying numerous diets. Using energy psychology, he was treated for loneliness and feelings of rejection. After one session, he was motivated to begin his diet. He learned how to appropriately deal with his weight issues and used the treatments on a regular basis to help him maintain his diet and to lose weight.

Q: *How quickly do energy treatments work?*

A: The answer to this important question depends on the type of problem being addressed as well as the person who is receiving treatments. Some people will resolve their problem in one treatment; most will experience significant relief after their first treatment. In general, we recommend two weeks of daily treatments for any problem, although periodic follow-up treatments may also be needed. Once these treatments are learned, however, they only take a minute to complete and can be done almost anywhere.

Basically, there are two types of problems: those that are based on single events, such as if your house is robbed, and those that are interactive, such as relationship issues. If your house has been robbed, you know firsthand that it is a traumatic event. The good news is that it is a single event, i.e., your home is not robbed on a regular basis. If you address this event by using the treatment for painful memories (see chapter 10), it is very likely that you can experience significant relief from one treatment. You then can use follow-up treatments to reinforce your success.

Complex, interactive problems are more difficult and are addressed in the last several chapters of this book. You need to be patient when treating these types of issues, as they take more time to successfully eliminate. We consider weight loss, relationships, and addictive issues as complex and interactive problems. They are complex because there can be several reasons why they exist; they are interactive because these situations occur and reoccur on a regular basis, unlike single event traumas. For example, there can be several reasons for someone to be overweight, and yet they can encounter situations that can sabotage them every day.

The other factor that affects how quickly energy psychology treatment works is you. Every person is different. People with multiple problems, severe problems, or long-term problems need to be patient. Although some will feel relief quickly, for most, it will take more time and many treatments to help you to better cope with and/or eliminate your issues. If you believe that you have extremely low levels of energy, the healing process will take even longer.

CHAPTER 1

Energy Psychology: The Missing Piece to Your Success

Letting go of the emotions that trap you, painful memories, fears, depression, or anger, is the way to a longer and healthier life.

—Deepak Chopra, M.D.

In the last decade, the use of alternative medicine has made enormous strides as an effective, acceptable tool that helps people prevent or better cope with various health problems. Although the number of leading contributors in this growing area is quite large, the work of Deepak Chopra, Caroline Myss, and Andrew Weil is among the most prominent. Each of these individuals has helped people to better understand themselves and to recognize that they have more control over their lives than they previously may have thought possible. Through their work, people now have a better understanding of how their bodies are impacted by toxins that can come from air, food, water, and chemicals. These toxins can increase people's vulnerability to disease and even speed up the aging process.

Although all three authors explore and stress the importance of life force or the internal energy system, it is Caroline Myss' (1997) work that especially has helped many people to understand that they can alter their energy system and, by doing so, change their lives. She says that if you spend your energy continually dealing with and holding onto the negative aspects of your life, you will not have enough energy to ward off disease, to heal from illnesses, and/or to deal appropriately with other potential problems. Myss, Chopra, and Weil have developed distinctive approaches to the healing process, although all three of them stress the importance of letting go of your negative emotions. In the chapters that follow, we will teach you specific techniques that will help you to do this efficiently and effectively.

The Essence of Energy

Everything you see—the sun, the moon, planet earth, the solar system, the stars—is a form of energy. Whether you are male or female, strong or weak, angry or happy, in the end, when broken down to the simplest structure, you are energy. There is positive and negative energy in our world and it continuously affects us in millions of ways. Our thoughts are energy, our feelings are energy, even the actions required for you to read this book are all about energy. To read this page, for example, your mind told your hand to open up the book and turn the pages; next, your eyes send the images on the pages to your brain; then, your brain interprets the images so that you'll understand what you are reading. Now, think about the speed at which this process must happen again and again for you to read. It happens at the speed of energy. In fact, it is the power of energy in our lives that allows us to do most activities and yet, in many areas, energy remains an untapped resource.

Physicist David Bohm (1980) says that energy saturates every inch of space throughout the universe and that it is energy that connects us to each other and everything else in our world. Energy psychology is about the examination and development of techniques that will help you to manipulate and use your life energy to better deal with your physical and emotional problems.

In fact, energy psychology allows you to tap into your own energy system and, by balancing it, eliminate the causes of any psychological problems or impediments. The results: you feel better about yourself, you are more confident, you are better able to cope with a myriad of emotional problems, and you stop feeling as if you are "stuck" in your life.

> Energy psychology has developed techniques that
> can help you to manipulate and use your life energy to
> better cope with emotional problems.

Your Energy System Provides the Solutions

Because we all struggle with our personal issues, learning how to better manage our lives has become one of the dominant themes in our society. Energy psychology will help you to understand that the solutions to your problems are within your body's energy system. One of the most perplexing parts of having a problem is that often you don't understand why it exists. People are commonly taught to believe that if they had more knowledge or if they developed certain skills, their problems would go away. Unfortunately, this is not always true.

When people don't understand why a problem is affecting them, they are prone to blame themselves. This lowers their self-esteem, makes them feel "stuck," and contributes to their confusion about how they can be helped. One of the most attractive components of energy psychology is that you don't need to understand why you have a problem to treat it. The techniques in this book teach you the skills that are needed for you to "tap" your problems away. In energy psychology, we will take you through a step-by-step process that will enable you to treat problems without having to analyze and discuss every piece of your life.

Fears and Phobias: A Case Study

The fears and phobias that can be treated with energy range from simple to complex. For example, Bill is a teacher with a fear of heights. He is successful and competent in most aspects of his life, but he has a fear that he cannot control. It seems as if he has always had this fear. As a child he became aware of it when he couldn't climb high up a tree without getting anxious. As a teenager, he felt embarrassed when he couldn't climb a ladder. He had no idea why he had this fear, and he just learned to adjust to it, staying away from the situations that he knew made him anxious. As an adult, he was again faced with embarrassing moments, such as the time he went to a party in an eighteenth-floor apartment only to find that the people he wanted to socialize with were on the balcony. He had a drink and walked out on the balcony, but his fear soon had him feeling paralyzed. He looked for a seat away from the end of the balcony, but once he looked over the railing, his fear started to overwhelm him. There was an uncomfortable feeling and then a fleeting thought about jumping, and soon he felt compelled to go back inside.

Although Bill's fear of heights is a situation that he feels he can't change, energy psychology helped him confront and deal with his fear. Imagine that before the party, Bill thinks about his fear of heights and taps with two fingers several times on his eyebrow, under his eye, and under his arm. When Bill gets to the party, he goes out on the balcony and finds that, although he is not completely comfortable, he can stay out on the balcony, socialize, and enjoy himself. Later in the evening, Bill feels his fear starting to return. He uses another energy psychology technique and while feeling his fear, he discreetly touches the side of his hand, under his eye, under his arm, and under his collarbone. When he again goes out on the balcony, he finds that he can walk up to the railing and look down and see people walking on the sidewalk eighteen stories below him. The situation that used to paralyze him and force him to go inside no longer affects him. Bill still doesn't know why he has a fear of heights, nor does he need to. Instead, he has learned what is most important: how to manage his fear. In time, Bill will eliminate his fear of heights altogether. This is the world of energy psychology. Although tapping on your face or hands may seem a little strange, it will open the door for you to make changes in your life that you may not have thought possible.

Relationships: A Case Study

Your energy level affects all aspects of your life, including your relationships. Despite numerous best-selling books on how to resolve relationship problems, the divorce rate is still extremely high in the United States. What's happening? Are people having difficulty choosing the right person or are they sabotaging good relationships? There are many ways to create problem relationships, including ignoring the right person or chasing the wrong one.

For example, Ann always wants to be in control because she doesn't trust men. She chooses to date men who are needy—similar to children—and who depend on her. In her relationships, she is the caretaker, making most of the decisions. Most importantly, however, she is in control. The problem is that her relationships don't last. Although she has control, Ann also does all of the work in the relationship, which leaves her feeling angry and frustrated. She feels like giving up on men, because it appears that the only men whom she attracts and who are attracted to her are similar to the men in her past relationships. Ann really wants to change. She wants to find a man who she can trust, one who will share the workload with her, and also be able to take care of her. Unfortunately, Ann has an energy imbalance that sabotages her real goal and blocks her from finding the right man. In future chapters, you will learn more about this concept and how to correct it.

> If you reflect for a minute, you can probably think of a time when you sabotaged a situation in your life.

How Are Energy Imbalances Created?

While it is true that problems can occur due to no fault of your own, each person still is responsible for finding effective solutions to dealing with the challenges in their lives. If you have a chronic problem, do you have the knowledge, skill, or ability to help you to cope with the problem, or is it an energy imbalance? If you do not lack the knowledge, skill, or coping ability, then most likely the cause of your problem is an energy imbalance and a psychological reversal that prevents you from identifying or implementing appropriate solutions.

For example, millions of people struggle with problems such as weight loss, poor relationships, depression, and/or addictive behaviors. Our society, and too many people in general, seem chronically angry about life's small concerns and issues. Often, people struggle year after year with the same issues. It seems as though many people have accepted that they can't understand their own problems or develop effective strategies for change. Some experts and authors of self-help books imply that a lack of knowledge or skill is creating the problem. Yet, when people sincerely try to develop coping skills and implement self-help strategies, they frequently find that it doesn't work for them. This type of situation is the hallmark of an energy-related issue: you know how to solve the problems that you encounter, but for some reason you can't make yourself do what is needed.

When we examine the beliefs that clients share with us, the word *can't* is important because, as we contend, it isn't a lack of knowledge or skill that causes your problems. Instead, we believe that an imbalance in your energy system sabotages your ability to achieve certain goals in your life and/or be capable of moving on with your life after a traumatic event has occurred. Once your energy system is balanced, however, you will be able to develop the motivation and concentration that are required to accomplish your goals, and to do so with far less difficulty.

If you are struggling to accept the ideas that support the effectiveness of energy psychology, remember that new approaches are often confronted with skepticism. It wasn't that long ago, for instance, that chiropractic care was viewed as a strange alternative medicine. Today, however, it offers treatment to more than fifteen million people a year; it is one of the fastest growing professions in the country; and its services are covered by most insurance plans (Burton Goldberg Group 1993).

> The Chinese believe that all things have Chi, are Chi. If life
> is movement, then Chi is what makes things move. The ability to
> increase or decrease this energy is the basis for healing.

How Energy Levels Affect Your Life

Your personality is a complex and changing element of who you are and how you cope with problems. In every situation, you respond with a different set of emotions, some are constructive and others destructive. For example, did you ever wonder about those people who scream at other drivers when they're on the road? Those same people can go to work and deal with a complex situation using trust, clear communication, and understanding. It is amazing how people can behave differently depending on the particular problem. Much of this depends on a person's balance—or imbalance—of energy.

When you are involved in a situation that involves an energy imbalance, your energy level is not sufficient to cope, and you resort to behaviors that are associated with low energy. For example, at the moment when people experience "road rage," they are hateful, impatient, and very anxious. In fact, their behavior at the wheel can be self-destructive and vengeful. At times, they may even try to punish other drivers. Their rage seems to be fueled by the belief that they should be able to drive exactly the way they desire, which often means driving as fast as they want without interference. When another driver slows them down, it elicits feelings of rage. What is equally strange is that this behavior most likely is not that person's typical life-view. That is, once they step out of their car, they can leave that feeling of rage behind and almost immediately behave in a calm and thoughtful manner. The point is that you can behave differently in various situations depending on your level of energy.

Map of Consciousness

To better understand this concept, we use the Map of Consciousness developed by David Hawkins (1985). The map is a theory and should not be confused with the writings of Callahan and Callahan (1996) or Gallo (1998), which are based on extensive clinical experience. However, the map is a helpful guide to understanding energy psychology. It identifies emotions and related behaviors that are associated with specific energy levels.

For example, if you have an experience that severely lowers your energy, you are likely to endure lower energy level emotions and/or behaviors, such as shame or guilt. This can be confusing, because you can argue that a negative experience makes anyone feel bad and, depending on the experience, they could feel shame. It is clear, however, that energy imbalances come about when you can't change, when certain areas of your life are stagnant, or when emotions such as shame or anger regularly appear in your life.

People can also operate at different energy levels for various problems. This is why people can be angry in one situation and show acceptance and inner strength in another. Hawkins believes that few people reach the higher levels of consciousness and emotions, such as willingness. Instead, most people operate at the level of pride and anger. The map, however, should not be used to make judgments. Rather, it should be used as a guide to identify your energy level with regard to a particular problem. It will also help you to identify what issues you may need to address if you are to move to a higher level.

What follows is a brief explanation of each energy level, as defined by Hawkins. Your goal is to determine the lowest energy level(s) at which you operate when you attempt to solve a problem. Remember, even if you start at a higher energy level, it is important to identify the lowest energy level at which you operate for the given circumstance. For example, you may begin operating in a situation by being calm and trustful (neutrality level), trying to empower others to solve a problem. If eventually, however, you get frustrated and blame others for the problem, then for this particular situation, you are operating at the guilt level. This information will be used in the following chapters to help you decide which emotions you may need to treat to eliminate a problem.

As you review each of the levels identified below, keep in mind the following two questions:

1. Can you identify a problem you wish to resolve?

2. What is your energy level when you are dealing with that problem?

Lowest Energetic Emotional Levels

Shame, guilt, apathy, and grief represent the four lowest energy levels. Keep in mind that when your energy is operating at these levels, there are usually multiple issues and problems causing the energetic imbalance. In these circumstances, it generally will take more time and multiple treatments to rebalance your system.

Shame: Early traumatic life experiences, such as sexual abuse and abandonment, can lead to shame. In our critical society, however, physical imperfections, sexual orientation, and other unusual behaviors can also lead to feelings of shame. Situations that deal with shame create many problems with self-acceptance. This is one reason why shame most likely will create a psychological reversal. Shame is the most destructive energy level, often leading to many self-sabotaging behaviors.

Guilt: People whose energy has dropped to the level of guilt tend to develop manipulative and/or punishing personalities. They always behave as if they are a victim of life, and blame is one of their primary weapons. Those who have unconscious guilt or feel responsible for a traumatic situation tend to suffer from psychosomatic diseases.

Apathy: This is a state of helplessness where external energy is sought from caregivers. People operating at this energetic level are often felt to be a burden by those around them, as they are needy and may endlessly discuss their problems.

Grief: Often felt during times of sadness and loss, grief is a feeling that everyone experiences for short amounts of time during their life. However, people who grieve for extended periods of time (years) and continually operate within this level live a life of regret and depression. Grief also is the energy level of habitual losers and chronic gamblers, who accept failure as part of their lifestyle.

Middle Energetic Emotional Levels

The next four levels are fear, desire, anger, and pride. It is possible for people to have successful lives operating at these levels; the energy level is much higher and they tend to exhibit healthier behaviors. These levels, however, have their own particular concerns.

Fear: As you probably know, fear can be a healthy emotion, as it protects us from danger. As a life-view or continual state of being, however, it can lead to jealousy, chronically high stress, or a fear of success. Fear also limits the growth of the personality, because much energy is expended on dealing with fears.

Desire: The desire for money or power dictates the lives of many people and helps to drive the economy. Desire also is the energetic level of addictions, where craving becomes more important than an outcome. Unfortunately, as one desire is achieved, another often quickly replaces it.

Anger: Energy at this level can be either constructive or destructive. Anger can cause people to leave problem situations or deal with them. But, as a lifestyle, anger expresses itself as resentment or revenge. Angry people are irritable and explosive, can easily fall into rage, and tend to distance people from them.

Pride: People feel positive as they reach the level of pride, as they have attained some level of accomplishment in their lives. If pride originates exclusively from external forces, however, the inflated ego is vulnerable to attack. Also, if a loss of status occurs regarding pride, this energetic level can quickly move to shame. This is different from what we call a "healthy pride," which is closer to the description of neutrality that follows.

Highest Energetic Emotional Levels

The last group of emotional levels to be discussed is the beginning of a crossover point, where power—rather than force—is used to make decisions and create change in your life. At this level, there is a realization that your own empowerment and the empowerment of others are the true keys to success. This level includes courage, neutrality, willingness, and acceptance.

Courage: This is where the world starts to look exciting, challenging, and stimulating. At the lower levels, the world is seen as hopeless, sad, frightening, or frustrating. Courage begins the process of empowerment and the ability to cope and handle the opportunities of life. Courage brings out the capacity to face fear or our own character defects and grow in spite of them.

Neutrality: At this stage, the world is seen as a complex and changing place without simple answers or rigid positions. The world is no longer viewed as black or white. To be neutral means that not getting one's way is no longer experienced as defeating or frustrating. The view is rather, "If I didn't get this, then I'll get something else. Life has its ups and downs and I will be okay if I roll with the punches." People at this level are easy to get along with and not interested in conflict.

Willingness: People who have reached the level of willingness are genuinely friendly, and social and economic success is a part of their lives. They have the ability to overcome inner resistance and do not have any major learning blocks. Having let go of pride, they are willing to look at their own defects and learn from others.

Acceptance: Although there are higher levels, acceptance is the level, according to Hawkins, where there is the realization that the source of happiness is within oneself. Love is not something that is given or taken away by another, but is rather created from within. Long-term goals take precedence over short-term goals. Self-discipline and mastery are prominent.

Summary

The goal of this chapter was to introduce you to the development of energy work and provide you with some examples of how your energy can affect your behavior. As you can see, we believe that most psychological problems are maintained by an energy imbalance. The key to eliminating these types of problems is to balance your energy. Energy imbalance is the reason why you have had so much difficulty dealing with problems in your life. After learning and utilizing the energy treatments in this book, you will be able to deal with most of your problems in an efficient and effective manner. Lastly, remember that letting go of your negative emotions is one of the keys to good physical health.

CHAPTER 2

Your Energy Meridians

*Just because we cannot detect, perceive, or measure forces that
Chinese doctors say are important in managing illness does
not automatically mean that they do not exist.*

—Andrew Weil, M.D.

There are a number of ways to obtain energetic balance in your body and thus relieve emotional distress. In this book, we specifically cover a simple, highly portable method that can be used by anyone, in practically any place, at almost any time. In most instances, repeating the energy treatments one to three times will eliminate your problem altogether.

Energy Meridian Points

There are twelve major energy meridians in your body. They run from the top of your head, through your fingers, and down to your toes. *Meridians* are "vessels" or channels that carry subtle energy through the body. *Acupoints* or *meridian points* are specific points on the surface of the skin, many of which evidence lower electrical resistance relative to the surrounding skin surface. These are the points that you will tap on when doing the energy treatments described in this book. It is thought that subtle energy from the environment enters the body through these portals. The acupoints interconnect along the meridians.

To provide easy access to the treatment points, we will focus on the meridians that are in your face, upper torso, and hands. Starting with the meridian points on your head, we will describe the location of each meridian and the emotions and/or problems that are addressed when stimulating the point on that meridian. We will also provide the meridian points for treating psychological reversals, which will be addressed further in this chapter and in chapter 6. And, we will explore two additional treatments that are often used in conjunction with the primary treatments.

Seventeen meridian points are used in the treatment sequences in this book. They include:

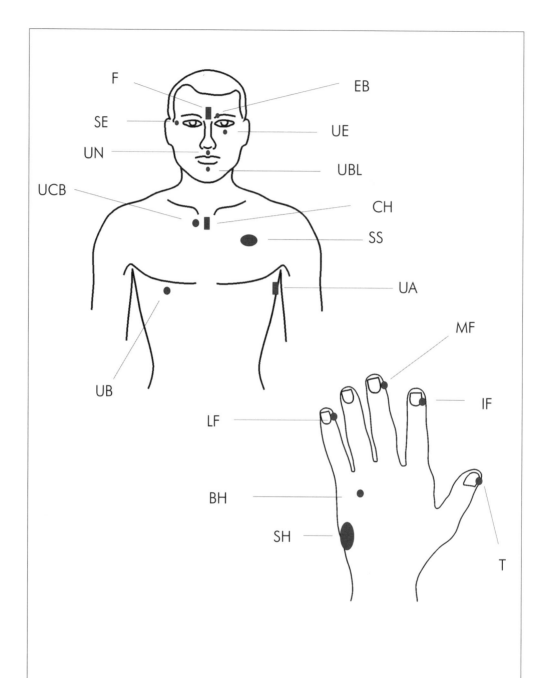

Diagram One: The Meridian Points Used in Energy Psychology

Eyebrow Point

The Eyebrow (EB) energy meridian point is located at the beginning of either eyebrow, near the bridge of the nose. The EB is often important in the treatment of trauma, frustration, and restlessness.

Side of Eye

The Side of Eye (SE) energy meridian point is located on the bony orbit of the eye at the side of either eye, directly below the end of the eyebrow. The SE is frequently helpful in alleviating feelings of rage.

Under Eye

The Under Eye (UE) energy meridian point is located on the bony orbit of the eye below either eye, directly under the pupil when the eyes are directed straight ahead. The UE is often used in the treatment of anxiety, nervousness, phobias, and cravings.

Under Nose

The Under Nose (UN) energy meridian point is located directly under the nose in the crevice above the upper lip. The UN is used to treat many conditions and is uniquely helpful for embarrassment. It is also used in treating what is referred to as deep-level psychological reversal.

Under Bottom Lip

The Under Bottom Lip (UBL) energy meridian point is located directly under the bottom lip, in the depression between the lip and the chin. The UBL is also used in the treatment of many problems and is specifically useful in alleviating feelings of shame. Additionally, it is used in treating some types of psychological reversal.

Under Collarbone

The Under Collarbone (UCB) energy meridian point is located directly under either collarbone, next to the sternum or chest bone. The UCB is easily found by placing a finger in the notch beneath where the Adam's apple is located (above the sternum), sliding the finger down one inch and then to the right or left approximately one inch. The indentation is the UCB. The UCB is used in the treatment of many conditions. It has specific relevance in the areas of anxiety and insecurity.

Under Arm

The Under Arm (UA) energy meridian is located on the side of the body, six inches under either armpit. Men can locate this point by raising an arm, placing the free hand on the breast nipple, and then sliding the hand directly under the raised arm. For women, the UA is located where the understrap of a bra meets the side of their body under either armpit. The UA is frequently used to treat anxiety, nervousness, and cravings. Sometimes, it is used to treat self-esteem issues as well.

Under Breast

The Under Breast (UB) energy meridian point is located directly under either breast, approximately where the rib cage ends. The UB is often useful in treating feelings of unhappiness.

Little Fingernail

The Little Fingernail (LF) energy meridian point is located on the inside tip of either little (pinkie) finger, where the fingernail joins the cuticle. The LF is easily located by extending the little finger and touching the side of the fingernail that is facing the ring finger. The LF is important in alleviating feelings of anger.

Middle Fingernail

The Middle Fingernail (MF) energy meridian point is located on either middle fingernail, on the side closest to the pointer or index finger. The MF is often useful in treating jealousy and addictive cravings.

Index Fingernail

The Index Fingernail (IF) energy meridian point is located on either index finger, on the side of the fingernail closest to the thumb. The IF is useful in the alleviation of guilt feelings.

Thumbnail

The Thumbnail (T) energy meridian point is located on either thumb, on the side of the nail nearest the body and away from the other fingers. The T is useful in treating feelings of intolerance and arrogance.

Back of Hand

The Back of Hand (BH) energy meridian point is located on the back of either hand between the little finger and ring finger knuckles, in the direction of the wrist. The BH is helpful in the treatment of conditions such as physical pain, depression, and loneliness. The BH is also used during two additional treatments that are covered in this book: the Brain Balancer (BB) and the Eye Roll (ER), both described later in this chapter.

Side of Hand

The Side of Hand (SH) energy meridian point is located on the little finger side of either hand. The SH is easily located by looking at the palm of your hand, finding the palm crease that is closest to the fingers, and noting where the crease crosses the edge of the hand closest to the little finger. This point is important in the treatment of sadness and in the correction of several types of psychological reversals.

Forehead

The Forehead (F) energy meridian point is located above and between the eyebrows on the forehead. It easily is located by placing a finger between your eyebrows and sliding the finger upwards approximately one inch. The F point is useful in treating a wide variety of problems, including trauma, anxiety, addiction, and depression.

Chest

The Chest (CH) energy meridian point is located on the chest, between and slightly down from the Under Collarbone points. The CH is useful in improving the functioning of the immune system and a wide variety of other problems.

Sore Spot

On the left side of your chest, at the midpoint of your collarbone and down toward your breast, is a tender spot. Sometimes it's actually quite sore, even painful. This spot is a pressure point or reflex along the lymphatic system, and it is referred to as a neurolymphatic reflex. For simplicity, however, we call it the Sore Spot (SS). It is not a meridian point, although it seems to affect the energy system. The SS is used to treat certain types of psychological reversals. Instead of tapping on this point, it is rubbed briskly with your fingertips. After locating the SS, press on it with your fingertips and quickly rub in a clockwise direction for several seconds. Although we identify the location of SS in each treatment diagram, its location may be a little different for each person. The SS is useful for treating massive psychological reversals.

Summary of Treatment Points

Meridian Point	Treats these emotions or symptoms
Eyebrow (EB)	Trauma, Frustration, Restlessness
Side of Eye (SE)	Rage
Under Eye (UE)	Anxiety, Nervousness, Phobias, Cravings
Under Nose (UN)	Embarrassment, Deep-Level Psychological Reversals
Under Bottom Lip (UBL)	Shame
Under Collarbone (UCB)	Anxiety, Insecurity
Under Arm (UA)	Anxiety, Nervousness, Cravings, Self-Esteem

Meridian Point	Treats these emotions or symptoms
Under Breast (UB)	Unhappiness
Little Fingernail (LF)	Anger
Middle Fingernail (MF)	Jealousy, Addictive Cravings
Index Fingernail (IF)	Guilt
Thumbnail (T)	Intolerance, Arrogance
Back of Hand (BH)	Depression, Loneliness, Physical Pain
Side of Hand (SH)	Sadness, Psychological Reversals
Forehead (F)	Trauma, Anxiety, Addiction, Depression
Chest (CH)	Improve Function of the Immune System
Sore Spot (SS)	Psychological Reversals

Locating and Tapping Meridian Points

By participating in the following exercise, you will become more familiar with the location of the energy meridian points and how to balance your energy:

Step One

Think of something that causes you a minimal level of emotional discomfort. Do not focus on something complex at this time. Perhaps you could think of an old argument that you've had that still causes you to feel a little angry.

Step Two

Now, rate the level of discomfort that you feel while thinking about the situation (for example, the old argument). This should be the level of distress you are experiencing right now as you think about the issue. It may not be the same level of distress that you experienced when you last encountered the situation. Rate your discomfort on a scale from 0 to 10:

- **Zero** means that the issue does not bother you at all; you're completely relaxed.

- **Two** means that the issue causes slight discomfort, but you're in control.

- **Four** means that although you can tolerate the distress, you are uncomfortable.

- **Six** means that you're highly uncomfortable.

- **Eight** means that the distress is very severe.

- **Ten** means that the distress is the most extreme imaginable.

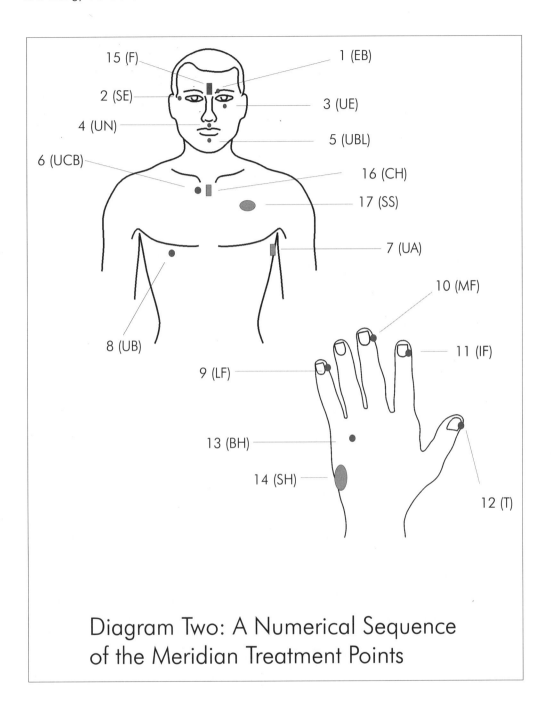

Diagram Two: A Numerical Sequence of the Meridian Treatment Points

Step Three

Use diagram 2 and follow the numbered sequence below. Beginning with number one, find each energy meridian point and tap lightly with two fingertips on each point five times.

1. Eyebrow (EB)

2. Side of Eye (SE)

3. Eye (UE)

4. Under Nose (UN)

5. Under Bottom Lip (UBL)

6. Under Collarbone (UCB)

7. Under Arm (UA)

8. Under Breast (UB)

9. Little Fingernail (LF)

10. Middle Fingernail (MF)

11. Index Fingernail (IF)

12. Thumbnail (T)

13. Back of Hand (BH)

14. Side of Hand (SH)

15. Forehead (F)

16. Chest (CH)

17. Sore Spot (SS)—Instead of tapping, rub this spot.

Step Four

Next, think about the issue or event that originally caused you emotional discomfort. Rate the level of your discomfort again on a scale from 0 to 10. Is it lower than it was before you did the above treatment sequence? Usually, it is. If the discomfort isn't completely eliminated, you may need to tap the sequence one to three more times. If there is little or no change in the way you feel, this may be due to a number of factors (e.g., psychological reversals, switching) that will be addressed later in this chapter.

Commonly, after doing the above treatment, it is difficult to fully think about the issue that caused you discomfort in the first place. That is, it often feels as if the event is simply a vague distraction in your mind. If you take the time to really bring the issue to mind, however, you usually will find that you do not become upset by it. In most instances, this absence of distress persists into the future. Many people come to realize that prior to doing this simple treatment sequence, they always or almost always felt upset about the issue that now no longer upsets them.

Most people report that they feel calm and relaxed, or even energized and tingly, after tapping on these seventeen energy meridian points. As a matter of fact, this tapping sequence is one method that you can use to become relaxed whenever you need it. That is, whenever you are feeling stressed, for whatever reason, take a 0 to 10 rating and then tap on all of these points, in numerical order, until the stress is entirely gone. Generally, the relief lasts for an extended period of time. Although tapping on all of the seventeen energy meridian points is often effective in treating many different problems, the process can become somewhat cumbersome. In Part II of this book (chapters 6 through 14), you will learn how to apply concise treatment recipes that are specifically designed to treat various conditions.

Psychological Reversals

As previously discussed, a psychological reversal is a disruption in your body's energy system that serves to sabotage your efforts at getting what you *really* want. Although everyone becomes reversed at times, we don't always know why it happens. Unfortunately, whenever there is a psychological reversal present, energy psychology treatments are not effective. As a matter of fact, it is unlikely that any therapy will work when you are in a state of psychological reversal. Therefore, it is extremely important to eliminate these blocks. Further details about psychological reversals as well as specific treatment sequences that are used for eliminating them are explored further in chapter 6.

Supplemental Treatment Strategies

Energy treatments (tapping on meridian points) are often sufficient on their own to treat a given problem. Following, however, are three supplemental treatments and an alternative to tapping on the meridian points. The Brain Balancer (BB) and Eye Roll (ER) are referenced in each of the treatment sequences in this book.

The Brain Balancer

The Brain Balancer (BB) is a treatment that is often used in combination with tapping on meridian points. The purpose of the BB is to activate various areas of your brain so that an energy treatment for a specific problem will be more effective. For instance, each of the various behaviors, such as moving your eyes in different directions, humming a tune, and counting, tends to stimulate different areas and functions of the brain.

The BB involves tapping on the Back of Hand (BH) meridian point (located on the back of either hand between the knuckles of the little finger and ring finger, midway between the knuckles and the wrist) while doing the following:

- rolling your eyes clockwise 360 degrees

- rolling your eyes counterclockwise 360 degrees

- humming a tune

- counting to five

- humming again

The BB is not always needed to bring about a therapeutic result. As a matter of routine, however, we include it in all of the treatments described in this book. Although you may personally determine whether it is necessary, it takes only a few seconds to do and it can't hurt. Give it a try now.

Eye Roll

Another treatment used throughout this book is the Eye Roll (ER). The purpose of this treatment is to strengthen the results of treatment sequences and to reduce any feelings of stress. The ER, like the Brain Balancer, also involves tapping on the BH. This time, however, as you are tapping, slowly and steadily move your eyes vertically from looking down at the floor to looking up toward the ceiling (without moving your head). Like the Brain Balancer, the ER is not always necessary, but we routinely include it in the treatment sequences. It only takes a few seconds to do and it usually feels good. The ER is a helpful, quick stress reducer. Try it now.

Switching

Sometimes treatments will not work to alleviate psychological issues due to a pervasive energy disruption referred to as *neurologic disorganization* or *switching*. When this condition exists, your energy system is disrupted significantly enough that the treatment sequences either will not work at all or will work far too slowly.

Some people experience a chronic degree of switching that requires ongoing and intensive treatment. In most cases, however, switching occurs directly in relationship to specific problems that are being treated. It also can occur temporarily for other reasons, such as high levels of stress; exposure to substances to which you are sensitive, such as foods and chemicals; or improperly executed physical exercises. For example, running with improperly fitted shoes or on highly irregular surfaces sometimes can cause switching.

Indications that your energy system is switched may include physical awkwardness and difficulties with coordination and spatial relations. Also, there can be a tendency to confuse words and concepts, such as saying "impossible" when you mean "possible," or saying "hot" when you mean "cold." As noted, another sign of switching is when you are trying to implement a treatment sequence and it is producing results very slowly or not at all.

There are a number of ways to treat switching, some of which are more complicated than others. One of the easiest is to do the *Over-Energy Correction* exercise. After doing this exercise for about two minutes, you can repeat treatment recipes and determine whether switching influenced their effectiveness. You may prefer to routinely do this exercise before attempting any treatment sequence, just in case you are switched at the time.

Over-Energy Correction Method:

1. Sit down in a comfortable chair.

2. Cross your legs at the ankles, left over right.

3. Extend your arms in front of you with the palms of your hands facing each other. Then, turn your hands over so that your thumbs are pointing down.

4. Raise your right hand up and over the left, and interlock your fingers.

5. Bend your arms so that your enfolded hands are now resting on your chest.

6. Place your tongue at the roof of your mouth, slightly behind the center ridge.

7. While maintaining this position, breathe deeply with your eyes closed for about two minutes.

Alternative to Tapping

Although we believe that tapping is the most effective way to stimulate a meridian point, there is an alternative. There may be times when you need to treat a problem, but you are at work or in a public area in which you don't feel comfortable physically tapping your meridian points. As an alternative, you can touch each meridian point while breathing deeply. That is, you can think about the specific problem or emotional distress you are treating, and then touch each meridian point with some pressure. At the same time, you take in a deep breath, hold it for a few seconds, and then release it. This method is also effective for treating energy reversals. As you touch the reversal treatment points, think to yourself, "I accept myself even though (name problem.)" Again, we do not recommend this method in place of tapping, but as an alternative method of treatment when you may feel uncomfortable tapping in public.

Summary

In this chapter we have provided an overview of the treatment points (i.e., acupoints) used in *Energy Tapping*. Additionally, a comprehensive treatment was introduced that can help you to reduce stress and to assist you in becoming familiar with all of the acupoints. Psychological reversals and other detailed treatment routines that are used throughout the book were introduced, including the Brain Balancer, the Eye Roll, Switching, and the Over-Energy Correction. To stimulate the acupoints, you can use an alternative technique of Touch and Breathe (Diepold 1999) if you are in public areas where you feel uncomfortable tapping. Before going into more detail about how to use energy psychology treatments for a wide array of problems, we will present the important phenomenon of energy toxins in the following chapter.

CHAPTER 3

Energy Toxins

Aging is accelerated by the accumulation of toxins in your body . . . eliminating those toxins will influence your biological clock in the direction of youth.

—Deepak Chopra, M.D.

Deepak Chopra (1993) believes that our biological system is continually eavesdropping on our thoughts. He believes that how we feel about ourselves can and will alter our immune systems and make us more vulnerable to disease. Feelings of hopelessness, says Chopra, can increase the risk of heart attacks and cancer, while joy and fulfillment will help to extend our lives. Andrew Weil (1995) supports this theory. In his approach to health and wellness, Weil encourages people to let go of their anger and express forgiveness to those who have made them feel angry. Weil also believes that healing depends on the efficient operation of our bodies' healing system, and that the toxins in our water, air, and food can create emotional and physical problems.

If your energy system is in balance, you will feel well, achieve your goals, and maintain healthy relationships. On the other hand, if your body's energy system is disturbed, many other areas of your life will be affected negatively. It is important to maintain a balanced energy system. Although painful emotional or physical experiences are among the more obvious causes of energetic disturbance, another energy disrupter is the foods you eat.

Interestingly, some of the foods that you find most enticing may be the very ones that disrupt your energy system so profoundly that you sabotage your life. That is, a food that you really enjoy eating may affect your internal thought process and cause you to make unhealthy emotional choices. (This will be addressed further in chapter 6.) In short, certain foods and beverages may be sending you on self-sabotaging missions.

One of the goals of this chapter is to help you to identify and guard against some of the environmental and substance toxins that may be interfering with your emotions, your relationships, and the achievement of your goals. This chapter also introduces the tools that you need to stabilize your body's energy system whenever it is out of balance.

Our bodies' energy systems can go out of balance for a variety of reasons. One of the major causes of imbalance is painful experiences or traumas. In these instances, treatment to restore balance simply involves focusing on past events and other triggers while tapping on the appropriate energy meridian points. With this method, the negative emotions associated with memories and other triggers are completely eliminated so that distress does not return again at any future time. In energy psychology, we call this *cure*.

Another cause of energy imbalance is heredity. For example, some people have a tendency to be anxious or to become depressed. This tendency often is seen in multiple members of one family, and not simply because of distressing childhood experiences. Rather, the tendency for the energy system to become imbalanced is inherited. In this respect, it appears that there are two kinds of heredity: genetic, which is related to genes and chromosomes; and energetic, which is related to disturbances in the energy system. Just as there are genes within the chromosomes of cells, the energy system can contain inherited energetic matter, i.e., genes of the energy system. **Note:** Even when the cause of an energetic disturbance is heredity, in most cases, it can be treated successfully by the methods discussed in this book.

The Impact of Toxic Substances

Another cause of energetic imbalance is *energy toxins*. This involves substances that, on exposure, alter your energy system. Toxins come in the form of certain foods, beverages, and other substances, such as perfumes and cleaning products. Exposure to electromagnetic pollution, such as high tension wires and the positive ions found in electromagnetic fields, seems to disrupt the body's energy system.

As you know, each individual is unique. What affects one person may not necessarily affect another. Or as the old saying goes, "One man's meat is another man's poison." Therefore, it is important to pay attention to how the foods and beverages that you consume affect you. Generally, within thirty to sixty minutes after consuming or being exposed to an energy toxic substance, symptoms of anxiety, nervousness, or fatigue will emerge. Substances that are especially toxic, such as nicotine and alcohol, will commonly disrupt your energy system even faster.

There are three concerns related to energy toxins. One is that problems that have been successfully treated by energy psychology may reemerge after exposure to the toxin, thus undoing successful treatments. A second concern is that toxins may initially block energy treatments from being effective, and you may mistakenly conclude that this approach doesn't work for you. Lastly, the toxin itself can be causing the problem, whether it is anxiety, depression, on any other emotional symptoms. Although abstract, intangible concepts are sometimes difficult to understand, the case study below further demonstrates how toxins may impact your energy system.

Sarah: A Case Study

Sarah had a severe fear of driving on freeways, which began after she was involved in a car accident. Since the accident, Sarah would sometimes experience panic attacks while she was driving on a freeway, and especially in heavy traffic. During these attacks, she would have to pull over to the side of the road. Sarah came in for energy treatments because her fear was becoming an increasingly debilitating problem, preventing her from traveling any distance and often interfering with work and family responsibilities.

After Sarah was treated with energy psychology methods, she could easily imagine driving in heavy traffic on a freeway without experiencing any anxiety. When she tried to actually drive in traffic, however, the anxiety and panic attacks returned. Each time Sarah was treated, she would feel much better, but then the symptoms would return. It became increasingly clear that something else was interfering with Sarah's treatments, as they are usually highly effective in relieving phobias, anxiety, and panic. We discussed various foods and beverages that Sarah simply loved to consume. One of her favorite foods was corn and she also drank a lot of a particular kind of tea.

We determined that the corn and tea were somehow interfering with Sarah's energy system. Her assignment was to eliminate these substances from her diet for a period of time until the accumulated energy toxins were adequately reduced. Approximately three weeks later, the energy treatments provided the results we wanted: no more anxiety and panic while driving. After this, it was possible for Sarah to occasionally eat corn and drink tea without creating an energetic disturbance.

Is Toxicity a Problem for You?

There are numerous symptoms that are a result of toxins, but you need only focus on those that are chronic. Some chronic symptoms include constant sneezing, runny nose, headaches, frequent mood swings, insomnia, bad breath, blotchy skin, blocked sinuses, fatigue, anxiety, and chronic aches or pains. If you have been experiencing any of these symptoms for a month or longer, you may want to consider the possibility that a food or inhalant toxin is negatively affecting you.

Identifying Energy Toxins and Allergens

Although each person is unique, there are a number of substances commonly known to disrupt the energy system. The list below includes some of these substances. **Please note**: Do not assume that each item on the list will negatively affect you:

Refined Sugar	Coffee
Artificial Sweetener	Tea
Alcohol	Caffeine
Wheat	Rice
Corn	Peas
Nicotine	Pepper
Legumes	Eggs
Tomatoes	Shellfish
Eggplant	Herbs
Detergents	Artificial Fibers
Pesticides	Cosmetics

Mold	Dust
Gasoline Fumes	Aftershave
Formaldehyde	Toiletries
Perfumes	

If you suspect that a substance is energy toxic to you, one of the simplest things to do is avoid it altogether. As we have noted, there are certain symptoms that will appear shortly after you consume a food that is toxic to you. The best way to identify these foods is to make mental notes (or better yet, written ones) after you eat. You can usually identify these substances by observing the patterns of emotional and physical effects they create. After consuming a food or beverage you suspect to be toxic, you may want to ask yourself the following questions:

- How did that food item make you feel?

- Did it energize you or did it make you feel tired?

- Did any other symptoms appear that made you believe that this food is not the best for you?

- Did your pulse rate increase significantly within thirty to sixty minutes after consuming the substance. If it has, one or more of the substances you consumed may be an allergen or energy toxin.

Although toxic substances are often the very ones to which you feel addicted, it should be noted that cravings can occur for good physiological reasons, such as low blood sugar; the need for minerals, such as iron and sodium; hormonal fluctuations in the brain; and more. Aside from these types of reasons, however, the foods and beverages that you crave the most are often those that can most readily disrupt your energy system. You may also find that these foods are the ones that you consume when you sabotage other goals in your life. Simply put, these foods weaken you and your body.

Eliminating Energy Toxins and Allergens

The goal is not to remove all the fun foods in your life, but rather for you to be aware of their impact. You may determine that it is better for you to cut back on—rather than completely eliminate—toxic foods. For most people, however, consuming toxins is a way of life. The good news is that your body has a high-functioning natural detoxification system.

Your liver is one of the hardest-working organs in your body, but it can use some assistance. Our recommendation is that if you have no additional health problems (if in doubt, consult your physician), you should detoxify your system. We are not suggesting anything radical. Most health food stores can recommend pills or powders that contain the fibers and herbs that are needed to detoxify your system without you having to severely change your diet. If you don't want to use any supplements, then you must increase the amount of fruit and water you consume, and reduce the amount of protein from foods such as red meat. There are a number of books at your local library or bookstore that address this topic.

Foods and other substances that cause allergic reactions are invariably energy toxic to the allergic person. An energy toxin by itself, however, does not necessarily cause an allergic reaction. That is, while allergen equals energy toxin, energy toxin does not always equal allergen. An allergen disrupts your immune system, causing your body to react as though the substance is a dangerous virus invader. An energy toxin, on the other hand, disrupts your energy system. In most instances, however, both allergens and toxins are examples of a threshold phenomenon: As the amount of the substance accumulates in your system, it reaches a point where the allergy or energy toxicity surfaces. This is why many people develop allergies later in life. This concept is known as the *barrel effect*, according to Doris Rapp (1991), the noted environmental physician who has seen a connection between allergies and conditions such as depression and Attention Deficit Hyperactivity Disorder. You can think of your body as a barrel. An allergy does not occur until the barrel (your body) is overflowing with the allergic substance. If you occasionally eat corn, for example, it is usually not a problem. If you regularly eat a lot of corn, however, in time, your barrel will overflow and you may develop an allergy to it.

One simple approach for detoxifying your system is offered by Andrew Weil (1995). He believes an effective approach is to drink a lot of water each day, take vitamin C and E and, at a different time of day, take selenium.

Summary

The main purpose of this chapter was to make you aware that toxins can affect energy work, including the energy psychology treatment methods in this book. This does not mean that you must detoxify your system. If you have any of the noted symptoms of toxicity, however, it might be a healthy choice for you to seek advice about this topic. Keep in mind, too, that you need to recognize and avoid the foods or beverages that weaken you. If you continually consume substances that are toxic to you, they may negatively affect your energy system.

CHAPTER 4

Beliefs That Hold You Back

Believe in yourself! Have faith in your abilities! Without a humble but reasonable confidence in your own powers you cannot be successful or happy.

—Norman Vincent Peale

The above quote was written more than thirty-five years ago in Norman Vincent Peale's best-selling book, *The Power of Positive Thinking* (1996). Peale was one of the first authors ever to encourage people to realize that their beliefs can affect their lives. His book was filled with statements such as, "We must expect to succeed if we are to do so." He challenged readers to closely examine their lives and to believe in their ability to make a difference.

Peale's ideas were a step away from the more prevalent, traditional beliefs of the time, which said that hard work—don't count on luck—was the way to make a difference in your life, and that confidence came from your work being recognized and rewarded by others. Instead, Peale said that you must first believe in yourself and that this belief will set the stage for your work to succeed. Although there is truth to Peale's adage, the problem is that while believing in yourself sounds great, it's difficult to sustain such a position when important parts of your life are not going well or as you planned.

What Is a Belief?

Beliefs don't have to be true or fact-based; they are merely perceptions. Amazingly, beliefs can be extremely complex, and yet operate with the precision of a surgeon's scalpel, defining your behavior in each situation. Appearance, for instance, is one way your beliefs operate. That is, when you meet someone, you may treat them differently based purely on their appearance. Most of us have experienced situations where two people are behaving exactly the same way, yet our response to each one is very different.

Every activity in which you participate is accompanied by a conscious or unconscious belief, positive or negative. A belief can be *global*, "I will fail at whatever I attempt"; *focused*, "I can park a car in a small space"; or *subjective*, "He always acts like a jerk." Your beliefs affect every aspect of your life. The beliefs you have about your own life will be explored in later chapters.

An early source of your beliefs came from your parents. One of their goals was to create beliefs that would protect you from danger. For example, "Don't talk to strangers!" This is a belief that almost everyone remembers as a child. Someone you trusted told you that it was dangerous to talk to or accept rides from people you did not know. You listened to stories about what happened to children who did talk to strangers: They were taken away and never seen again. These stories instilled in you a belief that strangers who offered you a ride or wanted to give you a gift were dangerous. You probably were also told, "Don't take candy from strangers." You responded by not trusting strangers and taking your parents' advice about whom to trust. As you got older, you learned to modify these beliefs and, based on your experiences and adult approval, you increased the circle of strangers that you could trust. This is an example of a complex belief about human behavior that affects you throughout your life. For example, you may still believe as an adult that if a stranger wants to give you a gift, they want something from you in return. As an adult, however, you ought to be able to determine when it is safe and reasonable for you to talk with and/or accept gifts from people you don't already know.

Social Change and Your Beliefs

Radical social changes can affect your beliefs. The events that occurred in the 1960s, for example, created and altered the beliefs of people for many generations. The trauma associated with the assassinations of John F. Kennedy, Robert Kennedy, and Martin Luther King, Jr. altered our society's beliefs about safety and created a sense of national grief that can still be felt more than thirty years later. Many other events from the 1960s still reverberate within the beliefs of modern society: The feminist movement sought equality for women in the workplace but, in the process, often created anger and alienation between the sexes. For the first time, a drug, marijuana, rivaled alcohol as a mind-altering substance. "Free love" dominated college campuses, changing the levels of acceptable sexual behaviors and leaving many people feeling confused about what was morally comfortable. The war in Vietnam divided younger and older generations, as hundreds of thousands of young men and their families were traumatized in a war that had no obvious noble purpose. These events of the 1960s coincided with a soaring divorce rate and the breakup of millions of families, a trend that continues to the present day. Further, while those events were taking place, television was becoming a dominant force. It created more passive interaction among family members, and parents spent less time learning about the beliefs governing their children's behavior.

Traumas that affect our society as a whole can create significant energy imbalances. This is particularly true when the events divide our country and attack individual beliefs, making self-acceptance much more difficult to attain. Perhaps this is one reason why, in a time of tremendous affluence, many people must struggle harder to be happy, and why, as a nation, we seem angrier and less respectful of others.

Moving Toward an Energy Approach

> It has been said that if you were to identify and write down all of your beliefs, you would see your life being played out before you.

Modern psychology supports the position that your beliefs can hold you back and prevent you from achieving your goals in life. Many popular self-help books exhort you to believe in yourself. When authors are on target, you may even experience an emotional cleansing while you are reading about a problem in your life and how you can overcome it. It's exciting to believe that your problem can be resolved; as long as the book is believable, it may help you to move in a positive direction, and reading it may be enjoyable. But did you really change? For a short time you may feel new energy, but in many instances, your old habits of thinking, feeling, and behaving eventually return.

A book can be intriguing, but it can't do the actual work that must be accomplished to change your life or make the process of change interesting. That takes time and effort. Generally, self-help books are designed to give you knowledge and help you develop the skills that are required for you to change some aspect of your life. If you can follow through on the suggestions, you will most likely succeed. Too many people, however, give up and don't implement the solutions that are provided by these secular bibles of our modern age. The reason most individuals don't follow through is due to an energy problem or energetic imbalance that must first be corrected before their efforts can be successful.

Alternative Approaches to Changing Beliefs

Many therapeutic strategies that are designed to help clients deal with their problems are effective. In fact, we believe your energy can be positively altered by other treatments; however, energy work is one of the most efficient, effective approaches available. In talk therapy, you are in the presence of a person who cares about you and is guiding you through a difficult situation. In effect, this person is helping you stop the negative habits that may be continually recreating your original problem. A good therapist is very supportive and provides you with a lot of positive energy. Over time, the goal of talk therapy is to change the energy around your issue from negative to positive. Additionally, if you talk about your problem, you focus on the issues at the crux of it. Learning to reframe problems or think differently about them frequently balances energy in a positive direction. The process, however, takes much longer and demands a lot more effort than energy psychology requires.

Following is a brief exploration of several strategies that can help you to better deal with your problems. These approaches can be very effective, especially when they are used in conjunction with energy psychology. One of the common goals is to remove the beliefs that create self-sabotage. People often find themselves unable to stop self-sabotaging behaviors. This is commonly caused by an energy imbalance that is at the source of their issue and can be identified by the presence of self-defeating beliefs and behaviors.

Energy imbalances also prevent many people from ever implementing new strategies or even taking the time to learn them. This is where most self-help approaches fail. Psychological reversals commonly leave people unable to use these approaches. As you learn how to treat your energy imbalances, traditional therapeutic strategies can be used to help eliminate your less desirable habits.

As you explore problems and/or try to change any of your habits that may create energy imbalances, we encourage you to utilize the strategies explored in the following sections, which include cognitive therapy, visualization, behavior and belief assessment, and releasing personal myths. Although energy treatments can correct a problem, imbalances can reoccur if you don't alter your old habits.

Cognitive Therapy

Cognitive therapy is currently one of the most popular strategies—especially in self-help books—that can help you to change your beliefs. Simply stated, this approach maintains that what you think affects how you feel and act. This strategy follows the logic that the mind controls our feelings and actions. With cognitive therapy, in addition to a stimulus (an event) and a response (your reaction to that event), a third intervening component—internal processing or self-talk (your interpretation of the event)—is added. According to cognitive therapy, your self-talk is creating the self-defeating belief and subsequent behaviors that prevent you from finding a solution to your problem. The therapeutic strategy is to identify and change the internal self-talk. This strategy, like many others, is much more difficult to accomplish than is energy work. Once your energy is balanced, however, you may find that these strategies are easier to implement and to use to help alter old habits.

For example, let us say that your boss' reaction to most problems is to become angry and yell, and your position in the company makes you a prime target for his behavior. When he behaves in this manner, you respond by withdrawing and feeling depressed. A cognitive therapist such as Albert Ellis (1995) would want to know what you believe about this situation. Most often your response would be similar to, "My boss should not (or must not) yell at me for every problem." Ellis believes that it is not simply the situation, but rather your irrational beliefs, that block your ability to change. The irrational belief is when you tell yourself that a situation should not occur when, in fact, it is happening. For example, while you are thinking that your boss must not yell at you, he still does. Ellis says that once you trap yourself with a "must" or a "should" thought, it leads to negative feelings, such as anxiety and depression, that, in turn, prevent you from exploring effective solutions to your problem.

In Ellis' view, the first step is to identify and dispute your irrational belief. That is, instead of saying, "My boss must not yell at me," you rationally reframe the belief and say, "It would be better for me, or it would be nice, if my boss did not yell at me. But if he does, it is his problem and it does not reflect on me." Ellis believes that once you eliminate the irrational belief, it frees you to move toward solutions.

The core of Ellis' work is to remove the block, i.e., the irrational belief that prevents you from changing. Cognitive therapy in general focuses on the idea that problems are created or perpetuated by a person's interpretation of a situation. By changing the beliefs, you can find most aspects of life acceptable and, therefore, not become terribly unhappy. It's helpful to become aware of the beliefs that trap you, and to realize that you can negate some of their effect by changing the way you think about and react to a situation.

Visualization

Another way to examine and affect your beliefs is through visualization. Unless you can clearly imagine a situation, e.g., completing a task or being promoted, then it is very unlikely that it will happen. Conversely, if you *negatively* visualize a situation, it speaks volumes about your self-sabotaging internal beliefs and feelings.

One of the most interesting studies in the area of visualization and sports was presented at the Ericksonian Approaches to Hypnosis and Psychotherapy Conference in 1986. After interviewing professional tennis players, Swedish psychologist Lars-Erik Unestahl (1988) studied videotapes of their game to determine what strategies they used to serve the ball on a consistent basis. In the interview, he asked them to close their eyes and describe what they did to serve well. Each described the position of their arm and body and exactly how they tossed the ball into the air to begin the serve. When the videotapes were examined, the psychologist met with the players again and told them that many times they served just the way they had described. At other times, however, the players' bodies were in different positions than they thought and yet, the ball still went to the corner where they were aiming. It's as if their bodies naturally compensated for the changes that occurred in their serving style.

Upon closer investigation, the psychologist found that the tennis players visualized where the ball was going before they actually hit it. He also found that the average player was less confident and often visualized the ball going into the net or going out of bounds. What happened was that the professional players believed that they could hit the ball over the net, so they could easily visualize and see the ball going over the net. The players who did not perform well were less confident about their ability to serve and hit the ball over the net, so their minds and bodies were not working together in harmony.

This doesn't mean that if you can visualize and see the ball going over the net and into the corner, you will reach the skill level of a professional player. We are limited by our natural abilities. What we are talking about, however, is reaching peak performance. To be at your best, you must believe that you can do what you are trying to achieve. As long as you choose realistic goals and are able to truly visualize them, you greatly increase your chances for success.

Visualization is simple, but it takes some work—you must visualize yourself achieving your goal. This does not mean that you simply and globally think about the overall situation or end point, such as scoring the winning point in a game. Instead, you spend time visualizing each component that is required for you to be successful. For example, professional golfers may walk a golf course while visualizing each swing. Visualization is a tool to help you identify a problem and/or improve yourself once you have treated your underlying belief issues. If anxiety is blocking your success, combining relaxation strategies with visualization can help you to improve your skills and more readily overcome problems.

Belief and Behavior Assessment

In the 1980s, Steve de Shazier (1988) wrote several books on therapeutic change that explored an interesting approach to looking at problems. He wanted to know how people "did" their problems. That is, he wanted to determine what the beliefs and/or behaviors were that people used to perpetuate a problem in their lives. He felt that people are often unaware of the specific beliefs or behaviors that create a problem, and instead focus on the problem itself.

For example, if you want to lose weight, being overweight is the problem. The solution is diet and exercise. The question posed by de Shazier would be, "What beliefs or behaviors prevent you from succeeding in losing weight?" The better you understand what beliefs and/or behaviors create how you "do" the problem, the easier it will be for you to use energy psychology to resolve it.

Teaching Approach

One strategy for understanding how you create or maintain problems is from a teaching approach. Although this may seem odd, imagine that someone wants to have your problem and they don't know how to "do" it. Using your life experiences as an example, your goal is to teach them how to recreate your problem. Normally, when you share a problem with someone, they listen and then solutions are offered on how you can solve it. In this situation, however, after you have shared your problem in detail, imagine that your friend says, "Wow! That's a great problem. I wish I had that problem. How do you 'do' it?" For example, if you are overweight, imagine talking to one of those thin people who claim that no matter how hard they try or how much they eat, they can't gain a pound. You would say, "But have you tried my approach?" At that point, you provide the detailed strategy you use to gain weight. Don't forget to include any negative beliefs that you use to diminish your self-esteem, or behaviors you use to put yourself in situations where you are likely to overeat or eat fattening foods. Once you have created this list of strategies, you will be consciously aware of the approach you use to create your problem.

Observing Exceptions

Another strategy of de Shazier's is looking for the exceptions to your problem. The goal is to identify an exception, when your problem doesn't occur. If you are helping to create or maintain your problem, then there should be a time when you are behaving in a manner that doesn't support it. For example, if you are eating too much of the wrong foods, determine when you are best able to stay on your diet. Who are you with and what are you doing? Sometimes exceptions are hard to recognize, but they usually exist. Once you identify an exception, you need to do more of that behavior. For the teaching approach and exception strategies to be successful, you must take the time to write down the details.

Releasing Personal Myths

Caroline Myss (1997) explores people's beliefs by looking at the personal myths that they hold onto, such as "My life is defined by my wound." She believes that after people experience a traumatic event, there is a tendency for them to look at their lives through the lens of the wound that was created by the event. Holding on to negative or traumatic events long after they have occurred greatly diminishes a person's vital life energy. Interestingly enough, Myss believes that holding on to good times as well as bad times can be costly. An example is a high school football star who still lives in the past and does not accept that he is fifty years old, overweight, and a couch potato.

In Myss' view, accepting who you are is one key to maintaining your healthy energy. No matter what stage of life you're in, you must consciously accept it and fully live it. That doesn't mean the high school football star has to be a couch potato; he could still exercise and be a competitive athlete. He has to let go of the mind-set, however, that he is eighteen years old and a football star. Once you consciously accept your life the way it is now, you will stop wasting your energy and find many ways to enjoy who you are.

Summary

This chapter explored how your beliefs contribute to your problems. Beliefs are divided into two groups: sabotaging beliefs that are the result of energy reversals, and beliefs that are bad habits. Although you most likely developed bad habits because of an energy imbalance, you can use the suggestions provided in this chapter to further help you deal with your problems.

In energy psychology, you can often treat a problem without understanding its roots. The better you understand the beliefs or behaviors that create that problem, however, the better equipped you will be to direct the energy treatments at their specific causes, and the less likely it is that an energy imbalance will reoccur. This is especially true of complex problems, such as alcoholism, where multiple beliefs and behaviors are at the source of the problem.

In conjunction with using energy psychology, you may want to utilize the following self-help strategies:

1. Examine your internal self-talk and dispute irrational beliefs.

2. Use visualization to test your internal beliefs about a situation.

3. Determine how you "do" a problem via your behaviors or beliefs.

4. Accept who you are at this time in your life.

CHAPTER 5

Identifying Problems That You Want to Resolve

Insecurity is the negative expected.
What are you doing about what bothers you?

—Merle Shain

To effectively use energy psychology, you need to be clear and specific about each problem that you want to change in your life. Although believing that your entire life is a mess may be a real feeling, it is too general and abstract to be affected by energy psychology techniques. Do not worry that there is a specific order in which your issues need to be addressed. Often what happens is that as you treat one problem, another problem is revealed that is also affecting that situation.

As you identify and treat each problem, you will begin to see a change in your life, and your outlook on related situations will improve. Although some problems are very straightforward, such as a fear of insects, others are more complicated, such as addictive behaviors.

Once you learn the process of energy psychology, you will be able to treat each problem in a fast and efficient manner.

Developing Your Personal Profile

The goal of developing a personal profile is to identify each situation, behavior, or belief that you believe is creating disruptions in your life. It also provides a solid opportunity to identify any ongoing themes or chronic problems you may have. Your personal profile is not a comprehensive, onetime list of every issue affecting your life. In our experience, we have found that whatever you think of first should be treated first. Then, once you have successfully treated those problems, you can repeat the process. As you are engaged in this process, problems that you were not consciously aware of may become apparent.

Review the areas of concern that are listed below and write down any that you feel you need to treat. Do not rely on your memory. Sometimes important problems are elusive, i.e., they surface to your conscious awareness, but then are quickly forgotten. The impact they have on your behavior, however, can remain active and significant.

1. **Childhood memories**. Can you identify any childhood memories or events that you feel could be creating problems in your life? If you have a memory, but you are not sure how or if it is affecting your present life, list and treat the memory anyway. As we have mentioned, you don't have to remember all the details at once. Memories will surface when you are ready to treat them.

2. **Associated beliefs**. Can you identify any beliefs that you have that were created as a result of these childhood memories?

3. **Fears**. Can you associate any fears that you have with any of the problems in your life? Remember, fears can be straightforward, such as a fear of insects or public speaking; or they can be more complex, such as a fear of being intimidated, or relationship and/or sports performance fears. There should be at least one fear on your list, as everyone is fearful of something.

4. **Controlling your emotions**. Can you identify any uncomfortable, yet common, emotions that you experience regularly? For example, do you often find yourself in situations in which you respond with anger, or feel alone or lonely? Other emotions of which to be aware include embarrassment, shame, rejection, frustration, and guilt.

5. **Painful memories**. In addition to your childhood memories, are there painful events that you have experienced as an adult? Identify any that you believe are related to or are negatively affecting your adult behaviors or beliefs.

6. **Depression**. This feeling is usually the culmination of many other unresolved issues. You can treat depression with energy psychology. To prevent depression from continually reoccurring, however, it is most important to identify and treat the underlying problems that are causing it.

7. **Eating**. Your inability to control what you eat is often related to unresolved emotional problems. What beliefs or behaviors are blocking you from achieving your goals regarding your eating or weight concerns?

8. **Addiction problems**. Smoking, alcohol, drugs, and gambling are the most common addiction problems. You can use the treatments in this book to treat these and any other addictions, such as an addiction to sex. For long-term success, it is important to identify what is missing in your life, as addictions are usually filling a void of some sort.

9. **Relationships.** This is the most complex issue presented in this book, as the source of relationship problems can be related to any of the previous problems you have listed. The goal here is to identify your current relationship situation, what you would like the relationships in your life to actually be, and what relationship-specific concerns currently exist.

10. **Common issues or patterns**. Identify any patterns or reoccurring situations that can help to guide you and to determine which problems need to be treated.

Using Energy Psychology for Your Specific Issues

After reviewing the questions above, you should now have a *written* profile (list) of the problems you hope to address as well as some idea of how these problems have an impact on your life.

Treatment Sequence Overview

In the chapters that follow, you will learn specific treatment sequences that address various types of problems. Generally, the process is very simple: Each sequence includes the following steps:

1. Identify a problem, such as a fear of insects, or a feeling, such as being angry. Now rate the amount of distress the problem causes on a scale of 0 to 10, with 0 indicating no distress and 10 indicating the most amount of distress.

2. Identify and treat any self-sabotaging beliefs (i.e., reversals).

3. Identify the appropriate treatment and tap those meridian points using a number sequenced diagram. All you have to do is look at the diagram and tap the numbered meridian points in the indicated order.

4. Again, rate your distress on a 0 to 10 scale (a number should just pop into your mind). If there is no decrease, repeat steps 2 and 3.

5. Next, do the Brain Balancer, which is explained in each treatment sequence.

6. Repeat the treatment sequence.

7. Again rate your distress on a 0 to 10 scale. It should be lower yet. When your distress is within the 0 to 2 range, go to step 9. Sometimes the treatment needs to be repeated several times before relief is felt from the distressful situation.

8. As long as the distress continues to decrease, continue with the treatment sequence until there is no distress remaining. If the treatment stalls at any point, this indicates a mini-reversal. Treat this by tapping on the Side of Hand (SH) while saying three times, "I deeply accept myself, even though I still have some of this problem."

9. When the distress is in the 0 to 2 range, consider doing the Eye Roll, this technique will also be explained in each treatment sequence.

The basic steps listed above are generally all you will have to do to eliminate most problems. Again, it is normal to repeat the treatment sequence two to three times to completely eliminate the problem. The entire process, however, rarely takes more than five minutes once you know what you are doing.

Summary

At this point, you should have developed a profile of your problems and have some idea of how they are contributing to the creation of certain situations in your life. As you engage in energy work, more unresolved issues that have been affecting your life will become part of your conscious memory. Eventually, you will eliminate the impact these problems have and will have to deal only with current issues in your life. We must emphasize: Do not avoid the process of identifying a personal profile. Your problems affect you in many ways and are connected to all aspects of your life. Although in many cases it is true that a specific treatment will eliminate the associated problem, developing a profile and working on all of your issues is the best way for you to achieve success with this approach.

PART II

Energy Treatments for Specific Problems

CHAPTER 6

Understanding Psychological Reversals and Self-Sabotage

We cannot change anything unless we accept it.
Condemnation does not liberate, it oppresses.

—Carl Jung

This chapter begins the treatment section of *Energy Tapping*, where specific problems are examined and appropriate treatment sequences are provided. The first step in applying energy psychology is to eliminate any psychological reversals. The simplest definition of a psychological reversal is that your energy system elicits thoughts and behaviors that are the opposite of what one would normally believe about life situations. For example, if you were asked if you want to be happy, the expected response would be "yes." But experience has proven that when people are psychologically reversed, deep inside (unconsciously) they are choosing to be miserable. There is a conflict between their internal beliefs and what they are trying to achieve. For instance, perhaps you don't believe that you deserve to be happy or perhaps you did something that you are ashamed of and can't accept in yourself.

When people are psychologically reversed, they often sabotage their lives. For example, they may try to resolve a problem with someone they love and, in the process, behave in a manner that is destructive and needlessly hurtful. Or, if a psychologically reversed person is applying for an employment position for which they are qualified, they may freeze up and act confused in the interview.

Although it is not readily apparent as to what physically occurs when your energy is reversed, it is clear that when you have sabotaging beliefs or behaviors, you literally act in opposition to what you are consciously trying to attain. Sabotaging beliefs, for example, are probably a major reason why people stay in abusive relationships, and also why partners are abusive in the first place. If an abused individual's underlying beliefs (such as, "I am not good enough") were treated with the techniques provided in this book, they would realize that they need to leave the abusive situation, and their partners would realize that they are only angry at themselves. (See chapter 14 for more on relationships.)

An energy reversal blocks you from seeing solutions even when you have the knowledge, or it prevents you from implementing the solution even though you have the ability. This is a core point of energy psychology. It is a reversal in your energy that prevents you from accomplishing your goal and it is an energy imbalance that creates faulty ideas or weak willpower. Once reversals are treated, you will experience the difference. In theory, when you correct a psychological reversal you are reconnecting the mind (beliefs) with the body (energy) so that you can again create positive energy in the previously reversed areas of your life. Once this is done, you will stop making the wrong decisions and start moving toward a successful lifestyle.

> An energy reversal blocks you from seeing solutions even when you have the knowledge, or it prevents you from implementing the solution even though you have the ability.

Six Types of Self-Sabotage

Throughout this book, we will stress the importance of identifying and treating psychological reversals. There are six common types of reversals that are at the core of all sabotaging beliefs or behaviors. When an energy treatment doesn't work, a psychological reversal is frequently the culprit, and it must be treated. Following is a brief description of these six types of reversals. Once you are familiar with them, you can assess yourself to determine if you are reversed in relation to a particular problem. You will find that you can be psychologically reversed with one problem and not another. Energy treatments are not effective until reversals are corrected.

Massive Reversal

Massive reversals affect major aspects of your life, especially in those areas where everything seems to go wrong all of the time. People who experience this type of reversal appear as if they want to live a miserable life. Although they consciously believe that they want a happy life, their behaviors create the opposite of what they seek. People who are massively reversed often reject or pass up potentially good opportunities. Unfortunately, they can't recognize them and instead often focus on the one negative aspect of that opportunity. They are unable to identify situations and people that are good for them and, in the worst cases, they actively seek out negative situations. People who continually have bad relationships, chronic depression, or ongoing addiction problems are usually massively reversed.

Deep-Level Reversal

Deep-level reversal affects people who want to change, but believe that their problem is too powerful or too much a part of their life for them to eliminate. With this type of reversal, a person expresses a sincere desire to deal with and eliminate their problem, yet at an unconscious level they hold the belief that, "There is no way I'm going to get over this problem." Usually, a lack of confidence and an inability to visualize their life without this problem helps perpetuate it.

Specific Reversal

Specific reversals are the most common and are usually limited to particular situations, such as a fear of heights or a fear of public speaking. With specific reversals, there are no other major issues to address, except the particular problem (e.g., fear of heights) you wish to eliminate. The central question of specific reversals is whether you are ready to eliminate the problem *now*. Although you might want to get over the problem, you may be blocked on letting it go at the present time. You may also be blocked on whether you are ready to eliminate the problem in its entirety.

Criteria-Related Reversal

The fourth type of reversal, criteria-related reversal, also deals with specific issues or beliefs. This type of reversal centers on issues such as whether you believe you *deserve* to get over a problem or whether you will *allow* yourself to get over a problem. For example, people who suffer from severe guilt may want to get over the guilt, but they may unconsciously believe that they deserve to feel guilty. In this case, the issue of what they believe they *deserve* must be treated before further treatments can be effective.

Mini-Reversal

A mini-reversal can occur after there is treatment progress. In this case, you experience considerable progress in getting over a problem but then, at some point, the progress comes to a halt. Some of the problem remains and the treatment sequence stops being effective. Most likely, you are not ready to completely let go of the problem. Mini-reversals can appear in the form of specific, deep-level, or criteria-related reversals. In these situations, you must determine which of the reversals is preventing you from completely eliminating your problem.

Recurring Reversal

When you experience significant progress in eliminating a problem but then a resurgence of your original level of distress occurs, it frequently indicates a recurring reversal. This is not merely a halt in progress, as is the case with mini-reversals, but rather a recurrence, often at the level of distress prior to the treatment. This is important to recognize because you can make the mistake of thinking that a treatment process isn't effective. Patience is required with recurring reversals, as you must start again and complete the entire treatment sequence from the beginning. You must also reexamine the possibility of each type of reversal and treat any reversal that you believe is blocking your success.

Once you understand the various types of reversals, you will be able to identify the specific ways that you sabotage situations in your life. The mind/body relationship is very concrete. Therefore, the more specific you are, the better the results will be. In general, repeated treatment for psychological reversal is necessary for addictive problems, for very competitive people, or when the problem has resulted in a very low energy level. If your problem involves shame, guilt, apathy, or long-term grief, your energy level is most likely very low in that area. This will require you to have patience. You must be willing to treat yourself on a daily basis for several weeks to eliminate the problem. While you are doing this, however, you will continue to receive some benefits from your treatment.

Treating Psychological Reversals

As we have been discussing, prior to using one of the treatment sequences in the chapters that follow, you need to determine if a psychological reversal exists, as it will block the successful elimination of a problem. When you are reversed, the first step is to accept yourself and the fact that you have the problem. This doesn't mean that you aren't going to change. Before you can change, however, you must accept yourself with your flaws.

The following questions are designed to help you to determine which type of reversal may be affecting you. Many of these questions are directed at your unconscious mind, so don't let yourself hesitate when responding. Most likely, the first answer you choose is the correct one. The purpose in completing the analysis is to help you understand the underlying beliefs that may prevent you from achieving your goals. If you have an energy reversal in a particular area, it will impede treatment. It is essential that these beliefs be explored with each problem you try to eliminate. You may find that you have different beliefs associated with different problems.

Once you have completed the analysis for a particular problem, use the treatments that are provided to correct any reversals that are sabotaging your life. Then, immediately locate and use the treatment sequence for that particular problem. If you wait—even for five or ten minutes—before using the treatment sequence, the reversal may reoccur and block the treatment. Once you treat the imbalance in your energy, it is far less likely that the reversal will reoccur. If there is a delay after you treat a reversal, just treat it again before using the appropriate treatment sequence.

After you treat a reversal, you must immediately go to the treatment sequence and treat the problem that is causing you distress.

Determining Massive Reversal

a. Think about your life in general over the last year. Do you feel you have been:

____ miserable

____ happy

____ not sure

b. Are two or more major parts of your life negative, such as your work and relationships?

c. Have you been chronically depressed?

d. Do you have a long-term addiction or an "addictive personality"?

e. Are feelings of shame, guilt, apathy, or long-term grief major problems for you?

If you answered "yes" to any one of the questions, this may indicate that you have a massive reversal (whole-life reversal), where many aspects of your life are negative. Its presence is supported by the fact that the problems are chronic and multifaceted.

Treatment

Find the Sore Spot (SS) on the left side of your chest (see diagram 3). Rub that spot while thinking or saying to yourself three times, "I deeply and profoundly accept myself with all of my problems and limitations." Even if you don't believe it right now, say it to yourself anyway. In fact, the more you don't believe it, the more important it is that you do this treatment. You need to repeat this treatment daily and always before you use any of the treatments in the following chapters.

Once a massive reversal is treated, it is common for other reversals that also must be treated to become apparent. It will take many treatments of massive reversals before the energy remains increasingly positive. You will, however, feel some progressive relief and change each time you treat it. The concern is that massive reversals tend to repeatedly reoccur. They also require numerous treatments. In fact, daily treatments for massive reversal are needed before you can be sure that you have eliminated this problem.

Determining Deep-Level Reversal

Which of the statements below accurately defines your belief about the problem you want to treat?

____ I will get over this problem.

____ I will continue to have this problem.

If your answer was, "I will continue to have this problem," a deep-level reversal may be present. This means that at a deep level you may believe you are unable to get over your problem. To help you change this belief, you must build your sense of pride and your confidence.

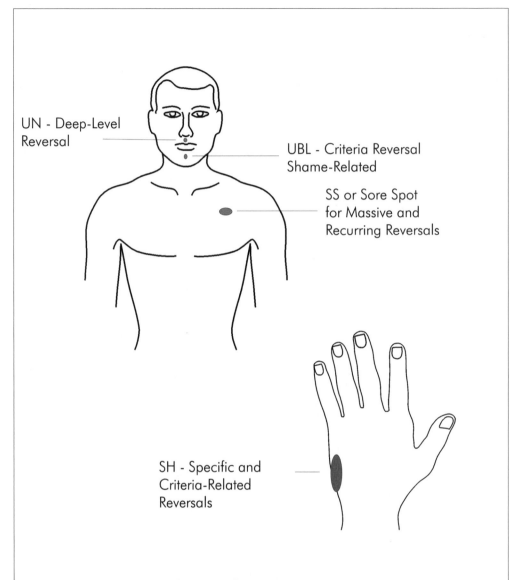

UN - Deep-Level
Reversal

UBL - Criteria Reversal
Shame-Related

SS or Sore Spot
for Massive and
Recurring Reversals

SH - Specific and
Criteria-Related
Reversals

Diagram Three: The Treatment Points for Specific Types of Reversals

Treatment

While you are thinking about a situation where your problem occurs, tap above your upper lip, directly under your nose (UN), and say three times, "I accept myself even if I never get over this problem."

Determining Specific Reversal

Which of the statements below accurately defines your belief about the problem you want to treat:

_____ I am ready to eliminate this problem.

_____ I am not ready to eliminate this problem.

Sometimes there are several problems going on at once. In some instances, you may not be ready to eliminate one of them. If you answered, "I am not ready to eliminate this problem," you may want to make a list of your problems, ranking them in the order you think would be best to solve them. Don't necessarily start by treating the problem that annoys you the most. That is, it may be easier to begin by treating the less frustrating issues.

Treatment

Think about a problem or situation where this problem happens and then tap on the Side of Hand (SH) while thinking or saying to yourself three times, "I deeply accept myself even though I have this problem."

Determining Criteria-Related Reversals

Determine which of the following statements accurately define your beliefs about the problem you want to treat.

1.

_____ I deserve to get over this problem.

_____ I don't deserve to get over this problem.

2.

_____ I feel it's safe to get over this problem.

_____ I feel it's not safe to get over this problem.

3.

_____ I am scared to try to deal with this problem.

_____ I am not scared to try to deal with this problem.

4.

_____ I will feel deprived if I get over this problem.

_____ I will not feel deprived if I get over this problem.

5.

_____ I will allow myself to get over this problem.

_____ I will not allow myself to get over this problem.

6.

_____ I will do what is necessary to get over this problem.

_____ I will not do what is necessary to get over this problem.

Treatments

Select the belief questions above that you feel best identify your problem and match its number to the statements below. While thinking about your problem or about a situation where your problem occurs, tap on the Side of Hand (SH) and think to yourself three times:

"I deeply accept myself even if":

1. I deserve to have this problem.

2. It's not safe for me to get over this problem.

3. I'm scared to get over this problem.

4. I will feel deprived if I get over this problem.

5. I will not allow myself to get over this problem.

6. I will not do what is necessary to get over this problem.

Psychological Reversal Sample Treatment

Imagine that you have experienced too much rejection in your personal life and you are feeling frustrated or angry about a current social life event. After reviewing the belief questions on reversals, you decide that not only are you feeling rejected, but you believe that you will continue to have this problem (deep-level reversal). Your reasoning is that although you are experiencing rejection, you are confused because you don't know why it occurs or how to stop it. Not understanding what you are doing wrong or how to change a problem is very common when you are reversed.

To treat a deep-level reversal, tap above your upper lip directly under your nose (UN) and say to yourself three times, "I accept myself even if I never get over this problem." You can personalize the statement and say, "I accept myself even if I never stop being rejected."

Although this sounds like an odd treatment, you must accept your situation, i.e., getting rejected, before you can create change in your life. Once you have treated yourself for the reversal, you are ready to use the specific treatment sequences for rejection, and eliminate the energy imbalance that is causing your problem. If you are still feeling angry about past situations, you will need to use the treatment sequence for anger as well.

You may need to repeat this treatment to ensure long-term, permanent success, although you will immediately be more confident and less likely to seek out people who will reject you. You will also be able to better handle rejection and to focus on supportive people and situations in the future.

Once you have identified any of the above reversals and treated yourself for them, you may be able to identify other beliefs that may be blocking you from changing. Once again, identify the type of reversal and treat it.

Summary

You cannot change a problem in your life unless you are willing to accept that, to some degree, you are involved in creating it. A problem can occur in your life without it being your fault; however, your response to it is key to your ability to cope with that problem. The core of a psychological reversal is that if your energy levels become very low due to problems in your past, your energy about a specific situation can become negative. Once that happens, your view of that or another situation and your idea of how to resolve a problem can become distorted. If you are reversed, you will actively sabotage a goal that you are consciously seeking to achieve. Your behaviors and beliefs at the time, however, will feel appropriate. That is why it is essential to treat any possible reversals before you employ a specific energy treatment.

If an energy treatment is not effective, a psychological reversal is usually the culprit. This chapter has examined the main types of reversals and their matching treatments. Once you learn how to treat reversals, you are ready to read the chapters about specific problems and to utilize the corresponding treatment sequences to eliminate them. Remember, if you are reversed, the energy treatments for specific problems will not be effective. Therefore, always treat yourself for reversals before using other treatment sequences to eliminate specific problems.

CHAPTER 7

Everyone Is Scared of Something

There are two fears really. The original wound from way back when and the fear of giving up our defenses and having to face the pain, so our fear becomes a roadblock that we service and maintain.

—Merle Shain

"No Fear!" and "Just Do It!" are two popular product slogans that exemplify a commonly accepted cultural idea that you aren't supposed to think of yourself as phobic or as having fears. The message is that you should be able to handle your situation, block out the fear, get out there, and make it happen. We have learned, however, that being fearless in one part of your life doesn't mean that you are immune to fears in other areas. For example, a firefighter will voluntarily enter a burning building to save another person's life, which is admirable and courageous. The same firefighter, however, may become paralyzed with fear at the thought of flying in an airplane.

Many situations, such as flying, which can easily be handled by most children, can cause serious panic for individuals who are fearless in most areas of their life. This is the nature of fears and phobias: What causes panic in one person has no effect on another. Fears and phobias have little to do with whether a person is weak or lacks courage. Instead, they are about energy imbalances. Once these imbalances are treated, you will be able to better cope with the presence of fear in your life.

A common strategy for coping with fears is learning to avoid the situations that create them and trying to accept this part of you. Unfortunately, your fears and phobias are not overcome easily, and their reason for existing has very little to do with logic. The result is that people tend to feel ashamed that they can't overcome their fears, especially if their fears are not socially acceptable. In truth, most people are not going to learn how to overcome their fears without some form of therapeutic help.

In this chapter, we will help you conquer your fears using energy psychology. We will address common phobias, such as a fear of insects or flying, as well as the fears that affect your ability to be successful in sports, at work, and in various intimidating situations.

How Do Fears Get Started?

Some fears can be traced to a single traumatic incident, others seem to be learned, and still others exist as part of our natural defense mechanisms. You might be able to trace a fear, such as imagining monsters in the closet. When you are in the dark, your diminished ability to interpret noises and the shapes created by shadows or objects can elicit a response of fear because your primary sense—vision—is incapable of determining if you are safe. Isn't it mysterious that children who have never seen a monster (and no matter how many times you check the closet) believe that something dangerous exists? Most people have a natural fear of the unknown, a safety device that is designed to protect us.

Fears can also develop from a single traumatic incident. If a person is in a car accident, for example, they may develop a fear of driving or even riding in a car. This type of fear is easily understood. That is, if someone has been in a severe car accident, being in a similar situation understandably recreates feelings that existed at the time of the initial trauma.

Other fears are learned and are commonly reflective of societal beliefs. For example, some people have a fear of alien abduction. In these cases, accurate information and experience can often help to erase the fear. All too often, however, people are ashamed and don't seek outside help that can help them to eliminate their fears.

An energy-related theory about fears is that they can be inherited by way of subtle energy. One way of looking at this is to imagine that your great-great-great-great grandfather suffered a traumatic event that has been passed on to you as a phobia or fear. For example, if he had a fall from the top of a tree and from then on avoided high places, the initiation of the problem may have begun with that incident. Generations later, you now have a fear of heights for no good reason of which you are consciously aware.

William McDougall (1938) conducted one of the longest experiments in the history of psychology. It lasted more than fifteen years and strongly suggested that animals can develop fears in this manner. So why not people, too? Whether or not you believe in subtle energy transference, do keep in mind that it's often impossible to determine the cause of any fear or phobia. No matter what theory you try to employ, you will find many holes in it. What holds true for one person doesn't always affect another.

Have you ever thought about why your fears exist? In some cases, fears prevent people from achieving important goals in their lives. For example, having a fear of success may be reflected in the fear of behaving responsibly. That is, once a certain income or position is achieved, the person may feel that they will be obligated to assume more responsibilities. By avoiding the success as well as the responsibilities, fear becomes a vehicle of self-sabotage.

Although the origin of your fears and phobias can be complex, the good news is that with energy psychology, you don't need to understand your problems to successfully eliminate them. If you simply treat your fears one at a time, you will eventually get to the root of your problem, and eventually eliminate that as well. Energy psychology doesn't require you to reexamine your life. Instead, it is a simple and rote process that will be effective once you identify the fears in your life.

Identifying Your Fears

Identifying and dealing with fear is generally a lifelong process. As you deal with one fear, your growth and development will lead inevitably to other fears that you must address and deal with as well.

There are a number of ways to identify the fears that block your growth. Jeffers (1987) divides fears into three levels:

1. Level one includes fears that happen to you, such as aging or dying, and fears that require action, such as test taking.

2. Level two fears involve your sense of self, and include fears such as rejection or dealing with intimidating people.

3. The last level is what underlies all fears: the belief that you can't handle the situations in your life.

According to Jeffers, level three is the core of all fears. She uses the phrase, *"I can handle ..."* to examine fears. For instance, if someone is going on a job interview and has a fear of not getting the job, this is translated as, *"I can't handle* not getting this job." According to Jeffers, it is your fear of not being able to handle the situation that creates your fear sensations. Although we agree with this position to some extent, we believe that ultimately it is an underlying energy disruption that causes fear and fearful thoughts. The goal of this chapter is to help you learn to eliminate the anxiety and the sensations that are associated with your fears.

From an energy psychology viewpoint, people who become stuck in levels one and two may have criteria-related or specific reversals, while level three most likely is reflective of a massive reversal. The reversals at the root of these levels must be treated before using the energy treatments. Otherwise, as noted previously, the treatment sequences won't be effective.

You should identify and write down the fears that are affecting your life as well as a brief example of the fear situation. It can be as simple as, "I'm embarrassed that I can't do (something)." Or, it can be a fear that blocks you from achieving an important goal in your life. If your fear is complex, you should identify and write down all of the fears that are contributing to the overall presence of your complex fear. For example, if you have a fear of getting old, you may also fear dying, lost opportunities, or the reality that certain desired events are not going to happen in your life. With complex fears, you may be required to treat each problem individually to experience relief.

Four Phobias and Fears

In the following pages, fear is divided into four groups and each is addressed individually. It is not that these groups are radically different from each other. However, to achieve results with energy psychology treatments, it is important to be as specific as possible. The four groups of fears include:

1. Basic phobias, i.e., fear of insects, animals, elevators, heights, flying

2. Related fears, i.e., test taking, fear of success, public speaking, meeting new people

3. Intimidating situations

4. Panic attacks

The treatment section is also divided into four areas. Although they overlap, the goal is to provide treatments that encompass most of the fears that people encounter. If your specific fear is not listed, locate the group that best matches your fear and then use that group's treatment sequence to address your specific fear. It is important to note that energy psychology will rid you only of *unrealistic* fears. Fear is a healthy reaction to have when you are in dangerous or truly life threatening situations.

Basic Phobias and Fears

The first group of fears includes fear of insects, animals, heights, elevators, and/or flying. The treatment for each of these is identical. We will briefly discuss each situation and then provide the relevant treatments.

Fear of Insects

It is embarrassing when a warm day arrives and you inevitably find an insect in your house or, worse, it finds you. If you are allergic to insect bites, such as bee stings, your fear is natural and understandable to some extent. We still assume that your goal is to not panic, as panicking only increases your chances of getting stung. However, if your fear extends to all insects, even those that cannot harm you, your fear is irrational. Most fears regarding insects are irrational.

Fear of Animals

This fear is very similar to fearing insects, especially in that it's an unrealistic or irrational fear. It's natural to be nervous about large, barking dogs that can physically reach you, but panic will not help you and will most likely make the situation worse. So, you have to evaluate the situation. Can the animal you are fearing hurt you? Is it probable that the animal will hurt you? Remember, energy psychology will rid you only of *unrealistic* fears. For example, large, dangerous, barking dogs will still be cause for concern. The good news is that you can eliminate the unrealistic fears you have about animals, such as mice, cats, and dogs, that are not dangerous.

Fear of Heights

A fear of heights is a very common fear that most people manage by avoidance. In fact, sometimes people have trouble getting in touch with their feelings of fear because they have avoided them so well. In that case, you may need to find a safe situation that sparks that fear again to help you treat it. What generally happens with a fear of heights is that when you go out on a balcony and get near the railing, you start to feel sensations that (to you) imply that you are losing control. One reason for this feeling may be that as you peer over the edge, lines from the structure that you are looking down from converge as they approach the ground. These converging lines of perspective can create disturbing sensations. At the same time, you may have intrusive thoughts of falling or jumping. These sensations create the negative thoughts that are scaring you.

The goal of treating fear of heights is to eliminate the negative feeling associated with this sensation. Once you have accomplished this, the negative thoughts will be less likely to appear. You can use the same sequence that is offered for all phobias and fears. However, you will not only treat for fear of heights in general, but will also treat the disturbing sensations you experience, such as your fear of jumping or falling and your fear of losing control. If you think about each one and rate your feelings, you can judge which needs to be treated.

The outcome will be different for each person. For some people, ongoing treatments are needed because the visual stimulus that creates the fear of heights is very strong. Regardless, the treatment, which only takes a minute to complete, will provide relief. If you know that you are going to be in a situation that involves heights, be sure to treat yourself beforehand. And, as always, treat yourself for reversals first.

Fear of Elevators

You must clearly identify your fear of elevators. Is it a matter of being out of control? Are you afraid of being in an enclosed space (claustrophobia)? Is your fear based on the sensation that occurs while riding in an elevator? Are you imagining that something bad will happen, such as getting stuck between floors and being trapped? The better you are at identifying the thoughts and beliefs associated with your fear, the faster and more thoroughly you can resolve it by employing energy psychology treatments.

Fear of Flying

This situation is similar to fear of elevators, although a number of additional elements come into play. You should treat each possible reason for your fear, such as the fear of taking off and landing, fear of being out of control, fear of flight turbulence, fear of feeling stuck in an enclosed area, or any form of catastrophic thinking. Although some people think that fear of flying is the same as fear of heights, they are actually quite distinct. Most people who have fear of heights are amazed that they do not experience that fear when looking out the window of an airplane. This is because the proximity of converging lines of perspective (which is the primary cause of fearing heights) is not present.

Treatment Sequence for Basic Fears

1. Think about a situation that scares you. It should be a single, specific event, such as a bee in your bedroom, being in an enclosed place, or riding in a car. Try to be as specific as possible. For example, it would be more effective to treat for a fear of German shepherds rather than for fear of all dogs. Rate your level of fear on a scale of 0 to 10, with 10 representing the highest level of distress and 0 indicating no stress.

2. Treat for the possibility of reversal by tapping repeatedly on the Side of Hand (SH) or rubbing the Sore Spot (SS) while thinking or saying three times,

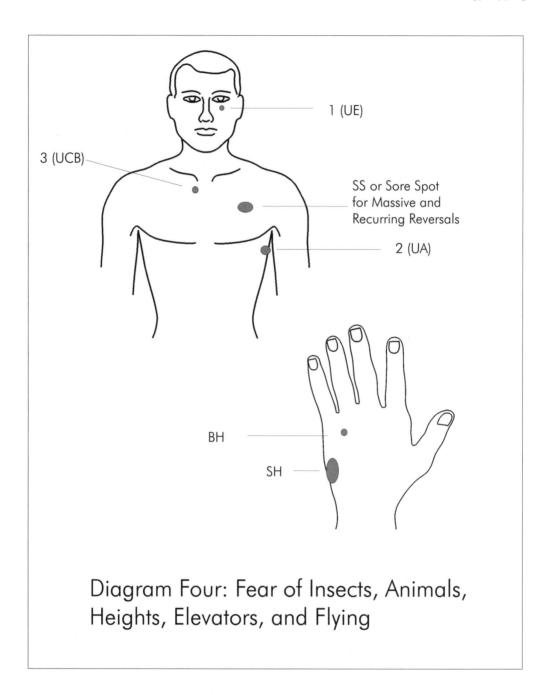

Diagram Four: Fear of Insects, Animals, Heights, Elevators, and Flying

Treatment Sequence for Basic Phobias and Fears

Meridian		Location
Under Eye (UE)	1	Under the center of the eye on tip of bone
Under Arm (UA)	2	Six inches below and under the armpit
Under Collarbone (UCB)	3	One inch under collarbone near throat

"I deeply accept myself even though I am scared of (name your fear)." It also may be helpful to tap the SH or rub the SS while saying, "I accept myself with all my problems and limitations."

3. Look at the chart and at diagram 4 to identify the locations for the meridian points for Under Eye (UE), Under Arm (UA), and Under Collarbone (UCB). While thinking about the feared item (don't get into it so much that you experience any major discomfort during the process), tap five times at each of these meridian points. Tap them in the following order: 1→2→3. Tap only hard enough to feel it. The tapping shouldn't cause any pain.

4. Again, rate your distress on a 0 to 10 scale (a number should just pop into your mind). If there is no decrease, go back to step 2 and cycle through the sequence again. If there is not a decrease after three attempts, this is probably not an appropriate sequence for this event, or else there is another sabotaging belief (i.e., reversal) that needs correction. (See step 8.)

5. Next, do the Brain Balancer (BB) by tapping repeatedly at the Back of Hand (BH) while rotating your eyes clockwise, rotating your eyes counterclockwise, then humming a tune, counting to five, and humming again.

6. Repeat the tapping sequence 1→2→3.

7. Again, rate your level of distress from 0 to 10. It should be lower yet. When the distress is within the 0 to 2 range, go to step 9. Sometimes you'll need to repeat the treatment several times while you are imagining your fear—or even while you are in the actual situation—before you feel complete relief from the distressful situation.

8. As long as there is a decrease in the level of fear, continue with the sequence until there is very little or no fear remaining. If the treatment stalls at any point, this indicates a mini-reversal. Treat this by tapping on the little finger Side of Hand (SH) while saying three times, "I deeply accept myself, even though I still have some of this problem."

9. When the distress level is 0 to 2, consider doing the Eye Roll (ER) to lower the distress further or to complete the treatment effects. To do this, tap on the Back of Hand (BH), hold your head straight, and, moving only your eyes, look at the floor and then slowly raise your eyes up toward the ceiling.

Although it has been our experience that one treatment will work to remove most fear-based problems, we have also found fears that need to be treated several times over a two- or three-week period before they are completely eliminated. It is also a good idea to treat yourself anytime that you know you are going to encounter a fear-arousing item or situation. Once you memorize a treatment sequence, you will be able to treat yourself for that item or situation even if your fear starts to come back.

The first step is always to attempt to treat the fear/phobia itself. If, after several attempts, the treatment sequence doesn't create the results you desire, then we encourage you to examine your beliefs: What are you telling yourself about your fear? Do you believe you can be hurt? Are you imagining the worst that can happen to you in a fear-based situation? Having awareness about your beliefs will help you to break any habits that are helping to perpetuate the problem. However, it will be much easier to change your beliefs once you have completed energy treatments on the most obvious aspects of your fear.

Testing Treatment Effectiveness

It is important to test the effectiveness of a treatment. For most situations, you can easily do this with a friend. For example, once you have treated a fear, place yourself in a situation where it is comfortable for you to test it. If you have a fear of elevators, for example, you can get on an elevator with a friend and ride the elevator up or down only one floor. An exception to this strategy is airplanes. In this case, you can prove the effectiveness of this technique by using it for another fear and testing that result. Or, you can go to an airport and think about flying while you are watching planes take off and land. Once you see the positive results of energy treatments, your confidence will grow and you'll realize that you have a technique that can help you in even the most anxiety-provoking situations, such as flying. **Please note**: Reversals are very common with fears, especially fears that you don't have the opportunity to experience regularly. Therefore, always treat yourself for a reversal before each treatment.

Treatment for Special Considerations

There are specific phobias that may require a more vigorous treatment approach. These include claustrophobia, fear of spiders, and anxiety related to flight turbulence. You may need to repeat this sequence three times before you feel complete relief from your distress. You still use the same treatment points listed on diagram 4, but you need to tap the points in the following order:

Treatment Sequence for Special Consideration Phobias and Fears

Meridian		Location
Under Eye (UE)	1	Under the center of the eye on tip of bone
Under Collarbone (UCB)	2	One inch under collarbone near throat
Under Arm (UA)	3	Six inches below and under the armpit
Under Collarbone (UCB)	4	One inch under collarbone near throat
Under Eye (UE)	5	Under the center of the eye on tip of bone

Related Phobias and Fears

The second group of fears includes test taking, public speaking, and meeting new people. Each of these situations involves a fear of how we will be evaluated or judged by others.

Test Anxiety

Tests are a very real and powerful tool that can have a strong impact on your life. They are also a huge business. Each year, for example, millions of students take college entrance exams, such as the Scholastic Aptitude Test (SAT), Graduate Record Exam (GRE), Law School Admission Test (LSAT), and Medical College Admission Test (MCAT). Many people must take exams that are required for specific licenses, certifications, and, in some cases, employment. Unfortunately, simply complaining that tests are "unfair" won't help you. At some point, tests are going to have an impact on your life. Don't allow anxiety to prevent you from doing your best.

First, determine which of these statements about test anxiety apply to you:

1. You know the material, but when you take the test you freeze.

2. You don't know the material and you freeze when you take the test.

The first statement indicates pure test anxiety. In this situation, you know the material, you may have taken preparation courses (for the SAT, LSAT, etc.), and you have studied on your own. You have evidence that you know the material, but when you take the test, your mind seems to go blank. The result is that you can answer the easier questions, but you cannot focus and solve the moderate and difficult questions. This means that anxiety is blocking you from taking the test to the best of your ability and you should treat yourself for test anxiety.

If your text anxiety is caused by the fact that you don't know the material and you don't study for the test, you must determine what life circumstances and/or beliefs cause you to behave in this manner. There are several possible reasons for your behavior, and you must examine each before you can ascertain which one is blocking you. It is appropriate to experience some anxiety when you must take a test for which you have not studied and don't know the material.

Our experience indicates that a number of issues can exist that create test anxiety in these categories. In the first situation, it may be pure test anxiety, as you know the material, but start to panic in a test situation. In the other situation, however, you may have been sabotaging your chances for success by not studying for tests, by being impatient, or by fearing success. If you find it difficult to study for extended periods of time, it may be helpful to do the following treatment sequence before treating yourself for test anxiety.

Treatment for Impatience When Studying for a Test

Imagine you are going to study for two hours. Tap under your nose (UN on diagram 5) and say three times, "I accept myself even though I can never study for two hours at one time." Then, tap the Side of Hand (SH) or rub the Sore Spot (SS) and say three times, "I accept myself even though I get impatient with studying and quit." Next, tap five times on your Eyebrow (EB). If this does not significantly reduce your impatience, then use the treatment for impatience and frustration in chapter 12. Lastly, complete the treatment sequence for test anxiety.

Test Anxiety Treatment

1. Identify the example below that best describes your situation:

a. When you take the test, you become so anxious that you can't perform to your actual ability.

b. You anticipate failing at some level or will not accept yourself if you score below a certain number. For example, you believe, "If I don't score 1100 on the SAT, then I am a failure."

Now, think about the situation that creates anxiety and rate your level of test anxiety on a scale of 0 to 10, 10 representing the highest level of distress and 0 indicating none.

2. Treat for the possibility of reversals by tapping repeatedly on the Side of Hand (SH) or rubbing the Sore Spot (SS) while thinking or saying three times, "I deeply accept myself even though I freeze when I take tests." Or, "I deeply accept myself even if I don't score high enough on this test." It also may be helpful to tap the SH or rub the SS while saying, "I accept myself with all my problems and limitations." It is always best to try and put the statement into your own words.

3. Look at the chart below and at diagram 5 to identify the locations for the meridian points for the Under Eye (UE), Under Arm (UA), and Under Collarbone (UCB). While thinking about the test anxiety (don't get into it so much that you experience any major discomfort during the process), tap five times at each of these meridian points. Tap them in the following order: 1→2→3. Tap only hard enough to feel it. The tapping shouldn't cause any pain.

4. Again, rate your distress on a 0 to 10 scale, (a number should just pop into your mind). If there is no decrease, go back to step 2 and cycle through the sequence again. If there is not a decrease after three attempts, this is probably not an appropriate treatment sequence for this event, or else there is another sabotaging belief (i.e., reversal) that needs correction. (See step 8.)

5. Next, do the Brain Balancer (BB) by tapping repeatedly at the Back of Hand (BH) while rotating your eyes clockwise, rotating your eyes counterclockwise, then humming a tune, counting to five, and humming again.

6. Repeat the tapping sequence 1→2→3.

7. Again, rate your level of distress from 0 to 10. It should be lower yet. When the distress is within the 0 to 2 range, go to step 9. Sometimes you'll need to repeat the treatment several times while you are imagining your fear—or even while you are in the actual situation—before your test anxiety no longer affects your performance.

8. As long as there is a decrease in the level of test anxiety, continue with the treatment sequence until there is very little or no anxiety remaining. If the treatment stalls at any point, this indicates a mini reversal. Treat this by tapping on the little finger Side of Hand (SH) while saying three times, "I deeply accept myself, even though I still have some of this problem."

9. When the distress level is 0 to 2, consider doing the Eye Roll (ER) to lower the distress further or to complete the treatment effects. To do this, tap on the Back of Hand (BH), hold your head straight, and, moving only your eyes, look at the floor and slowly raise your eyes up toward the ceiling.

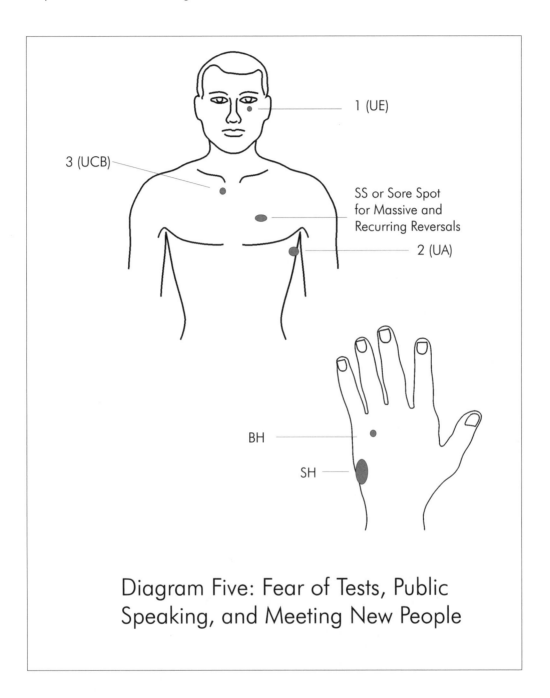

1 (UE)

3 (UCB)

SS or Sore Spot
for Massive and
Recurring Reversals

2 (UA)

BH

SH

Diagram Five: Fear of Tests, Public Speaking, and Meeting New People

Treatment Sequence for Test Anxiety

Meridian		Location
Under eye (UE)	1	Under the center of the eye on tip of bone
Under arm (UA)	2	Six inches under the armpit
Under Collarbone (UCB)	3	One inch under collarbone near throat

Public Speaking and Meeting New People

Although we have not directly addressed public speaking or meeting new people, the formula and treatments are identical to those used for treating anxiety. As we briefly address each topic below, remember that a fear of success is a reversal and should be treated as such because it blocks you from succeeding and may be how you sabotage yourself.

Public Speaking

When you speak in public, you are taking a risk and allowing yourself to be evaluated by the audience. You may also have had a negative experience in the past, such as freezing up or feeling your mind go blank. You may fear that this will happen again or you may be concerned that the audience will not like your speech. You must identify and treat each sabotaging belief before you begin the treatment sequence. For example, tap on the Side of Hand (SH) while saying three times, "I deeply accept myself even though I am afraid the audience will not like my speech." Then think about the situation of speaking in public and rate your anxiety. Next, use the treatment sequence for test anxiety, substituting the test anxiety statements with ones specific to your public speaking engagement.

Meeting New People

When you are meeting a new person, you are being evaluated. You must decide what you want from this encounter. Do you want to be liked by the person or do you want them to do you a favor? Although a date is different from a business meeting, the feelings are often the same. Again, the first step is to identify any sabotaging beliefs, such as "I'm not good enough." Or, "This never works for me." Once you treat any reversals, employ the treatment sequence for test anxiety. If you do not experience any decrease in distress, it may be because you feel intimidated when you meet new people in a particular setting. In that case, use the treatment sequence for intimidation that is outlined in the next section.

Intimidating Situations

One of the hardest situations to overcome is not being true to yourself when you're in an intimidating situation. This covers many types of circumstances, but they are essentially caused by the same idea: You believe that you can get hurt. It is easy to feel embarrassed or ashamed when you believe that you have not been true to yourself. Most likely, however, these feelings are caused by old, unresolved emotional wounds. Typically, emotional wounds occur when you are, or think you are, helpless. Later, even if you have developed the resources and/or skills to deal with similar situations, you react the same way you did when you were traumatized during the original experience. It is important to remember that emotional wounds create an energy imbalance that prevents you from being the most that you can be in these situations. In fact, you most likely are better able to cope with intimidating situations than you may believe.

A secondary consideration in successfully dealing with intimidating situations is that an unidentified fear has affected your sense of self, which has, in turn, produced an ongoing roadblock in your life. In this case, determine what the fear or intimidating situation has prevented you from achieving. You should treat any related problems that you can identify.

Treatment for Intimidation

As always, you must attempt to be as specific as possible when using energy psychology treatments. You may want to think about "how you do" intimidating situations. That is, what are the ingredients that create intimidation for you? Here are some examples:

- Someone has power over you emotionally or physically.
- Someone has the ability to provide you with something you want.
- You give a person power over you and respond accordingly.
- Someone is aggressive and is not respectful toward you.
- You believe that you cannot be successful.

1. Think about a situation that you find intimidating. The first question to ask yourself is: How do I respond to an intimidating situation? Do I respond with anger, sit quietly, do what I am told, or become an active participant in something I don't want to do. There are many scenarios that could be examined, but the treatments are the same. This is about you and how you respond to a situation. There will always be intimidating situations in life, but once you identify your fears and the beliefs associated with them, you can eliminate these roadblocks to a better life.

   Select a specific problem and rate your feelings of intimidation on a 0 to 10 scale, with 10 indicating the highest distress and 0 indicating none.

2. Below are some examples of intimidating situations/beliefs. Treat for the possibility of a reversal by tapping on the Side of Hand (SH) or rubbing the Sore Spot (SS) while thinking or saying one of the following statements three times:

   a. "I accept myself even if I think people with power are better than me."
   b. "I accept myself even if I am not myself when I am trying to achieve/obtain what I want."
   c. "I accept myself even if I believe I will get hurt."
   d. "I accept myself even if I give them (or whoever) power over me."
   e. "I accept myself even if I am not good enough to succeed in (name/describe)."

   If you can identify any other intimidating situations/beliefs, include them. Treat for the possibility of reversals by tapping on the Side of Hand (SH) or rubbing the Sore Spot (SS) and saying three times, "I accept myself even though (describe intimidating situation)." It also may be helpful to tap the SH or rub the SS while saying, "I accept myself with all my problems and limitations."

3. Look at the chart below and at diagram 6 to identify the locations for the meridian points for the Eyebrow (EB), Under Eye (UE), Under Nose (UN),

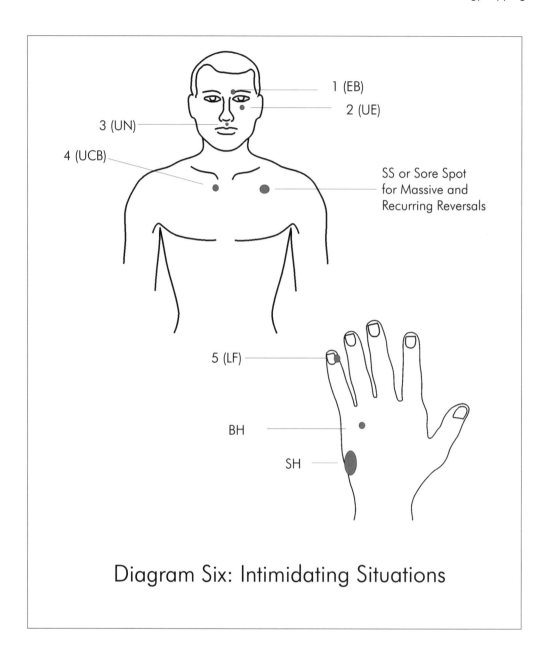

Diagram Six: Intimidating Situations

Treatment Sequence for Intimidation

Meridian		Location
Eyebrow (EB)	1	Beginning of the eyebrow near bridge of nose
Under Eye (UE)	2	Under the center of the eye on tip of bone
Under Nose (UN)	3	Above upper lip and below the center of nose
Under Collarbone (UCB)	4	One inch under collarbone near throat
Little Finger (LF)	5	Inside tip of little fingernail on the side

Under Collarbone (UCB), and Little Finger (LF). While thinking about the intimidating situation (don't get into it so much that you experience any major discomfort during the process), tap five times at each of these meridian points. Tap them in the following order: 1→2→3→4→5. Tap only hard enough to feel it. The tapping shouldn't cause any pain.

4. Again, rate your distress on a 0 to 10 scale (a number should just pop into your mind). If there is no decrease, go back to step 2 and cycle through the sequence again. If there is not a decrease after three attempts, this is probably not an appropriate sequence for this event, or else there is another sabotaging belief (i.e., reversal) that needs correction. (See step 8.)

5. Next, do the Brain Balancer (BB) by tapping repeatedly at the Back of Hand (BH) while rotating your eyes clockwise, rotating your eyes counterclockwise, then humming a tune, counting to five, and humming again.

6. Repeat the tapping sequence 1→2→3→4→5.

7. Again, rate your level of distress from 0 to 10. It should be lower yet. When the distress is within the 0 to 2 range, go to step 9. Sometimes you'll need to repeat the treatment several times while you are imagining your intimidation—or even while you are actually in the actual intimidating situation—before the problem is completely resolved.

8. As long as there is a decrease in the level of intimidation, continue with the sequence until there is very little or no distress remaining. If the treatment stalls at any point, this indicates a mini-reversal. Treat this by tapping on the little finger Side of Hand (SH) while saying three times, " I deeply accept myself, even though I still have some of this intimidation." Another type of reversal that occurs with intimidating situations deals with shame. If you have been demeaned in a situation, then you should treat for the possibility of a reversal. Tap under your bottom lip (UBL) while saying to yourself three times, "I deeply accept myself even though I feel ashamed."

9. When the distress level is 0 to 2, consider doing the Eye Roll (ER) to lower the distress further or to complete the treatment effects. To do this, tap on the Back of Hand (BH), hold your head straight, and, moving only your eyes, look at the floor and then slowly raise your eyes up toward the ceiling.

Panic Attacks

One of the scariest events in a person's life is to have a panic attack. As with most fears and phobias, there is often no rational reason why a particular situation causes a panic attack, or why a panic attack sometimes occurs "out of the blue." Yet it is all very real for people who suffer from panic attacks and they commonly lose control over many physical functions. The response people have during a panic attack is similar to what people experience when they are in a terrifying situation; it is symbolic of their feelings of helplessness. The symptoms can be numerous and diverse depending on the situation or the type of attack a person experiences. Common symptoms include shortness of breath, rapid heart rate, disorientation, rapid pacing, tightening of the chest, a feeling of losing control, inability to breathe, intense feelings of anxiety, and thoughts of dying or going crazy.

These symptoms are part of your natural survival mechanism for dealing with imminent danger. It has been referred to as the "fight-or-flight mechanism." At such times, the adrenal glands rapidly secrete adrenaline to speed up your heart, allowing extra oxygen and nutrients to be available to specific areas of your body, such as your arms and legs. The tingling sensations experienced during panic are an indication that blood is being drawn away from the surface of your body so that if you were to incur a physical injury, you would not readily bleed to death. Stomach discomfort at such times is indicative of the digestive process slowing down to divert needed energy to your legs for running, arms for fighting, etc. A wide array of other symptoms that are in line with the intention of survival also occur. During a panic attack, however, these survival mechanisms are being erroneously triggered because the looming danger is being greatly exaggerated.

What appears to cause panic attacks is that anxiety-produced sensations and thoughts are interpreted catastrophically. Those false interpretations allow your thoughts and feelings to spin out of control. For example, it is normal for you to feel strange sensations while driving at high elevations, especially on curves where your view of the elevation is panoramically clear. Also, it is not that odd to have a scary thought at these times, such as the thought of crashing or falling off the bridge. The problem occurs when you take such notions seriously, can't let go of them, and they start to overwhelm you. Once you feel out of control, the door is open for a panic attack to occur.

The actual thoughts that cause a panic attack may not be at a conscious level. Sometimes a scary thought occurs, such as the possibility of losing someone dear to you, and the thought gets suppressed before you have had a chance to consciously register it. However, your survival mechanisms noticed it and interpreted it seriously as a danger, thus triggering anxiety sensations. In turn, you misinterpret the anxiety sensations as a sign that there is something dangerously wrong with you. This adds to the scary thoughts, resulting in your thought process spinning wildly out of control, and producing what is referred to as a panic attack.

Although scary thoughts are an aspect of panic attacks, such thoughts do not invariably produce panic. Many people have such thoughts and do not succumb to panic. The key is the energy imbalance, which allows such thoughts to become frightening.

Treatment for Panic Attacks

1. Think about a situation when you had a panic attack. It should be a single, specific memory, maybe your first panic attack or the worst one. For example, it may be a memory of feeling frozen and not being able to move. Try to be as specific as possible. The goal is to focus on an isolated, specific event, but don't focus on it so much that it could trigger an actual panic attack. Rate your level of distress about the panic attack on a scale of 0 to 10, with 10 representing the highest level of distress and 0 indicating no stress. (This treatment may be used to eliminate a panic attack while it is occurring.)

2. Treat for the possibility of reversals by tapping repeatedly on the Side of Hand (SH) or rubbing the Sore Spot (SS) while thinking or saying three times,

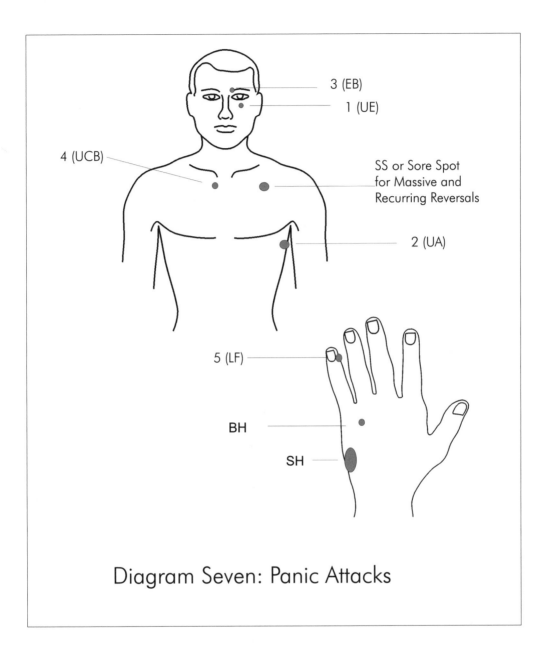

3 (EB)
1 (UE)

4 (UCB)

SS or Sore Spot
for Massive and
Recurring Reversals

2 (UA)

5 (LF)

BH

SH

Diagram Seven: Panic Attacks

Treatment Sequence for Panic Attacks

Meridian		Location
Under Eye (UE)	1	Under the center of the eye on tip of bone
Under Arm (UA)	2	Six inches under armpit
Eyebrow (EB)	3	Beginning of eyebrow near bridge of nose
Under Collarbone (UCB)	4	One inch under collarbone near throat
Little Finger (LF)	5	Inside tip of little fingernail on the side

"I deeply accept myself even though I have this panic problem." It may also be helpful to tap the SH or rub the SS while saying, "I deeply accept myself with all my problems and limitations."

3. Now look at the chart and at diagram 7 to identify the locations for the meridian points for Under Eye (UE), Under Arm (UA) Eyebrow (EB), Under Collarbone (UCB), and Little Finger (LF). While thinking about the panic attack (don't get into it so much that you experience any major discomfort during the process), tap five times at each of these meridian points. Tap them in the following order: 1→2→3→4→5. Tap only hard enough to feel it. The tapping shouldn't cause any pain.

4. Again, rate your distress on a 0 to 10 scale (a number should just pop into your mind). If there is no decrease, go back to step 2 and cycle through the sequence again. If there is not a decrease after three attempts, this is probably not an appropriate sequence for this event, or else there is another sabotaging belief (i.e., reversal) that needs correction. (See step 8.)

5. Next, do the Brain Balancer (BB) by tapping repeatedly at the Back of Hand (BH) while rotating your eyes clockwise, rotating your eyes counterclockwise, then humming a tune, counting to five, and humming again.

6. Repeat the tapping sequence 1→2→3→4→5.

7. Again, rate your level of distress from 0 to 10. It should be lower yet. When the distress is within the 0 to 2 range, go to step 9. Sometimes you'll need to repeat the treatment several times while you are imagining your problem—or even the actual situation—before you feel complete relief from your panic attacks.

8. As long as there is a decrease in the level of distress, continue with the treatment sequence until there are minimal feelings of panic. If the treatment stalls at any point, this indicates a mini-reversal. Treat this by tapping on the little finger Side of Hand (SH) while saying three times, "I deeply accept myself, even though I still have some of this panic problem." Then repeat the treatment sequence.

9. When the distress level is 0 to 2, consider doing the Eye Roll (ER) to lower the distress further or to complete the treatment effects. To do this, tap on the Back of Hand (BH), hold your head straight, and, moving only your eyes, look at the floor and then slowly raise your eyes up toward the ceiling.

If after three attempts, your distress level is not lower, there are two recommendations. First, your panic attacks may be based on a previous traumatic experience. If this is the case, you must use the treatment for trauma in chapter 10 before the treatment sequence for panic will be effective. Second, the alternate cluster of meridian points listed below may be required to effectively treat your panic problem.

Alternative Panic Treatment

Look at diagram 7 to identify the locations for the meridians for the Under Arm (UA), Under Eye (UE) Eyebrow (EB), Under Collarbone (UCB) and Little Finger (LF).

Use the same steps one through nine listed above, but use the alternate sequence order of 2→1→3→4→5.

Treating Yourself in Public Places

In some instances, you may be uncomfortable tapping a sequence when you are in public. Once you have successfully treated yourself using the suggested tapping treatment sequences, you can use the Touch and Breathe (Diepold 1999) technique briefly discussed in chapter 2. Instead of tapping, you can simply touch the meridian points to treat reversals and to eliminate your feelings of fear. When you use this technique, you will be in the situation that actually causes the distress, so there is no need to rate it. Inhale, touch the Side of Hand (SH), exhale, and say to yourself, "I deeply accept myself even though I still have (name your problem.)" Then, inhale and touch under your eye (UE) and exhale, then inhale and touch under your arm (UA) and exhale, and then inhale and touch under your collarbone (UCB) and exhale. Repeat this sequence until there is no more distress. You can use this approach with any of the treatment sequences in this book; remember, however, your problem must initially be treated by using the tapping treatment approach.

Further Reading

There are a number of books that go into great detail about how fears and phobias are created. Although you don't need to understand where your fears come from to successfully treat them, you may be interested in more information. We recommend *Anxiety Disorders and Phobias* by Beck and Emery (1985). Although this book is designed for clinicians, it does provide well-written explanations of the functions and relationships between anxiety and phobias. A more general book is *Feel the Fear and Do It Anyway* by Jeffers (1987).

Summary

There are many fears in our lives that can hold us back. If you still feel embarrassed about any of your past behaviors or beliefs, it's time to treat them and move on with your life. Your fears have never meant that you are any less of a person. Rather, fears indicate that you have had an energy imbalance that prevents you from being at your best in certain situations. Although some people have more fears than others, what is important is that you identity your fears and treat them. The more you grow and develop, the more new fears there will be to hurdle. By learning the treatment sequences in this chapter, however, you now have a new tool that will help you to successfully clear those hurdles.

CHAPTER 8

Overcoming Anger, Rage, Guilt, Shame, Embarrassment, Jealousy, Loneliness, and Rejection

*Anger is a passion that makes people feel alive and that they matter
and are in charge of their lives. So people often feel a need to renew their
anger long after the cause of it has died. It is a protection against the
helplessness . . . and for a while makes them feel less vulnerable.*

—Merle Shain

In this chapter we explore the emotions of anger, rage, guilt, shame, embarrassment, jealousy, loneliness, and rejection, along with treatments for each. In addition, we introduce a unique treatment that can be used with almost any problem. These treatments can be used alone or in combination with resolving other problems you want to eliminate.

All of the treatments in this book are only as effective as your willingness and commitment to apply them consistently to achieve the results you desire. If you read about a particular treatment and then apply it haphazardly, you won't experience much in the way of results. The treatments entirely depend on your *dedication*. If you have a tendency to not be diligent, you ought to suspect that you have a psychological reversal (see chapter 6). As always, it's advisable that you test for and correct psychological reversal before attempting any treatment sequence.

Releasing Anger

It's possible that anger is America's number one emotion. A recent survey found anger to be a significant problem within the work setting (*Wall Street Journal* 1999).When people get together with friends, they often share stories about the situations that upset them that day. These conversations are often a way to find relief by sharing feelings, and they give people a chance to find some humor in the situation. For some people, however, anger is a chronic problem. Situations at work or at home may instantly evoke their feeling of anger. Usually these people see themselves as victims of their life's events, and their anger is a response to their feelings of helplessness. This does not mean that all anger is unjustified; there is no shortage of unfortunate situations that cause legitimate anger, such as people whose behavior is rude or cruel.

The best strategy for interacting with anger is to accept and deal with the situations that caused it. For some people, however, once they are angered, they behave irrationally, leaping into the fight, and often making the situation worse. It is clear that the more time you spend being angry about situations you cannot control or change, the more you reinforce your tendency to use anger (even if this solution never works to your advantage).

Carol and Helen: A Case Study

What follows is a description of how energy treatments helped a family situation that was creating a great deal of anger. Carol was angry with her mother-in-law, Helen, whom she felt was self-centered and who often made cruel remarks about Carol's husband Mark. The real issue was that Mark had a poor sense of self and drank too much, especially to deal with problems. Carol largely blamed Helen for these behaviors. Also, during the years of their marriage, Helen would often exclude Carol and the children from extended family gatherings. Even the mention of Helen immediately made Carol defensive.

Carol's resentment toward Helen was also interfering with her marriage, and possibly preventing Mark from dealing with his alcohol problem. At the very least, it gave him an excuse to go out drinking, because they would have frequent arguments about his mother.

The solution was not to be found in simply discussing the reasons why Carol ought to overcome her anger. Any attempts to talk along these lines were met with a tremendous amount of resistance, as would be expected. Therefore, it was suggested to Carol that energy treatments might at least help to take the edge off the emotional upset she felt toward Helen. This way, if Carol absolutely had to be around Helen for some unforeseen reason, she would be better able to cope. Carol agreed.

After taking Carol through a rather extended energy treatment for this problem—about twenty minutes—her response to thoughts about Helen changed rather dramatically. The change occurred in layers: Initially she felt anger and resentment; after a few rounds of the anger-releasing treatment, she felt a reduced degree of irritation; next, Carol's irritation dissolved into feelings of sorrow; and finally, she felt a sense of relief. After the energy treatment was completed, Carol said, "I guess Helen just can't help herself. I wonder if she's struggled with this problem, too." From then on, Carol found it much more comfortable to be around Helen. In time, their relationship even improved and Carol and Mark were regularly invited to family events. Carol also learned how to apply energy treatment to her relationship issues with Mark, and their relationship improved as well.

Forgiveness

Many people who have experienced trauma and other negative events understandably harbor anger about the incidents and those who caused them. Once a person has been violated, every conscious and even unconscious review of the event causes emotional upset. Anger is one of the principal emotions here, and it is associated with blaming as well as the inability to forgive the circumstances, the other people involved, and even oneself.

It is normal to object to the idea of forgiving someone who has wronged you. In fact, you may feel that your forgiveness would be equivalent to saying that what the person did was okay. However, this is not what forgiveness is about. When you forgive someone, you still recognize that what the other person did was wrong—otherwise, forgiveness would make little sense. When you forgive, you are not condoning the other person's behavior. The behavior is obviously wrong. For example, you would not condone the behavior of a burglar, a rapist, or someone who severely mistreated you. It might be possible, however, to achieve another level of understanding and to forgive the person. When we forgive, there is a clear distinction between the person and the deed.

Still, some of you will strongly object to forgiveness. You may ask, for instance, how do you forgive someone for violating you or committing an atrocity? Or, how do you let go of the anger when anger seems to be so warranted? The idea of forgiving under such circumstances may cause you to shudder. There is another way to think about forgiveness, however.

Comedian Buddy Hackett said that he couldn't understand being angry at someone because, "While you're angry at them, they're out dancing." Guess who gets to suffer? Certainly not the person who did you wrong. Rather, you are the one who is stuck with the emotional consequences of remaining angry. And, as we all know, feeling angry isn't a pleasant or beneficial situation.

Emotions such as anger deprive you of your emotional, psychological, and physical well-being. There is even evidence that chronic anger can lead to cardiovascular problems, such as heart attacks and stroke (Johnson 1990). Therefore, for all intents and purposes, it is best to alleviate your anger. One way to accomplish this is through the acts of releasing and letting go; forgiveness can be a part of this.

Treatment for Anger

The following treatment sequence has been found to be highly effective in diminishing or even eliminating the feeling of anger. This treatment addresses the principal meridian involved in anger and forgiveness. When you are in a state of anger, this meridian is often out of balance. When you experience forgiveness, the imbalance in this meridian is removed. In addition, balancing this meridian makes way for forgiveness.

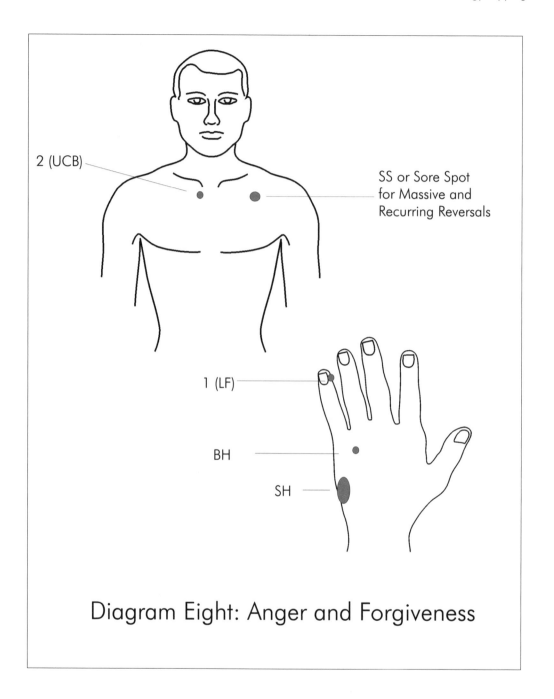

Diagram Eight: Anger and Forgiveness

Treatment Sequence for Anger

Meridian		Location
Little finger (LF)	1	Inside tip of little fingernail on the side
Under Collarbone (UCB)	2	One inch under collarbone near throat

1. Think about the person (it might be yourself) or a situation that angers you. It should be a single, specific person or event. Rate your level of anger from 0 to 10, with 10 representing the highest level of distress and 0 indicating no stress.

2. Treat for the possibility of reversal by tapping repeatedly on the Side of Hand (SH) or rubbing the Sore Spot (SS) while thinking or saying three times, "I deeply accept myself even though I'm angry at/about (person's name or event)." It also may be helpful to tap the SH or rub the SS while saying, "I accept myself with all my problems and limitations."

3. Look at the chart below and at diagram 8 to identify the locations for the meridian points for Little Finger (LF) and Under Collarbone (UCB). While thinking about the anger item (don't get into it so much that you experience any major discomfort during the process), tap repeatedly on LF while saying the following statement three times, "I release myself of this anger." (Alternative statements, depending on your preference, include the following: "I forgive (name the person, place, or circumstance), I know he/she/it couldn't help it." Or, "There is forgiveness in my heart." If you are angry at yourself, consider the following alternative statement, "I forgive myself, I'm doing the best that I can.") Next, tap on the UCB point five times. Tap the meridian points in the following order 1→2. Only tap hard enough to feel it. The tapping shouldn't cause any pain.

4. Again rate your anger on a 0 to 10 scale (a number should just pop into your mind). If there is no decrease, go back to step 2 and cycle through the sequence again. If there is not a decrease after three attempts, this is probably not an appropriate sequence for this event, or else there is another sabotaging belief (i.e., reversal) that needs correction. (See step 8.) Also consider the treatment for rage, which follows.

5. Next, do the Brain Balancer (BB) by tapping repeatedly at the Back of Hand (BH) while rotating your eyes clockwise, rotating your eyes counterclockwise, then humming a tune, counting to five, and humming again.

6. Repeat the tapping sequence 1→2.

7. Again, rate your level of distress from 0 to 10. It should be lower yet. When the distress is within the 0 to 2 range, go to step 9. Sometimes you'll need to repeat the treatment several times while you are imagining your anger—or even while you are in the actual situation—before you feel complete relief from the distressing situation.

8. As long as there is a decrease in the level of anger, continue with the sequence until there is very little or no anger remaining. If the treatment stalls at any point, this indicates a mini-reversal. Treat this by tapping on the little finger Side of Hand (SH) while saying three times, "I deeply accept myself, even though I still have some of this problem."

9. When the distress level is 0 to 2, consider doing the Eye Roll (ER) to lower the distress further or to complete the treatment effects. To do this, tap on the Back of Hand (BH), hold your head straight, and, moving only your eyes, look at the floor and then slowly raise your eyes up toward the ceiling.

If the anger should return at a later time, repeat these treatments. In time, anger about this issue will become less and less frequent.

Putting Out the Rage Fire

Rage is an even more intense emotional reaction than anger. Often, a different meridian is involved in rage as compared to anger, and this meridian can be balanced by tapping on the Side of the Eye (SE) (see diagram 9). Some people who have experienced a traumatic event experience chronic rage about the event itself and toward the people who were involved in it. If an event is involved, it is important to use the most complex trauma treatment for healing (see chapter 10) and then to specifically focus on and treat the rage with the following rage treatment sequence.

Rage can occur in many situations, but the most commonly discussed one is road rage. In this situation, people act as if they own the road and as if the other people driving on it are disobeying their driving rules. The reality is that most drivers are only vaguely aware of other drivers on the road. Drivers cut each other off or drive too slowly without even realizing it. Often what happens is that the person who is in a rage has a set of expectations about driving, and when those expectations are not met, that person blames the other driver. It's true that some people drive too slowly or are confused about where they are going, and they do slow other drivers down. However, there are also drivers who become impatient and honk if someone hesitates for a fraction of a second once the light turns green. It goes both ways, but the real issue is that road rage is about taking what other drivers do as a personal affront. It's not personal and, unfortunately, it has gotten out of hand and become dangerous. People have actually shot at other drivers. One man was convicted of murder after he became enraged over a minor incident and hit another driver with a tire iron.

In addition to treating rage with the treatment sequence that follows, imagery and visualization are also helpful. The next time you start to feel a sense of rage, for example, imagine that the person causing your emotional upset is someone you care about, such as your mother or a friend. This may help to break up your rage trigger.

For many people, road rage and other forms of rage are a habit. Once you are in certain situations, it triggers the rage response. If you consistently and with dedication use the rage treatment, you can break up this problem and eliminate it. As mentioned earlier, the operative word here is *dedication*. The treatment for rage, like many other treatments, can be used both to prevent situations that typically would trigger rage and to curtail a state of rage.

Treatment for Rage

1. Think about the person or situation that enrages you. It should be a single, specific person or event. Rate your level of rage between 0 to 10, with 10 representing the highest level of distress and 0 indicating no stress.

2. Treat for the possibility of reversal by tapping repeatedly on the Side of Hand (SH) or rubbing on the Sore Spot (SS) while thinking or saying three times, "I deeply accept myself even though I'm enraged at/about (person's name, event)." It also may be helpful to tap the SH or rub the SS while saying, "I accept myself with all my problems and limitations."

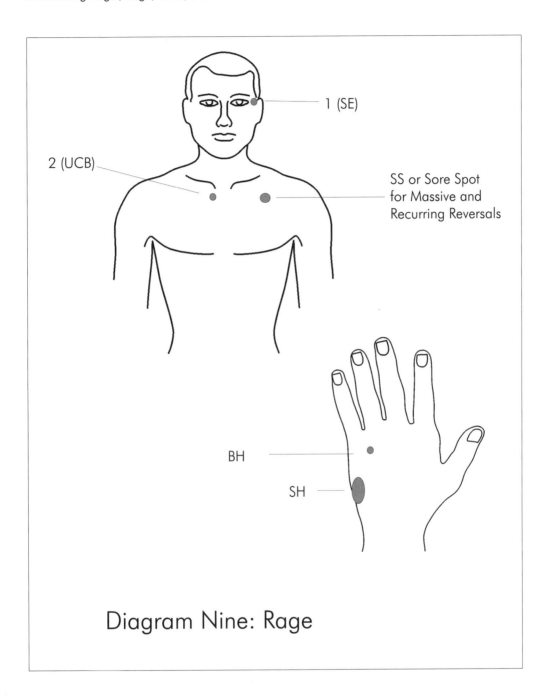

1 (SE)

2 (UCB)

SS or Sore Spot
for Massive and
Recurring Reversals

BH

SH

Diagram Nine: Rage

Treatment Sequence for Rage

Meridian		Location
Side of Eye (SE)	1	Side of eye on the bony orbit near temple
Under Collarbone (UCB)	2	One inch under collarbone near throat

3. Look at the chart and at diagram 9 to identify the locations for the meridian points for Side of Eye (SE) and Under Collarbone (UCB). While thinking about the rage item (don't get into it so much that you experience any major discomfort during the process), tap repeatedly on SE while saying the following statement three times, "I release myself of this rage." Then tap on the UCB point five times (see chart below). Tap the meridian points in the following order: 1→2. Tap only hard enough to feel it. The tapping shouldn't cause any pain.

4. Again, rate your rage on a 0 to 10 scale (a number should just pop into your mind). If there is no decrease, go back to step 2 and cycle through the sequence again. If there is not a decrease after three attempts, this is probably not an appropriate sequence for this event, or else there is another sabotaging belief (i.e., reversal) that needs correction. (See step 8.)

5. Next, do the Brain Balancer (BB) by tapping repeatedly at the Back of Hand (BH) while rotating your eyes clockwise, rotating your eyes counterclockwise, then humming a tune, counting to five, and humming again.

6. Repeat the tapping sequence 1→2.

7. Again, rate your level of distress from 0 to 10. It should be lower yet. When the distress is within the 0 to 2 range, go to step 9. Sometimes you'll need to repeat the treatment several times while you are thinking about your rage—or even while you are in the actual situation—before you feel complete relief from the distressing situation.

8. As long as there is a decrease in the level of rage, continue with the sequence until there is very little or no rage remaining. If the treatment stalls at any point, this indicates a mini-reversal. Treat this by tapping on the little finger Side of Hand (SH) while saying three times, "I deeply accept myself, even though I still have some of this problem."

9. When the distress level is 0 to 2, do the Eye Roll (ER) to lower the distress further or to complete the treatment effects. To do this, tap on the Back of Hand (BH), hold your head straight, and, moving only your eyes, look at the floor and then slowly raise your eyes up toward the ceiling.

If rage should return at a later time, repeat these treatments. In time, rage about this issue will become less and less frequent.

Overcoming Guilt

When our guilt system is operating properly, we feel guilt only for violating a closely held value or moral. When we have done something wrong the congruent feeling is that of guilt, which tells us to pay attention and change our behavior for the better. Often, however, guilt is not as simple as this. Sometimes, for instance, guilt is not triggered when it should be, and sometimes it is triggered when it is no longer necessary or for reasons that do not warrant guilt feelings. There is also evidence that certain medications, such as some blood pressure medications, can cause a feeling of guilt or even, more deeply, shame, when we're really very innocent. Therefore, if the treatments we suggest here do not alleviate your feelings of guilt, and you are taking prescription medications, you may want to consult your health care professional.

Although the treatment that follows is frequently effective in alleviating guilt feelings, the treatment will not make you immune to feelings of guilt altogether. Some people never feel guilt and, hence, take advantage of others. Many people with this condition are clinically referred to as antisocial personalities, sociopaths, or psychopaths. Many of these people end up in prison because they do not have much of a conscience; they violate laws and the rights of others without any sense of remorse. Our intention is not to produce such tendencies in our readers. Values and morals are direly important, and societies need to reinforce appropriate values in their citizens. To suffer chronic guilt, however, is an entirely different matter and serves no useful purpose. Once a lesson is learned, ongoing guilt feelings only get in the way of healthy psychological functioning.

Treatment for Guilt

1. Think about the person or situation about which you feel guilty. It should be a single, specific person or event. Rate your level of guilt on a scale of 0 to 10, with 10 representing the highest level of distress and 0 indicating no stress.

2. Treat for the possibility of reversal by tapping repeatedly on the Side of Hand (SH) or rubbing the Sore Spot (SS) while thinking or saying three times, "I deeply accept myself even though I feel guilty about (person's name, event)." It also may be helpful to tap the SH or rub the SS while saying, "I accept myself with all my problems and limitations."

3. Look at the chart and at diagram 10 to identify the locations for the meridian points for Index Finger (IF) and Under Collarbone (UCB). While thinking about the guilt item (don't get into it so much that you experience any major discomfort during the process), tap repeatedly on IF while saying the following statement three times: "I release myself of this guilt." (Alternative statements, depending on your preference, include the following: "I forgive myself, because I didn't do anything wrong." Or, "There is forgiveness in my heart." Or, "I forgive myself. I'm doing the best that I can.") Next, tap on the UCB point five times. Tap the meridian points in the following order 1→2. Only tap hard enough to feel it. The tapping shouldn't cause any pain.

4. Again, rate your guilt on a 0 to 10 scale (a number should just pop into your mind). If there is no decrease, go back to step 2 and cycle through the sequence again. If there is not a decrease after three attempts, this is probably not an appropriate sequence for this event, or else there is another sabotaging belief (i.e., reversal) that needs correction. (See step 8.)

5. Next, do the Brain Balancer (BB) by tapping repeatedly at the Back of Hand (BH) point while rotating your eyes clockwise, rotating your eyes counterclockwise, then humming a tune, counting to five, and humming again.

6. Repeat the tapping sequence 1→2.

7. Again, rate your level of distress from 0 to 10. It should be lower yet. When the distress is within the 0 to 2 range, go to step 9. Sometimes you'll need to

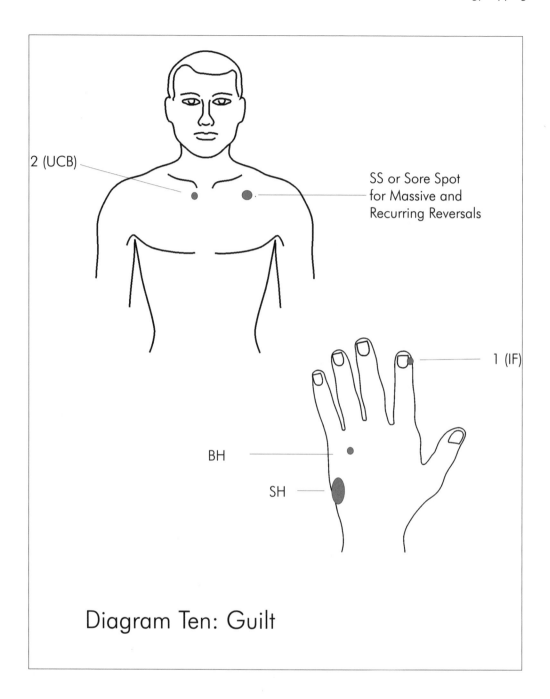

Diagram Ten: Guilt

Treatment Sequence for Guilt

Meridian		Location
Index Finger (IF)	1	Inside tip of index fingernail on the side
Under Collarbone (UCB)	2	One inch under collarbone near throat

repeat the treatment several times while you are thinking about your guilt—or even while you are in the actual situation—before you feel complete relief from the distressing situation.

8. As long as there is a decrease in the level of guilt, continue with the sequence until there is very little or no guilt remaining. If the treatment stalls at any point, this indicates a mini-reversal. Treat this by tapping on the little finger Side of Hand (SH) while saying three times, "I deeply accept myself, even though I still have some of this problem."

9. When the distress level is 0 to 2, do the Eye Roll (ER) to lower the distress further or to complete the treatment effects. To do this, tap on the Back of Hand (BH), hold your head straight, and, moving only your eyes, look at the floor and then slowly raise your eyes up toward the ceiling.

If guilt should return at a later time, repeat these treatments. In time, guilt about this issue will become less and less frequent.

From Jealousy to Security

Jealousy seems to be a combination of fear, hurt, insecurity, and anger, and sometimes can elevate to the level of rage. When you are jealous, you feel that someone is intruding on what is rightfully yours. Sustained jealousy is often associated with a trauma. In such instances, the trauma should be targeted and treated with the most complex trauma treatment in chapter 10. After the complex treatment, residual jealousy can be treated with the following therapeutic treatment sequence.

Treatment for Jealousy

1. Think about the person or situation about which you feel jealous. It should be a single, specific person or event. Rate your level of jealousy on a scale of 0 to 10, with 10 representing the highest level of distress and 0 indicating no stress.

2. Treat for the possibility of reversal by tapping repeatedly on the Side of Hand (SH) or rubbing the Sore Spot (SS) while thinking or saying three times, "I deeply accept myself even though I feel jealous about (name the person or event)." It also may be helpful to tap the SH or rub the SS while saying, "I accept myself with all my problems and limitations."

3. Look at the chart and at diagram 11 to identify the locations for the meridian points for Middle Finger (MF), Under Arm (UA), and Under Collarbone (UCB). While thinking about your jealousy (don't get into it so much that you experience any major discomfort during the process), tap repeatedly on the MF while saying the following statement three times: "I release myself of this jealousy." Then tap on the UA and UCB five times. Tap them in the following order: 1→2→3. Tap only hard enough to feel it. The tapping shouldn't cause any pain.

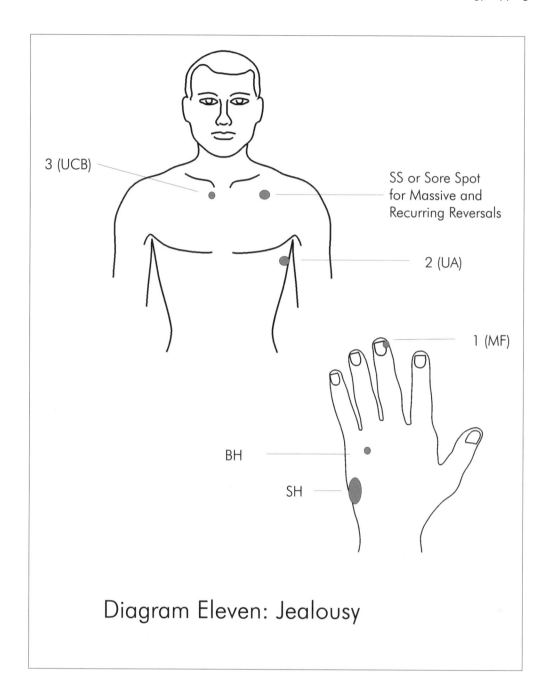

Diagram Eleven: Jealousy

Treatment Sequence for Jealousy

Meridian		Location
Middle Finger (MF)	1	Inside tip of middle fingernail on the side
Under Arm (UA)	2	Six inches under armpit
Under Collarbone (UCB)	3	One inch under collarbone near throat

4. Again, rate your jealousy on a 0 to 10 scale (a number should just pop into your mind). If there is no decrease, go back to step 2 and cycle through the sequence again. If there is not a decrease after three attempts, this is probably not an appropriate sequence for this event, or else there is another sabotaging belief (i.e., reversal) that needs correction. (See step 8.)

5. Next, do the Brain Balancer (BB) by tapping repeatedly at the Back of Hand (BH) while rotating your eyes clockwise, rotating your eyes counterclockwise, then humming a tune, counting to five, and humming again.

6. Repeat the tapping sequence 1→2→3.

7. Again, rate your level of distress from 0 to 10. It should be lower yet. When the distress is within the 0 to 2 range, go to step 9. Sometimes you'll need to repeat the treatment several times while you are thinking about your jealousy—or even while you are in the actual situation—before you feel complete relief from the distressing situation.

8. As long as there is a decrease in the level of jealousy, continue with the sequence until there is very little or no jealousy remaining. If the treatment stalls at any point, this indicates a mini-reversal. Treat this by tapping on the little finger Side of Hand (SH) while saying three times, "I deeply accept myself, even though I still have some of this problem."

9. When the distress level is 0 to 2, do the Eye Roll (ER) to lower the distress further or to complete the treatment effects. To do this, tap on the Back of Hand (BH), hold your head straight, and, moving only your eyes, look at the floor and then slowly raise your eyes up toward the ceiling.

If jealousy should return at a later time, repeat these treatments. In time, jealousy about this issue will become less and less frequent.

Why Be Embarrassed?

Mark Twain said, "Man is the only animal that blushes. Or needs to." You tend to feel embarrassed when you are "caught in the act" of doing something that you would rather others didn't know you were doing. That is, when you are embarrassed, others have seen you make a mistake, or they've gotten a glimpse of something about you that you would rather keep private. While Mark Twain's wit and wisdom are profound, we believe that most instances of embarrassment are based on "greatly exaggerated" thoughts about your normal human frailties. But even if embarrassment is warranted, why blush about something that has already occurred? It's over and done with. You might as well learn a needed lesson from your embarrassment and then tap the unwanted emotion away. The following treatment sequence eliminates embarrassment.

Treatment for Embarrassment

1. Think about the person or situation about which you feel embarrassed. It should be a single, specific person or event. Rate your level of embarrassment

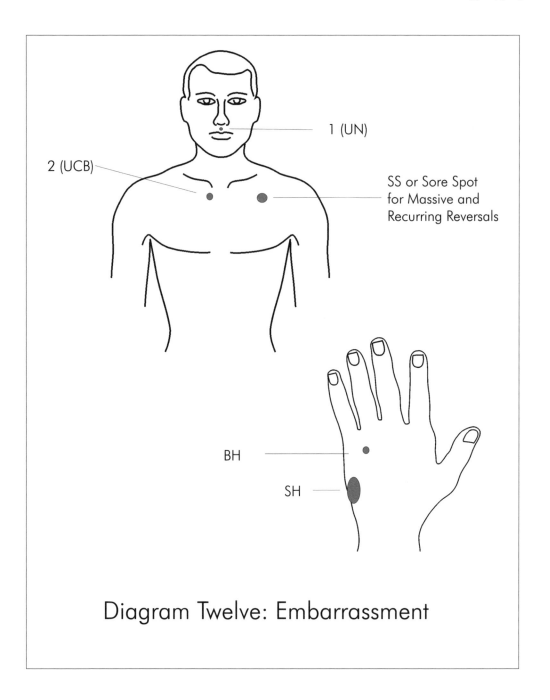

1 (UN)

2 (UCB)

SS or Sore Spot
for Massive and
Recurring Reversals

BH

SH

Diagram Twelve: Embarrassment

Treatment Sequence for Embarrassment

Meridian		Location
Under Nose (UN)	1	Above upper lip and below the center of nose
Under Collarbone (UCB)	2	One inch under collarbone near throat

on a scale of 0 to 10, with 10 representing the highest level of distress and 0 indicating no stress.

2. Treat for the possibility of reversal by tapping repeatedly on the Side of Hand (SH) or rubbing the Sore Spot (SS) while thinking or saying three times, "I deeply accept myself even though I feel embarrassed." It also may be helpful to tap the SH or rub the SS while saying, "I accept myself with all my problems and limitations."

3. Look at the chart and at diagram 12 to identify the locations for the meridian points for Under Nose (UN) and Under Collarbone (UCB). While thinking about your embarrassment (don't get into it so much that you experience any major discomfort during the process), tap five times on each of these meridian points. Tap them in the following order 1→2. Tap only hard enough to feel it. The tapping shouldn't cause any pain.

4. Again, rate your embarrassment on a 0 to 10 scale (a number should just pop into your mind). If there is no decrease, go back to step 2 and cycle through the sequence again. If there is not a decrease after three attempts, this is probably not an appropriate sequence for this event, or else there is another sabotaging belief (i.e., reversal) that needs correction. (See step 8.)

5. Next, do the Brain Balancer (BB) by tapping repeatedly at the Back of Hand (BH) point while rotating your eyes clockwise, rotating your eyes counterclockwise, then humming a tune, counting to five, and humming again.

6. Repeat the tapping sequence 1→2.

7. Again, rate your level of distress from 0 to 10. It should be lower yet. When the distress is within the 0 to 2 range, go to step 9. Sometimes you'll need to repeat the treatment several times while you are thinking about your embarrassment—or even while you are in the actual situation—before you feel complete relief from the distressful situation.

8. As long as there is a decrease in the level of embarrassment, continue with the sequence until there is very little or no embarrassment remaining. If the treatment stalls at any point, this indicates a mini-reversal. Treat this by tapping on the little finger Side of Hand (SH) while saying three times, "I deeply accept myself, even though I still have some of this problem."

9. When the distress level is 0 to 2, do the Eye Roll (ER) to lower the distress further or to complete the treatment effects. To do this, tap on the Back of Hand (BH), hold your head straight, and, moving only your eyes, look at the floor and then slowly raise your eyes up toward the ceiling.

If embarrassment should return at a later time, repeat these treatments. In time embarrassment about this issue will become less and less frequent.

Overcoming Shame

Shame is different from embarrassment or guilt. With guilt, you feel that you've *done* something wrong; when you experience shame, you feel that there is something essentially wrong about *you*, that is, something is wrong at the core of your being. This emotional state is also more profound than embarrassment. Many deep-seated psychological problems involve the sharp edge of shame.

When you experience profound shame, it is difficult—if not impossible—to look others in the eyes. The inclination is to hide, to avoid socializing. Experiencing feelings of shame can also be a side effect of certain medications, such as some that are used to regulate blood pressure. If you suspect that this may be the case, please check with your health care provider. Most shame, however, is rooted in experiences from your childhood. Somehow, you learned to be ashamed of yourself. Perhaps it is necessary to reach back into those formative experiences and eliminate the traumas. Additionally, you can use the following therapeutic treatment sequences to dissipate feelings of shame.

Treatment for Shame

1. Think about your feelings of shame. Rate your level of shame on a scale of 0 to 10, with 10 representing the highest level of distress and 0 indicating no stress.

2. Treat for the possibility of reversal by tapping repeatedly on the Side of Hand (SH) or rubbing the Sore Spot while thinking or saying three times, "I deeply accept myself even though I feel shame." It also may be helpful to tap the SH or rub the SS while saying, "I accept myself with all my problems and limitations."

3. Look at the chart and at diagram 13 to identify the locations for the meridian points for Under Bottom Lip (UBL) and Under Collarbone (UCB). While thinking about your shame (don't get into it so much that you experience any major discomfort during the process), tap five times on each of these meridian points. Tap them in the following order 1→2. Tap only hard enough to feel it. The tapping shouldn't cause any pain.

4. Again, rate your shame on a 0 to 10 scale (a number should just pop into your mind). If there is no decrease, go back to step 2 and cycle through the sequence again. If there is not a decrease after three attempts, this is probably not an appropriate sequence for this event, or else there is another sabotaging belief (i.e., reversal) that needs correction. (See step 8.)

5. Next, do the Brain Balancer (BB) by tapping repeatedly at the Back of Hand (BH) while rotating your eyes clockwise, rotating your eyes counterclockwise, then humming a tune, counting to five, and humming again.

6. Repeat the tapping sequence 1→2.

7. Again, rate your level of distress from 0 to 10. It should be lower yet. When the distress is within the 0 to 2 range, go to step 9. Sometimes you'll need to repeat the treatment several times while you are thinking about your shame—or even while you are in the actual situation—before you feel complete relief from the distressful situation.

8. As long as there is a decrease in the level of shame, continue with the sequence until there is little or no shame remaining. If the treatment stalls at

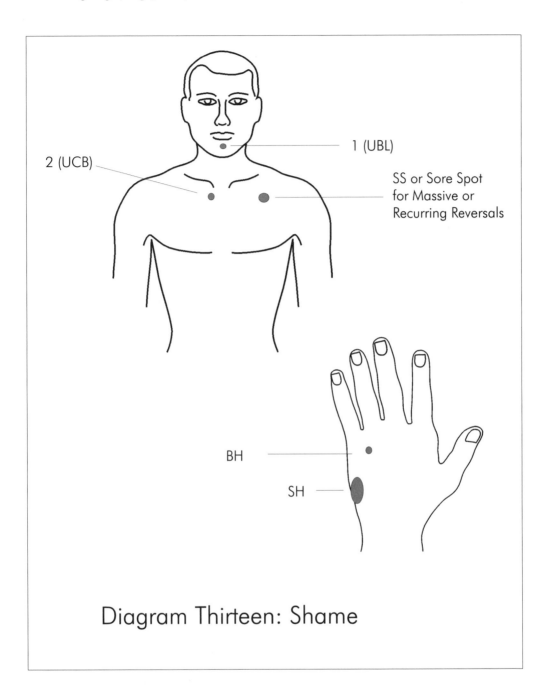

Diagram Thirteen: Shame

Treatment Sequence for Shame

Meridian		Location
Under Bottom Lip (UBL)	1	Under bottom lip in chin cleft
Under Collarbone (UCB)	2	One inch under collarbone near throat

any point, this indicates a mini-reversal. Treat this by tapping on the little finger Side of Hand (SH) while saying three times, "I deeply accept myself, even though I still have some of this problem."

9. When the distress level is 0 to 2, do the Eye Roll (ER) to lower the distress further or to complete the treatment effects. To do this, tap on the Back of Hand (BH), hold your head straight, and, moving only your eyes, look at the floor and then slowly raise your eyes up toward the ceiling.

If shame should return at a later time, repeat these treatments. In time, shame about this issue will become less and less frequent.

Loneliness

There is little doubt that human contact is an essential part of happiness. A recent national survey found that 36 percent of all Americans reported recent feelings of loneliness (Olds, Schwartz, and Webster 1996). Loneliness has two forms: emotional loneliness, in which you lack intimate contact, and social loneliness, in which you lack friends to share activities in your life. To clearly affect your loneliness, you must understand how your beliefs or actions create it in your life. This is not about blaming you or anyone else. Rather, it is about understanding what you have to do differently to change your life.

The mobile society in which we currently live often forces people away from their families and, in part, forces them to recreate a sense of community to ward off feeling lonely. For those who experience a chronic pattern of loneliness, however, there probably are multiple issues present, such as feelings of depression, shame, and rejection. Each of these must be treated before your pattern of loneliness can be broken. You should also look at how you escape from loneliness. For example, do you use drugs, watch an excessive amount of television, or even read too much?

If you become aware of your escape mechanisms, which are part of the way you sabotage yourself, then you can treat them as well. These escape mechanisms are another form of psychological reversals. Loneliness is not always a response to being alone. Some people feel habitually lonely in the company of others, whereas other people feel quite comfortable being alone.

Treatment Sequence for Loneliness

1. Think about your feelings of loneliness. Rate your level of loneliness on a scale of 0 to 10, with 10 representing the highest level of distress and 0 indicating no stress.

2. Treat for the possibility of reversal by tapping repeatedly on the Side of Hand (SH) or rubbing the Sore Spot (SS) while thinking or saying three times, "I deeply accept myself even though I'm lonely." It also may be helpful to tap the SH or rub the SS while saying, "I accept myself with all my problems and limitations."

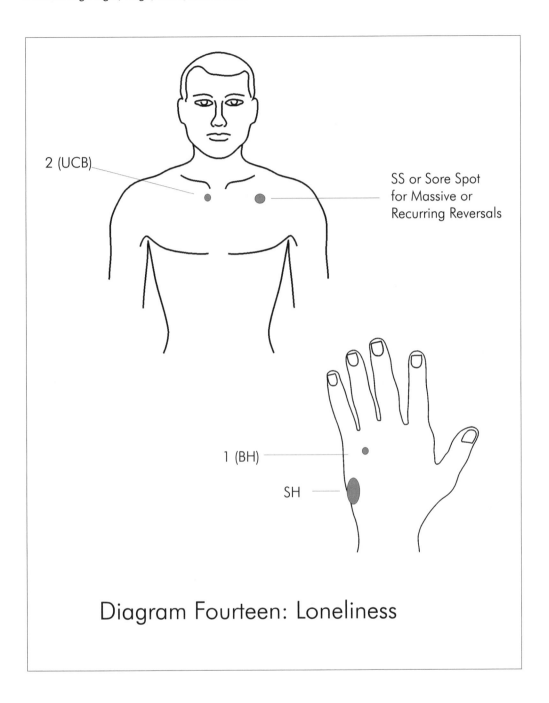

2 (UCB)

SS or Sore Spot
for Massive or
Recurring Reversals

1 (BH)

SH

Diagram Fourteen: Loneliness

Treatment Sequence for Loneliness

Meridian		Location
Back of Hand (BH)	1	Back of hand between little and ring fingers
Under Collarbone (UCB)	2	One inch under collarbone near throat

3. Look at the chart and at diagram 14 to identify the locations for the meridian points for Back of Hand (BH) and Under Collarbone (UCB). While thinking about your loneliness (don't get into it so much that you experience any major discomfort during the process), tap on the BH twenty to fifty times and then tap on the UCB five times. Tap them in the following order 1→2. Tap only hard enough to feel it. The tapping shouldn't cause any pain.

4. Again, rate your loneliness on a 0 to 10 scale (a number should just pop into your mind). If there is no decrease, go back to step 2 and cycle through the sequence again. If there is not a decrease after three attempts, this probably is not an appropriate sequence for this event, or else there is another sabotaging belief (i.e., reversal) that needs correction. (See step 8.)

5. Next, do the Brain Balancer (BB) by tapping repeatedly at the Back of Hand (BH) while rotating your eyes clockwise, rotating your eyes counterclockwise, then humming a tune, counting to five, and humming again.

6. Repeat the tapping sequence 1→2.

7. Again, rate your level of distress from 0 to 10. It should be lower yet. When the distress is within the 0 to 2 range, go to step 9. Sometimes you'll need to repeat the treatment several times while you are thinking about your loneliness—or even while you are in the actual situation—before you feel complete relief from the distressful situation.

8. As long as there is a decrease in the level of loneliness, continue with the sequence until there is very little or no loneliness remaining. If the treatment stalls at any point, this indicates a mini-reversal. Treat this by tapping on the little finger Side of Hand (SH) while saying three times, "I deeply accept myself, even though I still have some of this problem."

9. When the distress level is 0 to 2, do the Eye Roll (ER) to lower the distress further or to complete the treatment effects. To do this, tap on the Back of Hand (BH), hold your head straight, and, moving only your eyes, look at the floor and then slowly raise your eyes up toward the ceiling.

If the feelings of loneliness should return at a later time, repeat these treatments. In time, recurrence of loneliness symptoms will become less and less frequent.

Once you have treated the reversals surrounding your loneliness and their accompanying feelings and behaviors, it is time to make some changes in your life. That is, it's time to replace the behaviors you use to escape loneliness with healthy, more productive ones. If you like to read, for example, attend author events at your local bookstore and spend a few hours there. In time, you will begin to recognize other customers. Because you already have a common interest in reading, it will be easier to start a conversation. Another option is to take a class that teaches a topic in which you are interested. There are numerous classes available on almost every subject. The goal is to get out there and meet people who have similar interests as you. Once you do, you will expand your social life—and reduce your feelings of loneliness considerably.

Rejection

There is little doubt that rejection is one of the hardest feelings to accept, even though it happens to everyone. You can feel rejected when you are trying to sell a product for your business or an idea to your boss. Feelings of rejection can also surface when you ask someone out for a date or when you are not asked out for dates. Regardless of when the feeling arises, no one likes being rejected; it feels like you just got slapped and it hurts. The treatment sequence that follows will help you soothe feelings of rejection. If rejection is a pattern in your life, however, other issues are at hand and you need to figure out what you are doing to help create it.

Treatment for Rejection

1. Think about the situation for which you are feeling rejected. It should be a single, specific person or event. Rate your level of rejection on a scale of 0 to 10, with 10 representing the highest level of distress and 0 indicating no stress.

2. Treat for the possibility of reversal by tapping repeatedly on the Side of Hand (SH) or rubbing the Sore Spot (SS) while thinking or saying three times, "I deeply accept myself even though I feel rejected." It also may be helpful to tap the SH or rub the SS while saying, "I accept myself with all my problems and limitations."

3. Look at the chart and at diagram 15 to identify the locations for the meridian points for Eyebrow (EB), Under Eye (UE), Under Arm (UA) and Under Collarbone (UCB). While thinking about the rejection (don't get into it so much that you experience any major discomfort during the process), tap five times at each of these meridian points. Tap them in the following order: 1→2→3→4. Tap only hard enough to feel it. The tapping shouldn't cause any pain.

4. Again, rate your rejection on a 0 to 10 scale (a number should just pop into your mind). If there is no decrease, go back to step 2 and cycle through the sequence again. If there is not a decrease after three attempts, this probably is not an appropriate sequence for this event, or else there is another sabotaging belief (i.e., reversal) that needs correction. (See step 8.)

5. Next, do the Brain Balancer (BB) by tapping repeatedly at the Back of Hand (BH) while rotating your eyes clockwise, rotating your eyes counterclockwise, then humming a tune, counting to five, and humming again.

6. Repeat the tapping sequence 1→2→3→4.

7. Again, rate your level of distress from 0 to 10. It should be lower yet. When the distress is within the 0 to 2 range, go to step 9. Sometimes you'll need to repeat the treatment several times while you are thinking about your rejection—or even while you are in the actual situation—before you feel complete relief from the distressful situation.

8. As long as there is a decrease in the level of rejection, continue with the sequence until there are very little or no feelings of rejection remaining. If the

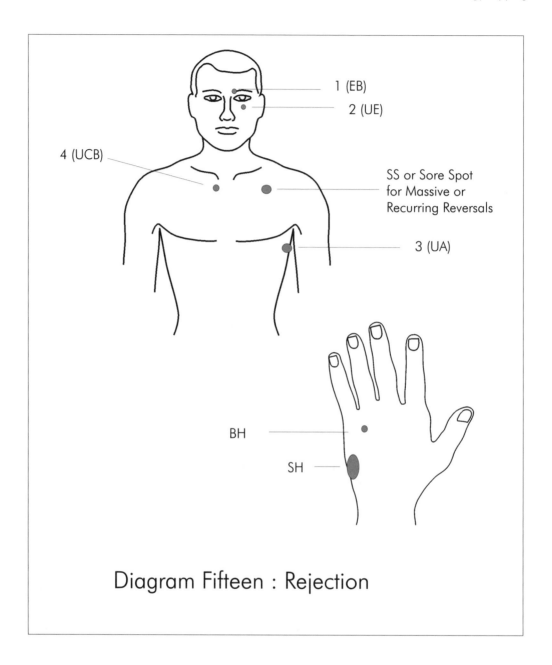

Diagram Fifteen : Rejection

Treatment Sequence for Rejection

Meridian		Location
Eyebrow (EB)	1	Beginning of eyebrow near bridge of nose
Under Eye (UE)	2	Under the center of eye on the tip of bone
Under Arm (UA)	3	Six inches under armpit
Under Collarbone (UCB)	4	One inch under collarbone near throat

treatment stalls at any point, this indicates a mini-reversal. Treat this by tapping on the little finger Side of Hand (SH) while saying three times, "I deeply accept myself, even though I still have some of this problem."

9. When the distress level is between 0 to 2, do the Eye Roll (ER) to lower the distress further or to complete the treatment effects. To do this, tap on the Back of Hand (BH), hold your head straight, and, moving only your eyes, look at the floor and then slowly raise your eyes up toward the ceiling.

If your feelings of rejection should return at a later time, repeat these treatments. In time, recurrence of rejection symptoms will become less and less frequent.

Once you have treated your feelings of rejection and any other related problems, you are ready to develop your new strategies. This may mean acquiring more knowledge or new tactics. The question you are always trying to answer is "Am I doing anything to sabotage myself and create this problem?" Once you treat any related reversals concerning rejection, you should be able to see new alternatives to your old approach.

Erasing Those Negative Feelings

The treatment sequences in this chapter are effective, but there is another treatment sequence that, in many cases, quickly erases negative feelings. This treatment is referred to as the Midline Energy Treatment (MET). The basic approach is similar to prior sequences with which you are already familiar.

Midline Energy Treatment (MET)

1. Think about the problem you want to treat. It should be a single, specific problem (e.g., behavior, emotion, limiting belief, etc.). Rate your level of distress on a scale of 0 to 10, with 10 representing the highest level of distress and 0 indicating no stress.

2. Treat for the possibility of reversal by tapping repeatedly on the Side of Hand (SH) or rubbing the Sore Spot (SS) while thinking or saying three times, "I deeply accept myself even though I have this problem." (Be specific.) It also may be helpful to tap the SH or rub the SS while saying, "I accept myself with all my problems and limitations."

3. Look at the chart and at diagram 16 to identify the locations for the meridian points for Forehead (F), Under Nose (UN), Under Bottom Lip (UBL), and Chest (CH). While thinking about the problem (don't get into it so much that you experience any major discomfort during the process), tap ten times at each of these meridian points. Tap them in the following order 1→2→3→4. Tap only hard enough to feel it. The tapping shouldn't cause any pain.

4. Again, rate your problem on a 0 to 10 scale (a number should just pop into your mind). If there is no decrease, go back to step 2 and cycle through the sequence again. If there is not a decrease after three attempts, this is probably not an appropriate sequence for this problem, or else there is another sabotaging belief (i.e., reversal) that needs correction. (See step 8.)

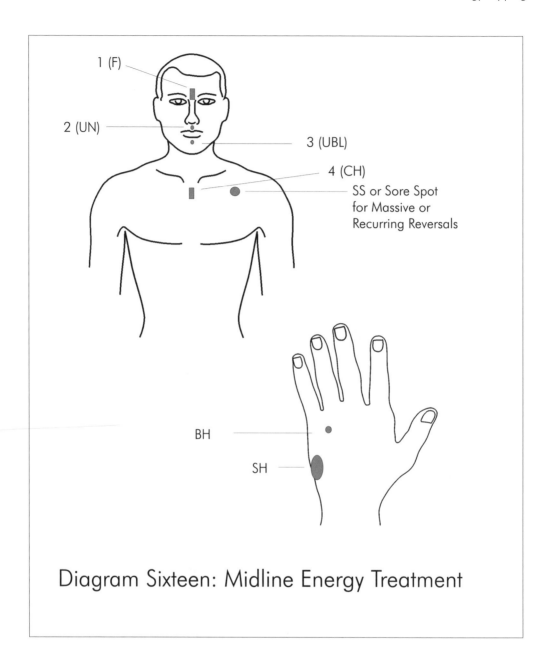

Diagram Sixteen: Midline Energy Treatment

Midline Energy Treatment (MET) Sequence

Meridian		Location
Forehead (F)	1	One inch above and between eyebrows
Under Nose (UN)	2	Under nose and above upper lip
Under Bottom Lip (UBL)	3	Depression between lip and chin
Chest (CH)	4	Upper section of your chest

5. Next, do the Brain Balancer (BB) by tapping repeatedly at the Back of Hand (BH) point while rotating your eyes clockwise, rotating your eyes counter-clockwise, then humming a tune, counting to five, and humming again.

6. Repeat the tapping sequence 1→2→3→4.

7. Again, rate your level of distress from 0 to 10. It should be lower yet. When the distress is within the 0 to 2 range, go to step 9. Sometimes you'll need to repeat the treatment several times while you are thinking about your problem—or even while you are in the actual situation—before you feel complete relief from the distressful situation.

8. As long as there is a decrease in the level of distress, continue with the sequence until there are very little or no feelings of distress remaining. If the treatment stalls at any point, this indicates a mini-reversal. Treat this by tapping on the little finger Side of Hand (SH) while saying three times, "I deeply accept myself, even though I still have some of this problem."

9. When the distress level is 0 to 2, do the Eye Roll (ER) to lower the distress further or to complete the treatment effects. To do this, tap on the Back of Hand (BH), hold your head straight, and, moving only your eyes, look at the floor and then slowly raise your eyes up toward the ceiling.

If the distress associated with the issue should return at a later time, repeat the MET sequence. In time, recurrence of the problem will become less and less likely.

Summary

The treatments in this chapter can be used alone or with other treatments described in this book. Traumatic events, for example, often involve feelings of anger, guilt, or shame. After treating the trauma with the treatments outlined in chapter 10, if you should continue to experience some negative emotion, the treatments in this chapter will help you to apply the finishing touches. Also, after treating any problem, such as a panic attack, you may feel guilty or angry with yourself for having had the problem in the first place. This can occur when the problem affects other areas of your life. If this is the case, you should treat these negative feelings with the treatments described in this chapter. Remember, if you don't treat these secondary negative emotions, over time, they can cause the original problem to return. This is especially true when dealing with anger or forgiveness. After successfully treating a problem, you may find it helpful to routinely forgive yourself for having had the problem in the first place. To do this, follow the treatment sequences for anger and guilt.

CHAPTER 9

Feeling Good Again

Although millions of Americans seem to be unhappy and may believe that they are depressed, there is a significant difference between clinical depression and what might be referred to as a "low mood." For the most part, the difference is determined by the degree of severity and longevity. A low, blue mood for a day, for example, regardless of its depth, does not qualify as clinical depression. Life invariably has its ups and downs. An unrelenting mildly low mood, however, can qualify as clinical depression. For example, if a low mood persists for at least two weeks and includes symptoms such as those listed below, clinical depression may be present and professional treatment is advisable. Generally the longer you are depressed, the more effort is required to resolve the depression.

Symptoms of clinical depression include:

- Difficulty concentrating

- Fatigue

- Low energy, or *anergia*

- Difficulty making decisions

- Trouble falling asleep

- Frequent awakening

- Early morning awakening

- Excessive sleep

- Low appetite

- Excessive appetite

- Loss of pleasure in previously enjoyable activities

- Feelings of hopelessness

- Feelings of worthlessness

- Ongoing guilt feelings

- Excessive thoughts of death

- Suicidal thoughts

The Drugging of America

There are a number of options for treating depression. Some physicians tend to rely heavily on antidepressant medication, including Tofranil, Sinequan, Prozac, Zoloft, Paxil, Serzone, Remeron, and more. Psychiatric medications, in fact, have become so popular and are in such high demand that many physicians may feel compelled to prescribe them even when they may not be entirely necessary. In addition to conventional medications, alternative antidepressants, such as *hypericum perforatum* or St. John's Wort, have been reported to be effective in treating clinical depression (Lockie and Geddes 1995; Linde and Ramirez 1996).

Used properly, medication can be a useful adjunct for treating certain kinds of depression. In most instances, however, depression can be successfully treated without antidepressant medication, or with very little or only short-term use of it. Most commonly, antidepressants do not *cure* depression because they only address one of its causes—a chemical imbalance. As a result, depression frequently returns after medication is discontinued, even when it is discontinued gradually. In the majority of cases where medication is deemed necessary, the best approach is to receive psychological treatment in conjunction with the medication.

Be aware: Certain physical illnesses are known to produce feelings and behaviors similar to depression. For example, an underactive thyroid gland, anemia, or nutritional deficiencies can cause sluggishness and fogged awareness. Before concluding that you are clinically depressed, be certain to examine all possible causes of how you are feeling.

What Causes Depression?

A number of factors affect depression. Certain areas of the brain, for instance, are intricately involved in depression, such as those that are instrumental in regulating emotional responses (e.g., the *amygdala* and *thalamus*). Additionally, there are chemical aspects to depression, such as the disruption of neurotransmitters (e.g., *serotonin* and *norepinephrine*), which serve as conductors of the electrical currents within our nervous system. Too little of these neurotransmitters and you become sluggish, uninterested, and perhaps anxious; you may also have a tendency to worry excessively. This is the cause of depression that antidepressant medications address. But neurotransmitters can often be increased by means other than medication, including aerobic exercise, proper nutrition, vitamins, full-spectrum light, and certain herbal remedies. The question, however, is what triggers depression in the first place? Surely, the brain and chemical changes associated with depression don't happen all by themselves. Something must set the proverbial ball in motion, rolling it down the hill toward the valley of depression.

In most instances, depression is triggered by recent or past events that are traumatic to some degree and involve real or anticipated loss of some sort. For example, the death of a loved one, the loss of a job, health problems, and the possibility of financial ruin all can instigate the onset of depression. For depression to result, however, you must believe that the events occurring are significantly negative. For instance, if you lost a job that you disliked very much, rather than feeling down or depressed about it, you might actually feel relief or joy. Conversely, when you feel depressed, you have negative, perhaps catastrophic thoughts about the loss. What you think about a situation, therefore, greatly affects your depression probability. (This is the core of cognitive therapy, which assumes that what you *think* directly figures into how you feel.)

So far, the depression chain of causes looks something like this:

1. A loss event occurs.

2. You have frequent unsettling thoughts about this event.

3. Next, certain instrumental areas of the brain that are involved in emotion become activated to produce negative emotions.

4. Additionally, certain body chemicals become imbalanced as disturbing thoughts are depleted.

5. Depression results.

This formula, however, is incomplete. Somewhere *energy* is involved. Energy operates your nervous system. For depressive thoughts to have an impact on certain areas of your brain and neurochemistry, the thoughts need to have within them certain electrical or electromagnetic features. These features, in turn, stimulate the brain centers and cause the depletion of neurochemicals. Energy (i.e., thought) is real; it interacts with your body in profound ways.

As an example, vividly imagine biting into a lemon or a lime. What happens? Most people report that they experience a bitter sensation on their tongue, even though there is no citrus fruit in reality, simply in thought. How does this happen? Where is the lemon or the lime? Your thinking about the citrus sends a message to the brain similar to sending electricity through a wire, which results in a puckering sensation. The same is true for experiences of anger, guilt, jealousy, anxiety, and even depression.

Given this, depression isn't simply a matter of the situation, the brain, the chemistry, or even your thoughts, although all four are important and can greatly affect depression probability. Instead, the thinking must carry certain electromagnetic charges so that the entire depression chain of causes can take place. Then, the specifically charged thought carries messages to your senses, throughout your body. The formula for depression, therefore, might be revised as follows:

1. A loss event occurs.

2. You have frequent unsettling thoughts about this event.

3. The thoughts are unsettling since they contain certain *disrupted energy* characteristics.

4. The electromagnetic features in thoughts produce negative emotions that activate certain areas of the brain involved in emotion.

5. Neurochemicals become imbalanced as disrupting thoughts deplete them.

6. Depression results.

Of course, this is not the only formula for depression. There are hereditary factors involved in some instances of depression. In fact, some studies of identical twin siblings indicate that heredity is the predominant predisposing factor of depression (Kendler, Walters, Truett, et al. 1994).

Energy Psychology Helps to Relieve Depression

When you feel depressed, your energy system is out of balance. It can be returned to balance by energy psychology treatments. These serve to remove the most basic cause of the depression, which is within the realm of energy. By tapping on specific energy points in specific ways, negative energetic features of thoughts are removed, your energy system becomes balanced, and the depression is relieved. Think of depression as being caused by an energy field—much like the magnetic impressions on an audiotape that produce the music when you play the tape. Stimulating the energy system causes that field to be erased, thus erasing the depression. Following are some examples of how this has worked for others.

Love, Fear, and Depression: A Case Study

David had been experiencing depression for more than six months. Although his physician placed him on an antidepressant medication, he found that it wasn't helping him much, if at all. He took the Beck Depression Inventory (BDI) test, which determined that his level of depression was severe. He decided to participate in psychotherapy, something he had not done before.

After discussing the various issues involved in his depression, David was advised to explore energy therapy. In David's first session, he was reminded that although there are chemical aspects involved in a depression, and this is why his physician had chosen to prescribe an antidepressant medication, depression is fundamentally caused by our disturbing thoughts about events in our lives. Further, he was told that his thoughts are not disembodied and that an electrical or electromagnetic aspect that is involved in negative thoughts can be relieved quite rapidly with certain techniques. It was also emphasized that David did not need to be caught in depression-producing thoughts. (This is an important consideration to take into account with any psychological problem.) In this regard, we emphasized that continuing to focus on negative issues causes energy imbalance, negatively affects the nervous system, produces a chemical imbalance, and more.

David took this advice to heart as he openly engaged in the energy treatment sequence for depression (provided later in this chapter). In less than five minutes, David's depression was gone. After the original treatment sequence, the importance of David not getting caught up in depressive thinking was reemphasized, and the treatment sequence was reviewed so that he could repeat it, if necessary, during the week.

When David returned for his session the following week, he again took the depression inventory (BDI), and notable improvement was evident. He no longer was severely depressed, although mild depression remained evident. The treatment sequences from the previous week were repeated and again the residual depression vanished.

During his third appointment, the depression inventory was administered again. At this point, there was no evidence of clinical depression. He was amazed at what had transpired in such a short period of time. He said, "It's uncanny!"

With the assistance of his physician, David's antidepressant medication was discontinued. A follow-up telephone contact six months later revealed that there was no recurrence of depression. David was doing quite well.

The Death of a Boyfriend: A Case Study

Jennifer was a high school junior. She had been dating nineteen-year-old Chris for more than two years when he developed a serious respiratory condition and deteriorated rapidly, eventually dying. Jennifer grieved deeply and soon became clinically depressed. She missed Chris, felt lost without him, and was plagued by images in her mind of when he was in his debilitated condition, suffering. Her physician put her on antidepressant medication. She also saw a therapist who encouraged her to discuss her grief, to review many of the events that transpired during Chris's illness, and to focus on her positive memories of him prior to his illness. Unfortunately, none of this helped Jennifer and, in fact, she became increasingly depressed. Psychiatric hospitalization was considered.

With energy psychology, Jennifer didn't have to focus on events from the past. The first objective was to have her briefly tune in to the images that were contributing to her depression, including symptoms of sleeplessness, loss of pleasure, crying, poor appetite, etc. She rated the distress at the time as being the highest level possible. Her visual image was one of Chris lying on the couch suffering as he was having difficulty breathing. Jennifer was taken through the highly complex trauma treatment (see chapter 10) and, within a matter of ten minutes, that image no longer caused her great distress.

Next, we focused on her residual feelings of depression. By this time, the feeling of depression had decreased significantly. Jennifer was encouraged to tap on the back of her hand between the little finger and ring finger (BH) while continuing to focus on the feelings of depression, which she described as being centered "in my heart." As her feelings of depression decreased, she was asked to tap under the collarbone (UCB) a few times and then return to tapping on the BH. Within a few minutes Jennifer was not experiencing any depression at all. Throughout the treatment she frequently exclaimed, "This is crazy. It's weird, but it's good."

When Jennifer was seen the following week she indicated that she had not felt depressed for three days after the initial treatment. In all, only a few visits were needed to help Jennifer improve her mood tremendously. She found it much easier to concentrate, she slept and ate better, and her interest in life and teenage activities returned. Her full-blown depression never returned. She became involved in social activities with friends and eventually started dating again. In consultation with our treatment of Jennifer's depression, her physician tapered her off the antidepressant medication.

Switching

As previously mentioned, sometimes treatment sequences will not work to alleviate depression due to an even more pervasive energy disruption referred to as neurologic disorganization or switching. If you find that the treatment sequences below do not alleviate depression or low mood, or if they are inefficient, correcting possible switching may be just what you need. See chapter 2 for more information on switching and an exercise to treat it.

Basic Treatment for Depression

1. Think about your feelings of depression. Rate your level of depression on a scale of 0 to 10, with 10 representing the highest level of distress and 0 indicating no stress.

2. Treat for the possibility of reversal by tapping repeatedly on the Side of Hand (SH) or rubbing the Sore Spot (SS) while thinking or saying three times, "I deeply accept myself even though I'm depressed." It also may be helpful to tap the SH or rub the SS while saying, "I accept myself with all my problems and limitations."

3. Look at the chart and at diagram 17 to identify the locations for the meridian points for Back of Hand (BH) and Under Collarbone (UCB). While thinking about your depression (don't get into it so much that you experience any major discomfort during the process), tap on BH fifty times or more until you notice a decrease in depression, and then tap on the UCB five times. Tap them in the following order 1→2. Tap only hard enough to feel it. The tapping shouldn't cause any pain.

4. Again, rate your depression on a 0 to 10 scale (a number should just pop into your mind). If there is no decrease, go back to step 2 and cycle through the sequence again. If there is not a decrease after three attempts, this is probably not an appropriate sequence for this event, or else there is another sabotaging belief (i.e., reversal) that needs correction. (See step 8.)

5. Next, do the Brain Balancer (BB) by tapping repeatedly at the Back of Hand (BH) while rotating your eyes clockwise, rotating your eyes counterclockwise, then humming a tune, counting to five, and humming again.

6. Repeat the tapping sequence 1→2.

7. Again, rate your level of depression from 0 to 10. It should be lower yet. When the depression is within the 0 to 2 range, go to step 9. Sometimes you'll need to repeat the treatment several times—while you are thinking about your depression—before you feel complete relief from the depression symptoms.

8. As long as there is a decrease in the level of depression, continue with the sequence until there is very little or no depression remaining. If the treatment stalls at any point, this indicates a mini-reversal. Treat this by tapping on the little finger Side of Hand (SH) while saying three times, "I deeply accept myself, even though I still have some of this depression."

9. When the depression level is 0 to 2, do the Eye Roll (ER) to lower the distress further or to complete the treatment effects. To do this, tap on the Back of Hand (BH), hold your head straight, and, moving only your eyes, look at the floor and then slowly raise your eyes up toward the ceiling.

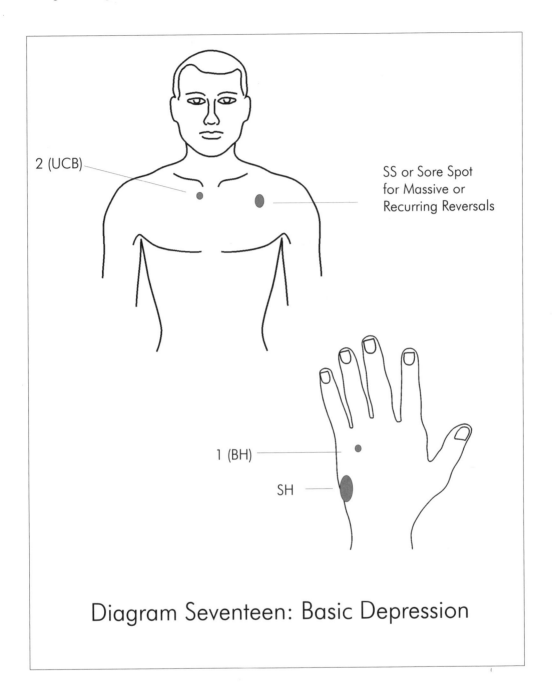

2 (UCB)

SS or Sore Spot
for Massive or
Recurring Reversals

1 (BH)

SH

Diagram Seventeen: Basic Depression

Basic Treatment Sequence for Depression

Meridian		Location
Back of Hand (BH)	1	Back of hand between little and ring fingers
Under Collarbone (UCB)	2	One inch under collarbone near throat

If the feelings of depression should return at a later time, repeat these treatments. In time, recurrence of depression symptoms will become less and less frequent. For many people, it will be unlikely for depression to recur at all.

Complex Treatment for Depression

When the Basic Treatment Sequence for depression does not alleviate your symptoms, it is likely that the depression is more complex. In some instances, this is due to another level of psychological reversal that must be corrected before the depression treatment will be effective (see chapter 6). For example, it may be necessary to tap at the Under Nose (UN), while saying, "I deeply accept myself if I never get over this depression." (Alternative reversals may also be involved.) In other instances, it is not a matter of a reversal, but rather that your energy system is more pervasively in a state of disruption, requiring more treatment points. Essentially, the Complex Depression Treatment Sequence involves combining additional treatment points with the Basic Depression Treatment Sequence. A detailed description of this process follows:

1. Think about your feelings of depression. Rate your level of depression on a scale from 0 to 10, with 10 representing the highest level of distress and 0 indicating no stress.

2. Treat for the possibility of reversal by tapping repeatedly on the Side of Hand (SH) or rubbing the Sore Spot (SS) while thinking or saying three times, "I deeply accept myself even though I'm depressed." It also may be helpful to tap the SH or rub the SS while saying, "I accept myself with all my problems and limitations."

3. Look at the chart and at diagram 18 to identify the locations for the meridian points for Eyebrow (EB), Side of Eye (SE), Under Eye (UE), Under Nose (UN), Under Bottom Lip (UBL), Under Arm (UA), Under Collarbone (UCB), Little Finger (LF), and Index Finger (IF). While thinking about your depression (don't get into it so much that you experience any major discomfort during the process), tap five times at each of these meridian points. Tap them in the following order: 1→2→3→4→5→6→7→8→9. Tap only hard enough to feel it. The tapping shouldn't cause any pain.

4. After completing the above sequence, identify the location for the meridian points for Back of Hand (BH) and Under Collarbone (UCB). While thinking about your depression, tap on BH fifty times or more until you notice a decrease in depression, and then tap on the UCB five times (see Basic Depression Treatment Sequence chart above).

5. Again, rate your depression on a 0 to 10 scale (a number should just pop into your mind). If there is no decrease, go back to step 2 and cycle through the sequence again. If there is not a decrease after three attempts, this is probably not an appropriate sequence for your depression, or else there is another sabotaging belief (i.e., reversal) that needs correction. (See step 9.)

6. Next, do the Brain Balancer (BB) by tapping repeatedly at the Back of Hand (BH) while rotating your eyes clockwise, rotating your eyes counterclockwise, then humming a tune, counting to five, and humming again.

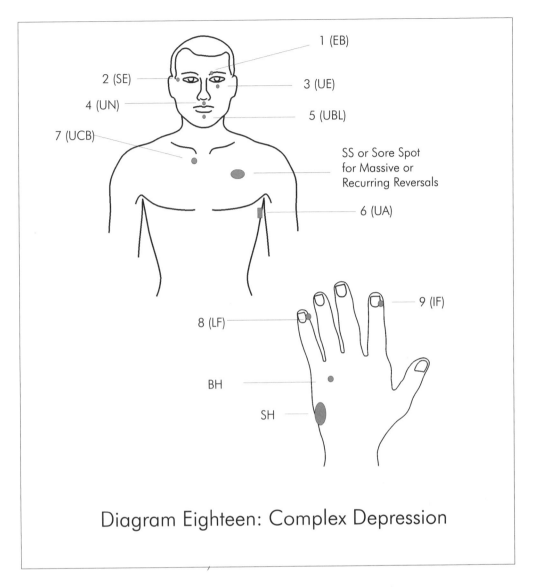

Diagram Eighteen: Complex Depression

Complex Treatment Sequence for Depression

Meridian		Location
Eyebrow (EB)	1	Beginning of eyebrow at bridge of nose
Side of Eye (SE)	2	Side of eye on bony orbit near temple
Under Eye (UE)	3	Under the center of eye on tip of bone
Under Nose (UN)	4	Above upper lip and below the center of nose
Under Bottom Lip (UBL)	5	Under bottom lip in cleft of chin
Under Arm (UA)	6	Six inches under armpit
Under Collarbone (UCB)	7	One inch under collarbone near throat
Little Finger (LF)	8	Inside tip of little fingernail on the side
Index Finger (IF)	9	Inside tip of index fingernail on the side

7. Repeat the tapping sequence 1→2→3→4→5→6→7→8→9, followed by the BH→UCB sequence.

8. Again, rate your level of depression from 0 to 10. It should be lower yet. When the depression is within the 0 to 2 range, go to step 10. Sometimes you'll need to repeat the treatment several times—while you are thinking about your depression—before you feel complete relief from the depression symptoms.

9. As long as there is a decrease in the level of depression, continue with the sequence until there is very little or no depression remaining. If the treatment stalls at any point, this indicates a mini-reversal. Treat this by tapping on the little finger Side of Hand (SH) while saying three times, "I deeply accept myself, even though I still have some of this depression."

10. When the depression level is 0 to 2, do the Eye Roll (ER) to lower the distress further or to complete the treatment effects. To do this, tap on the Back of Hand (BH), hold your head straight, and, moving only your eyes, look at the floor and then slowly raise your eyes up toward the ceiling.

If the feelings of depression should happen to return at a later time, repeat these treatments. In time, recurrence of depression symptoms will become less and less frequent. For many people, it will be unlikely for the depression to recur.

Depression Triggered by Anger

Many therapists believe—and in many cases it is true—that depression is "anger turned inward." That is, some undesirable event has happened in your life, and you beat yourself up by suffering an unhealthy dose of depression. In this case, attention to the events that have led to the depression is important. Referring to chapter 10, you can treat these events as traumas and also forgive yourself by using the anger and guilt treatments outlined in chapter 8. If the anger at yourself is extreme, the treatment for rage, also in chapter 8, may be needed.

Depression and Anxiety

Often depression and anxiety are intermixed. Anxiety is a feeling of dread, nervousness, and perhaps fear of the worst happening. Depression is a *down* or a *de-pressed* feeling and state of affairs. Also, you can often feel anxious about being depressed or feel depressed about being anxious. In such cases, it is important to treat the anxiety in addition to the depression. See chapter 7 for effective anxiety reduction treatments.

Losses That Cause Depression

Frequently, significant losses are involved in depression. If this is the case, it may be important for you to specifically target the loss as a trauma and neutralize it with one of the trauma treatment sequences. (See chapter 10 for more information.)

Massive Psychological Reversals

Massive reversal is commonly involved in depression (see chapter 6). Often, it is important to frequently repeat the massive reversal treatment throughout the day during the period when you are treating yourself for depression. The following more intricate treatment for massive reversal may prove beneficial if the standard treatment for massive reversal proves insufficient. You should repeat this treatment at least five times throughout the day:

1. Briskly massage the Sore Spot (SS) on the left side of your chest while saying or thinking three times, "I deeply and profoundly accept myself with all my problems and limitations, even though I'm depressed."

2. Then tap at the Under Nose (UN) while saying or thinking three times, "I deeply and profoundly accept myself with all my problems and limitations, even if I never get over this depression."

3. Tap at the Under Bottom Lip (UBL) while saying or thinking three times, "I deeply and profoundly accept myself with all my problems and limitations, even if I don't deserve to get over this depression."

Quit Thinking So Much

As noted, there are many causes of depression, although the energetic cause is the most fundamental. Nonetheless, your thinking is very much interrelated with your energy and you may have developed some "bad thinking" habits over the years. Even though you have balanced your energy, it is advisable to observe the connection between your thoughts and your feelings. Recognizing when you are entertaining thoughts that in the past fostered your depression is an important step. What you need are alternative solutions so you can readily dismiss such thoughts. For example, if depressive thoughts reoccur when you are alone too much, then you must take the time to develop a more active social life. This can be as simple as taking classes after work or learning new hobbies or skills. This will help you to remain in a more balanced state of mind and energy, aiding the specific energetic treatments provided in this book.

It also is important to note that dismissing depressive thoughts does not mean to suppress them. When you suppress, you're just trying to push the thought out of your mind, but you still essentially believe that what you are thinking is true. Instead, you need to make a shift in your understanding of depressive thoughts. That is, you need to recognize that the real cause of the depression is the connection between your thoughts and energy. As you allow such thoughts to evaporate, you will see that they were not the truth at all, but rather were a distorted way of thinking about your life and yourself. The thought only appeared to be true because your energy system was disrupted. In essence, the depressive thought is a mirage or an illusion, and you need to become *dis-illusioned* about it. Once you are able to see through it, your energy will be balanced.

Summary

In this chapter we have offered information about clinical depression and its treatment. Although we have provided detailed energy psychology treatments that have proven to be effective in the treatment of depression and related aspects of this disease, self-help is not always sufficient. If you find that you have been able to use these suggestions to alleviate depression, wonderful—keep it up. However, if the treatments have not proven sufficient for you, you are strongly advised against taking this as an indication that effective help is not available. Depression is eminently treatable. We strongly encourage you to contact a qualified mental health professional for assistance in general and to assist you specifically with regard to the energy approach described in this book.

CHAPTER 10

Resolving Trauma and Painful Memories Rapidly

We must rid ourselves of yesterday's negative thoughts to receive today's new and positive feelings.

–Sydney Banks

Painful memories are the result of experiencing traumatic events. Unfortunately, traumatic events are far too common in today's society and are the cause of many psychological problems and unhappiness. Many health care professionals also believe that trauma is a major contributing cause of many physical disorders, such as cancer and heart disease. When the distressing emotions attached to the memories of these traumas are eliminated, their negative effects dissipate as well. For example, relationships and emotional and physical health improve. The treatment sequences in this chapter will help you to eliminate the impact various kinds of trauma have had on your life.

Have you ever wondered why you consciously remember so little about your past? Whether you remember or not, all that information is nonetheless stored inside you, affecting the way you think, feel, and behave. This not only applies to your memories of traumatic events, but also to those that you remember as positive and neutral. Your *conscious* mind has a limited capacity for storing information. The majority of your life is stored as memories filed away in your unconscious mind. Current events or thinking about a specific time frame in your life may trigger these memories. If a memory pops up in certain situations or at certain times, it probably has meaning to you. You must evaluate the memory and determine if the event you remember had a traumatic impact on you. In most cases, the answer is self-evident.

Although this chapter primarily addresses the treatment of major traumas, you don't want to overlook other negative events that may have altered and shaped your life. These events, however, are usually not classified clinically as traumas. They can be events that occurred when you were much younger and now, as an adult, you believe that they should be viewed as trivial. At the time that the incident occurred, however, you did not have the coping resources now available to you. Therefore, the event may have left an emotional mark on you. That is, it may have lowered your sense of self or contributed to your not accepting a part of yourself. This is frrequently how energy imbalances and reversals are created.

It is amazing how a cruel remark made by an acquaintance or even a stranger may have a significant, long-lasting effect on you. One woman, for example, said that a remark made by a shoe salesman twenty years ago continued to affect the way she felt about herself today. It can be that simple. Of course, this doesn't mean that all negative events that happened when you were younger will have a lasting impact on you. But if an incident hurt your feelings or affected the way you feel about yourself, it's time to treat that memory with the techniques covered in this chapter.

There is no shortage of major traumas. Generally, the death of a child is the most traumatic. In 1997, in the United States alone, there were 28,000 infant deaths and an additional 46,000 deaths of children and young adults ages one to twenty-four (National Institute for Health Statistics 1997). Additionally, crime victims are traumatized, and the judicial process often retraumatizes them. Each year there are millions of reported crimes involving rape, robbery, and assault. Further, there are countless families traumatized by the 20,000 homicides and 30,000 suicides each year in the United States alone (National Institute for Health Statistics 1997). Other traumatic events include sexual abuse, incest, natural disasters, car accidents, and more. If you were traumatized by events such as these, you can use the treatments in this chapter to put these painful memories to rest.

Traumas and lingering painful memories can lead to secondary problems, such as an "unwillingness" to psychologically let go of the event. After some traumatic events, psychological reversal can set in and block your ability to see the situation from any perspective other than a distressing one. For example, if you were to lose a child, you might believe that if you allowed yourself to let go of the pain, it would mean that you didn't care about your child. Nothing, however, could be further from the truth. No matter what you do, you will always care about your child and you will continue to feel sadness and loss. Once your energy system is balanced about the event, however, the memory no longer will continue to overwhelm you or prevent you from moving on with your life.

Being assaulted also can provoke an "unwillingness-to-let-go-of . . ." response. If you were mugged or beaten, for example, you might feel that letting go of the trauma would either jeopardize your safety or be equivalent to absolving the perpetrator of any wrongdoing. Again, these types of thoughts are not accurate. Getting over a trauma such as assault does not invariably set you up to be assaulted again. Although resolving the trauma helps you to feel and function better, it does not cause you to forget what happened or to forget any useful information you gained from the experience. That is, if a specific person assaulted you, you would still know to avoid that person in the future. Also, as far as exoneration is concerned, what's right is right, and what's wrong is wrong. How you currently react to your memory of the event does not affect the fact that the perpetrator was nothing short of evil in his actions. When you resolve your painful memories, however, you become stronger and better able to deal with the traumatic memory.

Trauma can also lead to other problems, such as shame, self-blame, belittlement, powerlessness, and resignation. By reviewing the information in chapter 1, you can gauge the trauma's impact on your energy level. If you are feeling one of these strong emotions, it is possible that a psychological reversal has occurred, causing you to sabotage some area of your life. In this case, you will also have to treat the secondary problems, along with the painful memories, in order to resolve the problem. The treatments in this chapter will make this task easier.

The Treatment Process

Traumatic events are divided into three groups: simple trauma, complex trauma, and highly complex trauma. At times, resolution of traumatic issues may require the assistance of a qualified psychotherapist who is trained in energy therapy. In many cases, however, self-administering the treatment sequences in this chapter will yield positive healing results.

Self-Treatment

There are some instances when a traumatic memory will continue to bother you even after you have attempted to treat it. In these cases, simply assume that the trauma has not been completely treated and then cycle through the appropriate treatment sequence again. Be optimistic. Once the pain associated with the memory has been completely treated, it should never bother you again. There are instances in which severe psychological stress or energy toxins cause a thoroughly treated problem to return. This is rare, however, and your persistence in treating the traumatic memories with the sequences in this chapter will pay off in time.

Treatment for Simple Trauma

As was noted earlier in this chapter, simple traumas can be any event in your life that you feel is holding you back. They can involve cruel remarks, embarrassing situations, times when you were bullied, or perceived mistakes you made in life for which you continue to punish yourself. A single isolated event often can be treated with this sequence. If there is more than one part involved, however, each aspect should be treated individually, one at a time. For example, let's say that the event was an argument with a friend and that the friend said something insulting and then, later in the argument, did something else that was hurtful. The argument, i.e., the traumatic event, would involve two distinct aspects, and each would be treated separately.

As always, the first step in the treatment sequence is to remember the event. It's not necessary to experience any discomfort, except for a brief moment when the memory of the event is recalled. The purpose of recalling the event is twofold: to get a distress rating, and to make sure that the problem memory is tuned in so that it can be successfully treated. Concerning the latter, to simply go through energy psychology treatments without tuning in to the event possibly could result in a pleasant feeling of relaxation, but it would do nothing to resolve a specific problem. The problem must be brought to your awareness, although it need be only at the subtlest level.

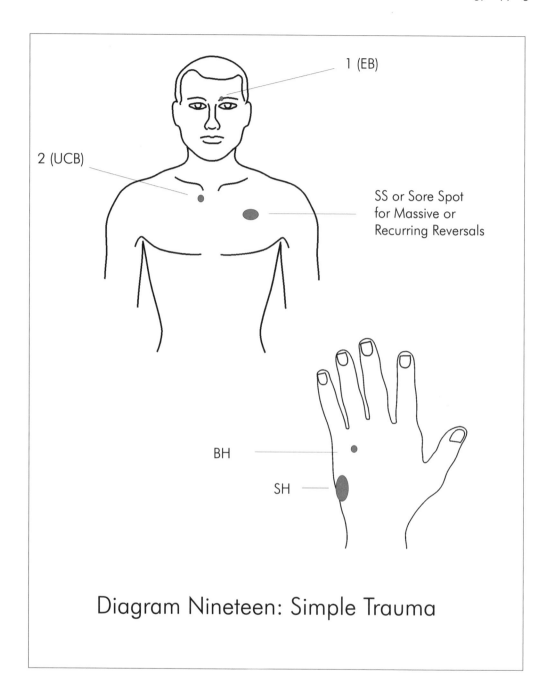

1 (EB)

2 (UCB)

SS or Sore Spot
for Massive or
Recurring Reversals

BH

SH

Diagram Nineteen: Simple Trauma

Treatment Sequence for Simple Trauma

Meridian		Location
Eyebrow (EB)	1	Beginning of eyebrow near bridge of nose
Under Collarbone (UCB)	2	One inch under collarbone near throat

1. Think about a traumatic or painful memory. It should be a single, specific event. Rate your level of distress on a scale of 0 to 10, with 10 representing the highest level of distress and 0 indicating no stress.

2. Treat for the possibility of reversal by tapping repeatedly on the Side of Hand (SH) or rubbing the Sore Spot (SS) while thinking or saying three times, "I deeply accept myself even though I'm upset." It also may be helpful to tap the SH or rub the SS while saying, "I accept myself with all my problems and limitations." You can be specific about the event.

3. Look at the chart and at diagram 19 to identify the locations for the meridian points for Eyebrow (EB) and Under Collarbone (UCB). While vaguely thinking about the event (don't get into it so much that you experience any major discomfort during the process), tap five times at each of these meridian points. Tap them in the following order 1→2. Tap only hard enough to feel it. It shouldn't cause any pain.

4. Again, rate your distress on a 0 to 10 scale (a number should just pop into your mind). If there is no decrease, go back to step 2 and cycle through the sequence again. If there is not a decrease after three attempts, this is probably not an appropriate sequence for this event, or else there is another sabotaging belief (i.e., reversal) that needs correction. Consider the Complex Trauma Sequence (in this chapter).

5. Next, do the Brain Balancer (BB) by tapping repeatedly at the Back of Hand (BH) while rotating your eyes clockwise, rotating your eyes counterclockwise, then humming a tune, counting to five, and humming again.

6. Repeat the tapping sequence 1→2.

7. Again, rate your level of distress from 0 to 10. It should be lower yet. When the distress is within the 0 to 2 range, go to step 9. Sometimes you'll need to repeat the treatment several times—while you are thinking about your trauma—before you feel complete relief from the distressing situation.

8. As long as there is a decrease in the level of distress, continue with the sequence until there is very little or no stress remaining. If the treatment stalls at any point, this indicates a mini-reversal. Treat this by tapping on the little finger Side of Hand (SH) while saying three times, "I deeply accept myself, even though I'm still upset."

9. When the distress level is 0 to 2, do the Eye Roll (ER) to lower the distress further or to complete the treatment effects. To do this, tap on the Back of Hand (BH), hold your head straight, and, moving only your eyes, look at the floor and then slowly raise your eyes up toward the ceiling.

In most cases, once a trauma has been treated successfully with this sequence, the distress will not return. If distress should return at a later time, repeat these treatments. In time, distress will become less and less frequent.

It should be noted that the trauma treatment sequences do not change the memories themselves. Rather, they eliminate the upsetting emotional elements of the memory. So, when you have successfully treated a trauma, notice that you will still be able to recall the event in detail, although you may feel rather detached from it.

Also, you may notice that you can actually recall the event more vividly than you could before doing the treatment. This is because you are no longer distracted by emotional upset, making it possible for you to look unwaveringly at the event and think about what happened. It's as though a memory has different tracks: visual, sound, emotional, and belief. Energy psychology treatments serve to erase the negative emotional track, not the visual or sound tracks. Because the belief track is generally attached to the emotional track, the treatment may affect your beliefs about the trauma, usually moving them in a more positive direction.

In some cases, however, people report that while the memory no longer bothers them, they are no longer able to recall the memory clearly. The image might be described as vague, unclear, disjointed, fragmented, etc. If this happens to you, it is not cause for concern. You might like to repeat the treatment, however, because the difficulty seeing and/or hearing the event is sometimes, although not always, an indication that the trauma has not been thoroughly treated. Repeating the treatment may result in an ability to clearly see and hear what happened in a calm, relaxed manner.

Complex Trauma

Generally, complex traumas involve traumatic or other painful memories that have many aspects and greater complexity in terms of emotional distress than do single-event focused simple traumas. The following two case studies will help you to understand the types of complex traumas that can be resolved by using energy psychology.

War Trauma: A Case Study

Bill was a Vietnam vet who was decorated with honor for his valor in combat. However, he bore the scars of the war: an amputated left leg above the knee, a respiratory condition due to Agent Orange, alcohol and drug dependence, and a whole host of traumatic memories that found their way into his dreams at night, and often surfaced during his waking hours as well. He suffered frequent flashbacks about fellow soldiers who were blown up in the war and the people he had to kill. He also maintained the belief that all is hopeless and that he was guilty of committing atrocities. Although he was only defending himself in battles, he nonetheless suffered guilt, including survivor's guilt.

Bill had been in psychotherapy before. He had tried group work, emotional reliving, numerous medications, alcohol and drug rehabilitation, and so on. He was barely getting by in life. When Bill's sister heard about energy psychology, she made a consultation appointment for him to see if it would be of any help. On the day of the initial session, Bill was exceptionally nervous. He expected therapy to proceed in the same way that he had previously experienced. He did not want to take trips back into the painful memories, reliving scenes that he would prefer had never occurred in the first place. In fact, he would like to forget about them altogether, although that was not possible at the time.

Most people receive optimal treatment if they are in a more secure mood. After becoming more relaxed, Bill described one scene that had continued to haunt him since his tour in Vietnam. He was engaged in hand-to-hand combat and that scene continued to be a source of distress. When Bill talked briefly about the event, he turned white and started to shake. Bill was told to tap on several specific meridian points. He repeated this and some other treatments several times and, within the course of approximately five minutes, the memory of that incident no longer bothered him. He could remember what happened clearly, but he no longer turned white, nor did he shake. Actually, he was quite calm. With some bewilderment in his voice, he stated, "It doesn't bother me. I can see what happened, but it doesn't bother me!"

After the treatment, Bill no longer felt guilty about the event either. He could see clearly that he had had no alternative other than to defend himself and his fellow soldiers in the war. Bill was seen many times over the next couple years and at no time did that particular memory bother him again. He has remained calm about it ever since. It should be noted, however, that resolving that particular combat memory was not sufficient to resolve all of Bill's problems. Treatment of many other traumatic memories and other issues was needed. He never experienced nightmares, flashbacks, and emotional distress about that specific memory again. Further, as his energy psychology treatments progressed, he experienced improvement in many other areas of his life as well.

Rape Trauma: A Case Study

When Barbara was thirteen years old, her eighteen-year-old boyfriend raped her. This trauma devastated her well into her early thirties. She had an extensive drug and alcohol problem and, in most respects, lived a notably anxious and depressive lifestyle. Over the years, she received treatment at a number of inpatient and outpatient psychiatric facilities. When she began energy psychology treatments, she was taking a regime of psychiatric medications, including Lithium, Prozac, and Desyrel. Even so, she was not doing well. During her first energy treatment session, Barbara discussed her rape incident; it was evident that she was traumatized. She cried deeply and, in many respects, seemed to be reliving the event in memory. She said that she was to blame, that she should have known better, that she had never listened to her mother. As she spoke, it was as though she were that thirteen-year-old girl once again.

Although not all of her psychological problems could necessarily be traced back to the rape, there was no question that the event was a significantly painful memory that had set her on a path of great misery. The energy trauma treatment took less than ten minutes and it completely resolved Barbara's painful memory. Not only did Barbara no longer feel painful emotions while reviewing the memory, but her belief about the situation and herself changed dramatically as well. Immediately after the treatment was completed, she was able to tell me with obvious conviction that the rape was "just something that happened" in her past and that she was "not to blame."

Both of the above situations are examples of a complex trauma. Remember, when treating this type of trauma, each aspect involved in the traumatic event should be treated individually, one at a time.

Treatment Sequence for Complex Trauma

1. Think about the traumatic event. It should be a single, specific event. Rate your level of distress on a scale from 0 to 10, with 10 representing the highest level of distress and 0 indicating no stress.

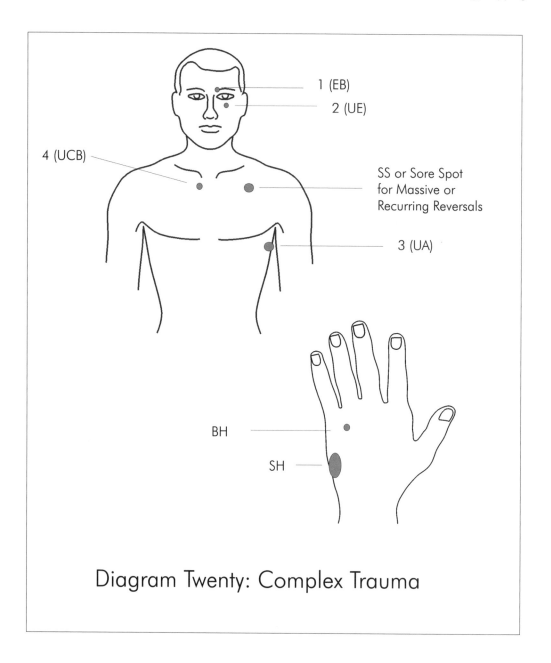

Diagram Twenty: Complex Trauma

Treatment Sequence for Complex Trauma

Meridian		Location
Eyebrow (EB)	1	Beginning of eyebrow near bridge of nose
Under Eye (UE)	2	Under the center of the eye on tip of bone
Under Arm (UA)	3	Six inches under armpit
Under Collarbone (UCB)	4	One inch under collarbone near throat

2. Treat for the possibility of reversal by tapping repeatedly on the Side of Hand (SH) or rubbing the Sore Spot (SS) while thinking or saying three times, "I deeply accept myself even though I'm upset about what happened." You can be specific about the event. It also may be helpful to tap the SH or rub the SS while saying, "I accept myself with all my problems and limitations."

3. Look at the chart and at diagram 20 to identify the location for the meridian points for Eyebrow (EB), Under Eye (UE), Under Arm (UA), and Under Collarbone (UCB). While thinking about the event (don't get into it so much that you experience any major discomfort during the process), tap five times at each of these meridian points. Tap them in the following order 1→2→3→4. Tap only hard enough to feel it. The tapping shouldn't cause any pain.

4. Again, rate your distress on a 0 to 10 scale (a number should just pop into your mind). If there is no decrease, go back to step 2 and cycle through the sequence again. If there is not a decrease after three attempts, this is probably not an appropriate sequence for this event, or else there is another sabotaging belief (i.e., reversal) that needs correction. As an alternative, consider the Highly Complex Trauma Sequence (later in this chapter).

5. Next, do the Brain Balancer (BB) by tapping repeatedly at the Back of Hand (BH) while rotating your eyes clockwise, rotating your eyes counterclockwise, then humming a tune, counting to five, and humming again.

6. Repeat the tapping sequence 1→2→3→4.

7. Again, rate your level of distress from 0 to 10. It should be lower yet. When the distress is within the 0 to 2 range, go to step 9. Sometimes you'll need to repeat the treatment several times—while you are thinking about your trauma—before you feel complete relief from the distressing situation.

8. As long as there is a decrease in the level of distress, continue with the sequence until there is very little or no stress remaining. If the treatment stalls at any point, this indicates a mini-reversal. Treat this by tapping on the little finger Side of Hand (SH) while saying three times, "I deeply accept myself, even though I'm still upset."

9. When the distress level is 0 to 2, do the Eye Roll (ER) to lower the distress further or to complete the treatment effects. To do this, tap on the Back of Hand (BH), hold your head straight, and, moving only your eyes, look at the floor and then slowly raise your eyes up toward the ceiling.

In most cases, once a trauma has been successfully treated with this sequence, the distress will not return. If distress should return at a later time, however, repeat these treatments. In time, the distress will become less and less frequent.

Highly Complex Trauma

One analogy or image for highly complex traumas is that of a cafeteria tray dispenser. As soon as you remove one tray, another pops into place. If the objective was to remove all of the trays, you would continue to remove trays, one after another, until the last tray had been removed. The same line of reasoning applies to many psychological and emotional problems. That is, after you treat one problem, another appears. Problems are often not just singular events, but are composed of many aspects. They can even be layered, one on top of another.

Arthur Koestler (1967) coined the term "holon" to describe this concept. A holon indicates a whole that is part of an even greater whole. If a trauma is composed of many holons, for instance, each element of the trauma both encompasses and goes beyond the one that came before it. Consequently, each individual holon, i.e., element of the trauma, needs to be treated before the trauma as a whole can be resolved.

One exception to this theory is if the trauma being treated is the earliest one in a series. Often, resolving the earliest trauma will also alleviate all of the later ones. In this case, each of the traumas is a holon to the network or series of interrelated traumas. One patient, for example, was physically abused by her father repeatedly when she was a child. The first incident of her trauma was when, at age seven, she incurred the physical wrath of her father after she accidentally dropped her baby brother, who cried, but was not seriously injured. She reported that after that particular trauma was resolved with energy psychology treatments, all incidents in which her father abused her no longer caused distress. She expressed the view that perhaps this was because the various events were so similar.

Please note: Even though simultaneous collapsing of related traumas frequently happens, this does not always occur. Therefore, when treating a disturbing memory, it is important to think about the event sequentially, from beginning to end, treating each aspect as you go along. In this way, you can be assured that the trauma as a whole has been successfully and thoroughly treated.

In some cases, the complex trauma treatments will totally eliminate the distress associated with the painful event, and repeating the treatment with each component of the problem will not be necessary. However, an untreated aspect may continue to stir up negative emotions, making it appear as if the treatment is not working. This is why it is important to break down the trauma into sequenced events and be prepared to treat each one. For example, one woman's husband committed suicide shortly after an argument with her. Her memory of the event had the following sequential aspects:

1. An embarrassing scene at a party

2. An ensuing argument upon returning home

3. Her husband threatening her with a gun

4. Her husband shooting himself

5. Calling her sister on the phone for help

6. Calling 911

7. The police arriving and accusing her of shooting her husband

8. Events related to the funeral, having to move, etc.

Each of the scenes in the woman's memory carried with it specific negative emotions, including embarrassment, anger, fear, and then panic. In treating this trauma, all of these aspects had to be treated thoroughly. That is, it was not enough to treat an aspect that was at a high level of distress and reduce it to a four or five; it had to get down to a 0 (no distress at all). Also, if an important aspect was not addressed at all, the patient would continued to experience distress. The following example illustrates the procedure and benefits of treating highly complex traumas.

The Death of a Child: A Case Study

Debbie had been suffering from trauma and depression ever since her infant died in the hospital a couple days after his birth. This had happened more than two years prior to our initial session. The trauma was taking its toll on her emotionally as well as on her relationship with Harold, her husband. They couldn't talk about the death of their child, and Harold's silence and seeming nonchalance suggested to her that he did not care about what had happened or about her. They were on the verge of a divorce.

Debbie and Harold entered treatment because of their frequent arguments. When the arguments occurred, Harold would often withdraw for days, frequently not coming home after work. Their relationship was on a downward spiral. It was apparent that neither of them had resolved the trauma concerning the death. Debbie's way of coping was to want to talk about it, whereas Harold's approach was to leave it alone.

Their first energy psychology session was taken up gathering details about their relationship and their problems. During the second session, however, it was explained to them that a significant aspect of their relationship difficulties could be the fact that they continued to feel distressed about the loss of their infant. Although obviously nothing could be done to bring their child back, energy psychology treatments could relieve the trauma and thus increase the chances of regaining a healthy relationship.

They were both treated in the office on the same day. Debbie was first. When she thought about the death she immediately began to cry. Within a few minutes of providing energy psychology treatments, she was able to think about the event in a much calmer manner. Although there was still sadness attached to the memory, the extreme distress had dissipated. It was explained to Debbie that this treatment might need to be repeated until all of the aspects were resolved.

Next, Harold was taken through the same type of treatment. At first he claimed that he felt no distress. While the energy psychology treatments were being provided, however, he started to cry. We discussed his emotions and he indicated that he did not realize that there was so much distress under the surface. Debbie had an opportunity to witness that he did care. With his permission, the treatments were again administered and he felt much better.

A follow-up visit the next week revealed a significant shift in both Harold and Debbie's distress levels regarding their infant's death. Although there was still sadness concerning the death of their child, they were finally able to lay their child to rest. They were now in a better position to deal with their relationship as a whole.

Highly Complex Trauma Treatment

A treatment sequence for highly complex trauma follows. Generally, this treatment works with traumatic or other painful memories that have many aspects and greater complexity in terms of emotional distress than can be resolved adequately by the previous treatment sequences. If there are a number of aspects involved in the traumatic event, each aspect should be treated individually, one at a time.

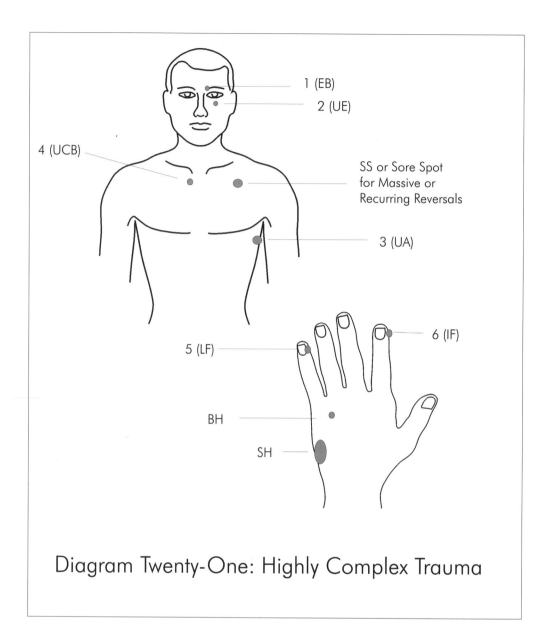

Diagram Twenty-One: Highly Complex Trauma

Treatment Sequence for Highly Complex Trauma

Meridian		Location
Eyebrow (EB)	1	Beginning of eyebrow near bridge of nose
Under Eye (UE)	2	Under the center of the eye on tip of bone
Under Arm (UA)	3	Six inches under armpit
Under Collarbone (UCB)	4	One inch under collarbone near throat
Little Finger (LF)	5	Inside tip of little fingernail on the side
Index Finger (IF)	6	Inside tip of index fingernail on the outside

1. Think about the traumatic event. It should be a single, specific event. Rate your level of distress on a scale of 0 to 10, with 10 representing the highest level of distress and 0 indicating no stress.

2. Treat for the possibility of reversal by tapping repeatedly on the Side of Hand (SH) or rubbing the Sore Spot (SS) while thinking or saying three times, "I deeply accept myself even though I'm upset." You can be specific about the event. It also may be helpful to tap the SH or rub the SS while saying, "I accept myself with all my problems and limitations."

3. Look at the chart and at diagram 21 to identify the locations for the meridian points for Eyebrow (EB), Under Eye (UE), Under Arm (UA), Under Collarbone (UCB), Little Finger (LF), and Index Finger (IF). While thinking about the event (don't get into it so much that you experience any major discomfort during the process), tap five times at each of these meridian points. Tap them in the following order 1→2→3→4→5→4→6→4. **Note:** The UCB appears three times in the sequence. Tap only hard enough to feel it. The tapping shouldn't cause any pain.

4. Again, rate your distress on a 0 to 10 scale (a number should just pop into your mind). If there is no decrease, go back to step 2 and cycle through the sequence again. If there is not a decrease after three attempts, this is probably not an appropriate sequence for this event, or else there is another sabotaging belief (i.e., reversal) that needs correction. Also there may be an earlier trauma that needs to be addressed.

5. Next, do the Brain Balancer (BB) by tapping repeatedly at the Back of Hand (BH) while rotating your eyes clockwise, rotating your eyes counterclockwise, then humming a tune, counting to five, and humming again.

6. Repeat the tapping sequence 1→2→3→4→5→4→6→4.

7. Again, rate your level of distress from 0 to 10. It should be lower yet. When the distress is within the 0 to 2 range, go to step 9. Sometimes you'll need to repeat the treatment several times while thinking about your trauma before you feel complete relief from the distressing situation.

8. As long as there is a decrease in the level of distress, continue with the sequence until there is very little or no stress remaining. If the treatment stalls at any point, this indicates a mini-reversal. Treat this by tapping on the little finger Side of Hand (SH) while saying three times, "I deeply accept myself, even though I'm still upset."

9. When the distress level is 0 to 2, do the Eye Roll (ER) to lower the distress further or to complete the treatment effects. To do this, tap on the Back of Hand (BH), hold your head straight, and, moving only your eyes, look at the floor and then slowly raise your eyes up toward the ceiling.

In most cases, once a trauma has successfully been treated with this sequence, the distress will not return. However, if distress should return at a later time, repeat these treatments. In time, distress will become less and less frequent.

Summary

This chapter has covered how to rapidly resolve traumatic and other painful memories. Many other conditions covered in this book, such as phobias, panic, depression, rage, and even negative beliefs about who you are and what you are capable of doing originate from experiences that can be effectively treated with these sequences. Weeding out the traumas of our lives is an important step toward becoming psychologically, emotionally, and physically healthy. Perhaps if these treatments were to be used on a widespread basis (for example, as the psychological equivalent of the Heimlich maneuver), many of the problems that we experience in society would quickly dissolve.

CHAPTER 11

Improving Your Sports Performance

The game of golf is 90 percent mental.

—Jack Nicklaus

The goal in an athletic event is to play to the best of your ability; that is, to maintain an energy level that allows your natural ability to come through without hesitation or doubt. This doesn't mean that you'll win—it means that you are giving yourself every opportunity to win. The key to doing this is to eliminate the self-defeating beliefs and anxiety that can cause mistakes and result in you playing at less than your ability.

Energy work will not compensate for a lack of ability or the practice required to excel at any sport. It can, however, help you to eliminate any sabotaging thoughts and excessive anxiety that prevent you from playing at your best, especially in crucial situations. When using energy psychology to improve your sports performance, you must factor in your skill level and mental attitude when evaluating your success. Additionally, you must be realistic about what you are trying to accomplish. For instance, a golfer who shoots in the 90s isn't going to make the pro tour just by using energy psychology methods, but that player can eliminate a lot of needless mistakes and probably shoot consistently in the 80s.

Athletes often lose their mental focus when playing a sport, especially if they have unrealistic expectations or feel that they are playing poorly. Energy work can help you to regain your focus, but you still need realistic expectations about your playing ability that day. For example, if you know from experience that you normally hit 70 percent of your free throws in basketball, then that is what you should expect to do in crucial situations. That means that even if you are focused and at your best, you can miss the shot. If the miss results in you becoming angry or losing your focus, this is a self-defeating behavior. When used regularly, energy psychology is a tool that can help you to improve your game. You will be less anxious in crucial situations and will remain focused and positive while you are playing.

> Energy psychology will not improve your natural athletic ability,
> but it certainly can help you to play consistently at your best.

The energy psychology techniques in this chapter can easily be applied to any athletic situation. If you play competitive sports, you know that some mistakes are created purely by anxiety. Most likely, you know the feeling as it occurs. It is obvious that an athlete is anxious, for example, when they cannot perform a task that is within their ability level. What really occurs when a professional basketball player shoots an air ball from the free throw line or a golfer repeatedly misses short putts? If it happens often or in crucial situations, anxiety, fear, and self-sabotaging beliefs are probably involved.

Managing Performance Anxiety and Fears

Choking in the sports world refers to an inability to manage anxiety and fears at crucial times during athletic events. Although anxiety is usually the central cause of choking, negative beliefs can also fuel this feeling. When you are too tense, for instance, your muscles tighten up and can cause you to lose the keen sense of touch and feel that is crucial in any athletic event. Once that subtle feeling is lost, you may try to compensate by doing something harder or faster, which is generally an ineffective solution.

When using energy psychology to improve your athletic performance, it is important to identify crucial situations in which you know that you have the skill to play better, and yet you regularly err. For example, a golfer most likely has an energy problem if 80 percent of the time that they are on the driving range they can hit the ball high and 140 yards with their seven iron, but when they are in front of a pond, they consistently slice the ball or hit it into the water. In this situation, the golfer's belief that they can't hit the ball over the water sabotages their game; they become so anxious in front of the water that it prevents them from completing their normal swing.

Focus

The most difficult task in many sports is maintaining focus. Many professional athletes have reported that energy psychology helps them to improve their focus significantly. There are two types of focus: mechanical and mental. Although they overlap, energy work primarily affects the latter. You need to work on your mechanical focus with a qualified instructor or coach. Mechanical considerations include physical skills, such as how you would stand and set up to hit or putt a ball. If you become too concerned about your mechanics during a game, however, it is difficult for you to focus mentally. This, in turn, limits your ability to relax and play at your best.

Energy psychology indirectly helps the mechanical part of your game. As you use energy work to decrease your anxiety and eliminate sabotaging thoughts, you will find it much easier to identify and correct your mechanical skills. For example, continually missing short- and medium-length putts will lead you to feel anxious and have no confidence in your game. Once you balance your energy and lower your anxiety, however, you will be better able to detect and resolve real performance issues that may, in part, be mechanical.

You must also have faith in yourself and not lose your focus because of any one particular performance. No athlete can perform at the same level every day. The goal is to stay focused no matter what happens and continue playing to your best ability. If you lack confidence or have unrealistic expectations, you will start to focus on your mistakes or bad breaks and put less focus on the task at hand.

Events that are not within your control can also alter the game. The key is to determine how you respond to a situation that's out of your control. Again, if you worry about what happened or dwell on bad outcomes, you will lose focus and minimize your chances for success. If you use energy work to accept these situations, you will stay focused. Your opponents may eventually encounter similar situations and lose their focus. You never know, even professional athletes "fumble the ball," so to speak. So, don't ever give up. Keep in mind that it is impossible to perform at your best skill level when you become angry or frustrated or blame outside situations.

In the treatment section that follows, we will examine the beliefs that create self-sabotage and provide treatment sequences that will eliminate sabotage and any accompanying anxiety. We will also help you to identify a single treatment point that will help to reduce anxiety and keep you focused while you are playing your sport of choice.

Creating Peak Performance in Sports

Self-acceptance is always a crucial element of success in sports. If you can't accept yourself or the situation when you make a mistake, you are less likely to succeed. This doesn't mean that you are not trying to improve or work harder. There is a big difference between players who think they can play better and those who become angry or blame others for their own poor performance.

Three Common Beliefs

There are three common beliefs that affect your sporting performance: a fear of success, overcompetitiveness, and outside influences.

Fear of Success

Fear of success centers around the fact that you don't think you are good enough to succeed. We're not talking about your athletic skills, but your overall sense of who you are. What would change if you became a great (at your level) athlete? People might think about you differently or treat you differently. Perhaps by self-sabotaging your skill, it helps you to maintain a certain belief you have about yourself, such as that you don't deserve to win, or that you aren't worthy of the situation.

Overcompetitiveness

Winning is an outcome, not a process. Those who are winners never lose the composure or focus that allows them to play at their best. If your focus becomes one of beating your opponent, rather than the strategy or activity that you must complete, you have a self-defeating behavior. There is a fine line between being a winner and wanting to win too much, but once you cross it, you are no longer focused on playing at the best of your ability.

Outside Influences, AKA "I'm Not Getting Any Breaks"

Here the athlete believes that they aren't lucky or that other athletes are lucky. Although perhaps this may be true to some extent, luck in sports usually comes from the athlete not making any crucial mistakes or not trying to accomplish goals that are beyond their ability level. If an athlete blames their game on outside influences, they usually lose focus and become angry or frustrated with the situation. Then they may believe that only something special will make the difference and therefore attempt a low percentage play or shot. Perhaps their belief is that it's their "turn to get lucky." In this case, the athlete has moved away from the central point of all athletic events: to stay focused and execute your role to the best of your ability.

You may be aware of other beliefs that limit your success in sports, and you can easily include them in the following treatment plan. Look for emotions or beliefs that make you lose your focus or prevent you from regaining it. Examples include emotions such as anger, frustration, and anxiety; or beliefs such as, "I can't win," "I don't care anymore," "I'm unlucky," or "I'm not good enough." While deep-seated beliefs such as "I don't deserve to win" may sound strange, they are very real and limit many athletes.

No matter what happens when you play, your ability to accept it and stay focused is the only way to play to the best of your ability each day.

Treatment Plan for Sports Issues

All energy treatments to some degree revolve around self-acceptance. When you are angry or lose trust in yourself, you are thinking that the situation should not happen. You can be so concerned about the outcome that you lose your focus. This, in turn, blocks your ability to reach your peak performance. On the other hand, once you accept yourself—even if you do not succeed—you have opened the door to change, enabling yourself to get back on track and regain your focus.

Although the examples in the following treatment focus on golf, the same concepts can be used in any athletic or performance situation.

1. Clearly define the problem that you want to resolve. It must be specific and within your current level of ability to achieve. For example, "When I become anxious I miss short putts that I easily make during practice." Remember to be specific and not to generalize, such as, "I stink at golf." You can, however,

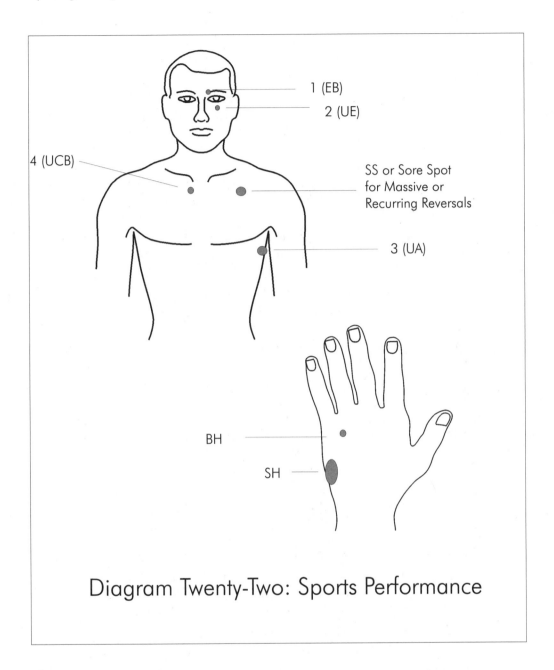

Diagram Twenty-Two: Sports Performance

Treatment Sequence for Sports Performance

Meridian		Location
Eyebrow (EB)	1	Beginning of eyebrow near bridge of nose
Under Eye (UE)	2	Under the center of the eye on tip of bone
Under Arm (UA)	3	Six inches below armpit
Under Collarbone (UCB)	4	One inch below the collarbone near throat

experiment with some generalizations, such as "I always make mistakes at crucial times." The more specific your statement, the better the outcome. Now rate your nervousness or level of tension on a scale of 0 to 10, with 10 representing the highest level of tension and 0 indicating no tension.

2. Identify any sabotaging beliefs or feelings that you think affect your performance. Don't be hesitant. If you think it could be a problem, treat it. It only takes a minute. In time, you will come to know which beliefs are most typical of you and need to be treated regularly. Treat each reversal by tapping on the Side of Hand (SH) or rubbing the Sore Spot (SS) while thinking or saying to yourself the sabotaging belief. Below are some examples:

   • I accept myself even though I am too competitive in sports.

   • I accept myself even though my anger makes me lose my focus.

   • I accept myself even though I think I'm not good enough to shoot in the 80s.

   • I accept myself even though I am too nervous when I putt.

   If you think your problem is a deep-level reversal (see chapter 6) and that you can *never* get over your problem, then tap under your nose (UN) while saying three times, "I accept myself even if I can never get over (name the situation)".

3. Now look at the chart and at diagram 22 to identify the locations for the meridian points for Eyebrow (EB), Under Eye (UE), Under Arm (UA), and Under Collarbone (UCB). While thinking about the situation and/or feeling, tap five times at each of these meridian points. Tap them in the following order 1→2→3→4. Tap only hard enough to feel it. The tapping shouldn't cause any pain.

4. Again, rate your level of distress on a 0 to 10 scale (a number should just pop into your mind). If there is no decrease, go back to step 2 and cycle though the sequence again. If there is no decrease after three attempts, this is possibly not the appropriate sequence for this situation, or else there is another sabotaging belief (i.e., reversal) that needs correction. (See step 8.)

5. Next, do the Brain Balancer (BB) by tapping repeatedly at the Back of Hand (BH) while rotating your eyes clockwise, rotating your eyes counterclockwise, then humming a tune, counting to five, and humming again.

6. Repeat the tapping sequence 1→2→3→4.

7. Again, rate your level of distress from 0 to 10. It should be lower yet. When the distress is within the 0 to 2 range, go to step 9. Sometimes you'll need to repeat the treatment several times while you are imagining your fear—or even while you are in the actual situation—before you feel complete relief from the distressful situation.

8. As long there is a decrease in your level of distress, continue with the sequence until there is very little or no tension remaining. If the treatment stalls at any point, this indicates a mini-reversal. Treat this by tapping on the little finger Side of Hand (SH), while saying three times, "I deeply accept myself, even though I still have some of this problem."

9. When the distress level is 0 to 2, consider doing the Eye Roll (ER) to lower the distress further or to complete the treatment effects. To do this, tap on the Back of Hand (BH), hold your head straight, and, moving only your eyes, look at the floor and then slowly raise your eyes toward the ceiling.

Note: Results sometimes do not happen instantly. In fact, it may be five or ten minutes before you are focused and playing better.

Visualization Practice

Visualization is usually a beneficial means of improving your performance in sports, as well as a number of other areas. The more confidently you can visualize accomplishing your goal, the greater your chances are of actually achieving it.

Some people have difficulty visualizing. One strategy that helps to enhance your visualization ability is to tap on the EB and the UA meridian points (see diagram 22) five times each, while thinking about your desired goal. Now visualize achieving your goal in as much detail as possible. You may need to repeat this process several times before you see results. You can also attach to your visualization any positive feelings that could be associated with your goal, such as sensations of confidence or pride in your hard work. Imagine, for example, that you need a five-foot putt to put you ahead in a golf match or to break a score of 90 for the first time. Now, imagine that you are feeling a little anxious in this situation, but also confident and focused. See yourself putt the ball and watch the ball go into the cup. Smile! Although each person differs in their ability to visualize, your mind/body knows what you are doing and even a vague image may be all that is required for you.

Golf is again used as the example in the treatment sequence below. Be sure to substitute appropriate phrases and mental images to match the sport of your choice.

1. Imagine yourself on the putting green attempting a difficult putt. Now, imagine that you have putted the ball, and see your ball rolling toward the hole. Did it go in? If yes, then continue to pick new situations. If you did not see the ball drop in the hole, then what do you think the problem is? Do you have doubts or are you feeling too anxious?

2. If you did not see the ball roll into the hole, tap on the Side of Hand (SH) or rub the Sore Spot (SS) while thinking or saying three times, "I accept myself even if my anxiety prevents me from sinking this putt."

3. Again, think about the problem and repeat tapping on the following meridian points: 1→2→3→4 (see diagram 22). Now imagine the situation again. In most instances, you will be able to see the ball roll into the hole. If the putt still doesn't go in, repeat steps 2 and 3. Then tap under your nose (UN) while saying three times, "I accept myself even if I never sink this putt." Next, repeat the tapping sequence: 1→2→3→4. In most instances, you should now be able to see the ball go in the hole. If not, another type of reversal may be interfering with your success (see chapter 6.)

You can also use this exercise to learn to cope with other anxiety-provoking situations, such as achieving a hit in baseball when the bases are loaded, hitting a good first serve in tennis, or hitting a ball over water in golf.

Key Meridian Points During the Game

The strategy at this point is to identify a *key meridian point* that helps you to focus at any point in your game when beliefs or anxieties are blocking your success. In most instances, when you tap on one of the four meridian points listed below, you will regain significant focus in a short period of time, assuming that you are not reversed. (See chapter 6 for more on reversals and self-sabotage.) You should experiment to determine which meridian points work best for you.

- Under Eye (UE)
- Under Collarbone (UCB)
- Under Arm (UA)
- Under Nose (UN)

Eliminate Self-Sabotaging Thoughts

Although this chapter has provided effective treatments for anxiety, your performance in any sport is a complex and interactive activity. This means that reversals and self-sabotage can frequently occur. If you are reversed, your original problem can reoccur over and over. It is very common to have reversals in crucial situations or when you are nearing a breakthrough goal. Therefore, significantly reducing instances of reversal will most likely require numerous treatments over an extended period of time. The good news is that if you are persistent, you will eliminate those sabotaging beliefs and reach your peak performance. (See chapter 6 for more information on reversals and self-sabotage.)

As we pointed out in the beginning of this chapter, people tend to quit when they don't receive immediate and long-lasting success with their mental element of sports. A strong mental component takes practice, work, and time to develop; it is complex, but once you learn to stay focused for long periods of time, you will be able to play more consistently at your highest skill level. The good news is that the more clearly you can identify your particular beliefs or issues, the easier it is to correct them.

Be aware of flashing thoughts when you are in the
middle of your game. If you have a negative thought
or visualize hitting the ball poorly, you have a self-sabotaging
thought or reversal that needs to be corrected.

When you sense that you are reversed, there are two common types of reversals. For the first, simply tap on the Side of Hand (SH) or rub the Sore Spot (SS) while thinking or saying three times to yourself, "I accept myself even though (name problem)." If that isn't effective, perhaps you believe that you can never eliminate the problem. To treat this type of reversal, tap under your nose (UN) while thinking or saying several times to yourself, "I accept myself even if I never get over (name problem)."

Then, tap on your key spot to regain focus and be ready to play more consistently at your best ability. After doing these exercises, you should be more relaxed and that should be reflected in your game and your ability to improve it.

Touch and Breathe

The Touch and Breathe method (Diepold 1999) should be used only after you first learn the treatment sequences by tapping on your meridian points. Once you have achieved success tapping, you are ready to try the Touch and Breathe technique. It is very simple: You use the same methods to treat your problem, but instead of tapping, you use two fingers to place mild pressure on the specific meridian point while taking in a deep breath, holding it, and releasing it. For example, if you feel that you are too nervous to sink your putt on the golf course or to successfully shoot a free throw, touch the Side of Hand (SH), while thinking or saying to yourself, "I accept myself even if I miss this putt (free throw)." Then touch your key point and, if you feel the need, touch the Under Nose (UN) while thinking, "I can make this putt (free throw)."

Specific Sports

Energy psychology can be used to deal with many sports-related issues. Following are some specific suggestions for basketball, baseball, tennis, and golf. It is best to start with a situation over which you have the most control, for example, free throw shooting in basketball, as your performance in these sports can depend on the ability and skill of your opponents.

Basketball

In basketball, improving your performance at the free throw line is the most effective place to begin using energy psychology to improve your game because your opponent does not affect your performance and you know your free throw shooting percentage. The question to ask yourself is does your anxiety affect your free throw? Nothing can create more tension in basketball than when your free throw will determine the final outcome of the game. Your anxiety level can skyrocket or your sabotaging beliefs can quickly surface. Other basketball-related situations that respond well to energy psychology include when you feel you cannot guard your opponent and when shots that you normally make are not going into the basket.

1. Think about a specific situation or belief that you have had while playing basketball that made you feel anxious and/or tense. Rate your level of distress on a scale of 0 to 10, with 10 representing the highest level of distress and 0 indicating no distress.

2. Treat for any sabotaging beliefs (i.e., reversals) by tapping on Side of Hand (SH) or rubbing the Sore Spot (SS) while thinking or saying to yourself three times something such as, "I deeply accept myself, even though I miss free throws at the end of the game." It is best to phrase the sentence in your own

words. It also may be helpful to tap the SH or rub the SS while saying, "I accept myself with all of my problems and limitations."

3. Now look at the chart below and diagram 22 (on page 141) to identify the locations for the meridian points Eyebrow (EB), Under Eye (UE), Under Arm (UA), and Under Collarbone (UCB). While thinking about the situation or feeling, tap five times at each of these meridian points. Tap them in the following order: 1→2→3→4. Tap only hard enough to feel it. The tapping shouldn't cause any pain.

Treatment Sequence for Basketball Performance

Meridian		Location
Eyebrow (EB)	1	Beginning of eyebrow near bridge of nose
Under Eye (UE)	2	Under the center of the eye on tip of bone
Under Arm (UA)	3	Six inches below armpit
Under Collarbone (UCB)	4	One inch below the collarbone near throat

4. Again, rate your distress on a 0 to 10 scale (a number should just pop into your mind). If there is no decrease, go back to step 2 and cycle through the sequence again. If there is not a decrease after three attempts, this is probably not the appropriate sequence for this event, or else there is another sabotaging belief (i.e. reversal) that needs correction. (See step 8.)

5. Next, do the Brain Balancer (BB) by tapping repeatedly on the Back on Hand (BH) while rotating your eyes clockwise, rotating your eyes counterclockwise, then humming a tune, counting to five, and humming again.

6. Repeat the tapping sequence of 1→2→3→4.

7. Again, rate your distress from 0 to 10. It should be lower yet. When the distress is within the 0 to 2 range, go to step 9. Sometimes you'll need to repeat the treatment several times while you are imagining your fear—or even while you are in the actual situation—before you feel complete relief from the distressful situation.

8. As long as there is a decrease in the level of distress, continue with the sequence until there is very little or no tension remaining. If the treatment stalls at any point, this indicates a mini-reversal. Treat this by tapping on the little finger Side of Hand (SH) while saying three times, "I deeply accept myself, even though I still have some of this problem."

9. When the distress level is 0 to 2, consider doing the Eye Roll to lower the distress further or to complete the treatment effects. To do this, tap on the Back of Hand (BH), hold your head straight, and, moving only your eyes, look at the floor and then slowly raise your eyes up toward the ceiling.

Repeat this treatment until you have little or no anxiety and then use the visualization exercises explored previously in this chapter. In a game situation, you can quickly treat your key point using the Touch and Breathe technique to help stay focused.

The goal of energy work is to help you to regain focus, play smart, and perform to the best of your ability that day. The result is that you stop making the same mistake repeatedly. That is, you eliminate any psychological reversals. No one plays at the same level in every game; you may need to adjust your game to compensate by passing more or requesting that your team help you on defense. Once you are thinking clearly and are not too tense, you will understand what is wrong and how to correct it.

Baseball

In baseball, pitching and hitting are two dominant components of the game. The pitcher is under pressure each time an opposing team member is batting. If you have flashing thoughts, such as the batter hitting a home run, this is a strong signal to treat yourself and reevaluate what you intend to do. After you treat any distress, you should be able to visualize your pitch to the plate and a successful outcome. Because the batter's skill is going to affect the outcome, even good pitches will be hit. The goal, as in basketball, is to play smart and not make crucial mistakes. Energy psychology will help you to achieve this.

Hitting is another situation that can be successfully addressed with energy psychology. As always, defining a situation is very important. For example, there are hitters who have a great batting average when no one is on base, but whose batting average drops significantly in situations with players on second or third base. Clearly there is more anxiety and pressure when other players are in scoring positions. Once you identify the specific situations and beliefs that are creating your anxiety, you can use the following treatment to address your fears. Then, when you are going to bat, touch your key point, take a deep breath, let it out, visualize what you want to do, and step up to the plate ready for success.

1. Think about a specific situation or belief that you have had while playing baseball that made you feel anxious and/or tense. Rate your level of distress on a scale of 0 to 10, with 10 representing the highest level of distress and 0 indicating no distress.

2. Treat for any sabotaging beliefs (i.e., reversals) by tapping on the Side of Hand (SH) or rubbing the Sore Spot (SS) and while thinking or saying three times something such as, "I deeply accept myself even though I rarely get hits with the bases loaded." It is best to phrase the sentence in your own words. It also may be helpful to tap the SH or rub the SS while saying, "I accept myself with all my problems and limitations."

3. Now look at the chart below and at diagram 22 (on page 141) to identify the locations for the meridian points for Eyebrow (EB), Under Eye (UE), Under Arm (UA), and Under Collarbone (UCB). While thinking about the situation or feeling, tap five times at each of these meridian points. Tap them in the following order: 1→2→3→4. Tap only hard enough to feel it. The tapping shouldn't cause any pain.

Treatment Sequence for Baseball Performance

Meridian		Location
Eyebrow (EB)	1	Beginning of eyebrow near bridge of nose
Under Eye (UE)	2	Under the center of the eye on tip of bone
Under Arm (UA)	3	Six inches below armpit
Under Collarbone (UCB)	4	One inch below the collarbone near throat

4. Again, rate your distress on a 0 to 10 scale (a number should just pop into your mind). If there is no decrease, go back to step 2 and cycle through the sequence again. If there is not a decrease after three attempts, this is probably not an appropriate sequence for this situation, or else there is another sabotaging belief (i.e. reversal) that needs correction. (See step 8.)

5. Next, do the Brain Balancer (BB) by tapping repeatedly at the Back on Hand (BH) while rotating your eyes clockwise, rotating your eyes counterclockwise, then humming a tune, counting to five, and humming again.

6. Repeat the tapping sequence of 1→2→3→4.

7. Again, rate your level of distress from 0 to 10. It should be lower yet. When the distress is within the 0 to 2 range, go to step 9. Sometimes you'll need to repeat the treatment several times while you are imagining your fear—or even while you are in the actual situation—before you feel complete relief from the distressful situation.

8. As long as there is a decrease in your level of distress, continue with the sequence until there is very little or no tension remaining. If the treatment stalls at any point, this indicates a mini-reversal. Treat this by tapping on the little finger Side of Hand (SH) while saying three times, "I deeply accept myself, even though I still have some of this problem."

9. When the distress level is 0 to 2, consider doing the Eye Roll (ER) to lower the distress further or to complete the treatment effects. To do this, tap on the Back of Hand (BH), hold your head straight, and, moving only your eyes, look at the floor and then slowly raise your eyes to the ceiling.

Tennis

Energy psychology can be quite effective in improving your tennis game. When you want to enhance your ability to receive a serve or to volley, you should use the same procedure as a baseball player at the plate (see above sequence). The more you do prior to the match, the easier it should be for you in an actual game. You should treat any anxious feelings or doubts and be able to successfully visualize how you want to serve and receive the ball. When it is your turn to play, the treatments and exercises that you did before the game will allow you more time and control. Then, just before serving or receiving the ball, touch your key point, take a deep breath, and let it out. You should now be focused.

Golfing

At the beginning of this chapter, Jack Nicklaus was quoted as saying, "The game of golf is 90 percent mental." One reason is the difficulty of staying focused over a long duration. When you play golf, you are on the course for four hours, but you actually golf for less than thirty minutes. You walk a lot, talk to other players, and then, you must stop, focus, and hit your ball. You have to do this again and again. Once it is your turn to hit the ball, many elements can negatively affect your game. The treatment sequences in this chapter all apply to the game of golf. Following, however, are golf-specific sequences and suggestions that may help you to further improve your game.

Practice Range Situations

1. Set up golf balls in reasonable locations where you are least comfortable for a par or a birdie. Now imagine a situation that could make you nervous. Rate your level of nervousness on a scale of 0 to 10, with 10 indicating extreme nervousness and 0 indicating calmness.

2. Treat for the possibility of reversal by tapping the Side of Hand (SH) or rubbing the Sore Spot (SS) while thinking or saying to yourself three times, "I accept myself even if I become nervous (put the statement in your own words.) when putting." It also may be helpful to tap the SH or rub the SS while saying, "I accept myself with all my problems and limitations."

3. Look at the chart below and at diagram 22 (on page 141) to identify the locations for the meridian points for Under Eye (UE), Under Arm (UA), and Under Collarbone (UCB). While thinking about the situation and/or feeling, tap five times at each of these meridian points. Tap them in the following order: 1→2→3. Tap only hard enough to feel it. The tapping shouldn't cause any pain.

Treatment Sequence for Practice Range Situations

Meridian		Location
Under Eye (UE)	1	Under the center of the eye on tip of bone
Under Arm (UA)	2	Six inches below armpit
Under Collarbone (UCB)	3	One inch below the collarbone near throat

4. Again, rate your level of distress on a 0 to 10 scale (a number should just pop into your mind.) If there is no decrease, go back to step 2 and cycle though the sequence again. If there is not a decrease after three attempts, this is probably not an appropriate sequence for this situation, or else there is another sabotaging belief (i.e., reversal) that needs correction. (See step 8.)

5. Next, do the Brain Balancer (BB) by tapping repeatedly on the Back of Hand (BH) while rotating your eyes clockwise, rotating your eyes counterclockwise, then humming a tune, counting to five, and humming again.

6. Repeat the tapping sequence 1→2→3.

7. Again, rate your level of distress from 0 to 10. It should be lower yet. When the distress is within the 0 to 2 range, go to step 9. Sometimes you'll need to repeat the treatment several times while you are imagining your fear—or even while you are in the actual situation—before you feel complete relief from the distressful situation.

8. As long there is a decrease in your level of distress, continue with the sequence until there is very little or no tension remaining. If the treatment stalls at any point, this indicates a mini-reversal. Treat this by tapping on the little finger Side of Hand (SH), while saying three times, "I deeply accept myself, even though I still have some of this problem."

9. When the distress level is 0 to 2, consider doing the Eye Roll (ER) to lower the distress further or to complete the treatment effects. To do this, tap on the Back of Hand (BH), hold your head straight, and, moving only your eyes, look at the floor and then slowly raise your eyes up toward the ceiling.

Practicing Long Putts

Practicing long putts (more than fifteen feet) is a good test to determine the strength of your mind/body connection. First, putt several balls until you start to feel the speed of the green. Then, go to a different hole, do your normal setup, and line up your putt. Once you have your line, take some practice swings beside your ball. Don't look down. Instead, look at the pin or the cup and let your arms swing back and forth in a putting motion. What should happen is that as you focus on the cup, your eyes should send signals back to your brain/body about how hard you should be swinging. Once you feel this, trust yourself. Set up as you normally would for a putt, and you should putt the ball with the correct pace. If you cannot do this, then you may still be too anxious and need to repeat the treatment sequence or treat for reversal.

Summary

As we have pointed out throughout this chapter, you will need to work on your mechanical skills as well as your mental game. Energy psychology will help you to be more focused and confident when you are playing your sport of choice. As a result, you most likely will become more aware of the mechanical flaws in your game that need improvement. You should also have less need to blame outside situations. As you eliminate self-sabotaging beliefs and anxious feelings, you may feel an increase in the amount of enjoyment that you receive from playing your sport.

CHAPTER 12

Developing an Effective Weight-Loss Strategy

During his morning commute, a man was talking to his friends about a book he was reading that was helping him to change his diet. Later, he mentioned that he had not eaten breakfast, so they stopped at a store. He saw a sign for fruit and picked up a banana, an apple, and a bottle of water. On the way to the counter, he saw a section full of cakes and doughnuts, and he proceeded to share his expertise on this subject. He picked out a box of chocolate-covered doughnuts and said, "Always get the ones with devil's food cake inside. They are much tastier than the white cake." Then he said that he had read that one shouldn't combine the fructose from the fruit with foods high in carbohydrates (and fat) such as chocolate doughnuts. He put the fruit back and bought a cup of coffee to go with his doughnuts. Clearly, that was not what the authors of the book he was reading had in mind.

Striving to Lose Weight

Have you ever made a decision to go on a diet, and then watched that decision crumble the moment you encountered foods that you love? The foods that are healthier and helpful to your weight-reduction plan are forgotten as soon as the cravings begin. If you haven't dealt with your food cravings, you will find a reason to eat that food—and you'll even find a way to make it seem rational. You may say to yourself, "I have to cheat sometimes!" "It won't hurt just this once!" "I feel bad, so I deserve this!" Or, "I'll start my diet tomorrow." The information in this chapter will teach you how to decrease your cravings for certain foods.

Interestingly, some of the foods that you crave are energy toxic and can create self-sabotage in many areas of your life. We believe, along with a growing number of authors on diet, nutrition, and weight loss, that the focus of losing weight must be on dealing with the emotional issues that sabotage your weight-loss goals. Overeating or an inability to diet is often a symptom of another problem that must also be treated. Once these issues are addressed, you will be able to create the changes that will help you to maintain a diet, lose weight, and get into the shape you desire.

If you are trying to lose weight, you aren't alone. The United States represents one of the most overweight societies in the world. In 1998, The National Heart, Lung and Blood Institute (NHLBI 1998) reported that 55 percent of all Americans are overweight or obese. In the last thirty years, the percentage of obese adults has almost doubled to 23 percent, and most of that increase occurred in the 1990s. To complicate matters further, people are becoming overweight at an increasingly young age. These data support our belief that the reason people cannot lose weight is an energy-related problem. It is unlikely that the problem is due to a lack of knowledge about dieting, because at least one new book on weight-loss strategies appears on the best-seller list every year.

American society perpetuates a myriad of contradictions about health and lifestyles. Fast-food restaurants have been a growth industry, yet the United States claims to be a very health-conscious society. The result is that diet books, magazines, health and diet foods, exercise programs, and health spas have flooded the market. Yet these products and all of the media attention about weight loss still have had a minimal effect on the majority of the population's commitment or ability to lose weight.

If you are one of the 97 million overweight adult Americans, then you have a higher risk of developing high blood pressure, gallbladder disease, and even certain types of cancer (NHLBI 1998). The correlation between heart disease—a major cause of premature death—and obesity is often ignored. It has also been suggested that the increase in American adults' consumption of sugar is related to the rise in the onset of adult diabetes.

However, the correlation between health problems and weight has had little impact on people successfully losing their unwanted and unhealthy pounds. Every time our society takes a healthy step forward with more emphasis on diet and exercise, it seems to take two steps backward as our consumption of fast food continues to grow.

Another discouraging fact is that most dieters gain even more weight after each diet attempt. And, for those who do lose weight, only a small percentage are able to maintain the weight loss for more than two years. For many Americans, especially women, it seems that they are forever going on and off diets (the yo-yo diet effect) and never succeeding in achieving their goal of substantial weight loss.

There are three main reasons why you can't lose weight or permanently keep the weight off:

1. There is a physical reason why you can't lose weight, and medical assistance is required.

2. You have insufficient knowledge about how to design an effective diet and lose weight.

3. You have an energy-related problem that triggers cravings and sabotages your attempts to implement any diet program. This means that you have an energy imbalance possibly due to a prior trauma and that self-sabotaging beliefs undermine your motivation and ability to diet successfully.

Any combination of the above concerns may apply in your individual case. The treatment sequences in this chapter, however, will focus on correcting energy-related problems, including frustration and impatience, food cravings, urge reduction, and more.

Physical Issues

If you have any health concerns or if you need to lose a significant amount of weight, you should definitely consult a health care professional to assist you in designing a diet that best suits your individual circumstances. You may have hormonal problems or ailments that necessitate medications or a specialized program to help you safely lose weight. Energy psychology will help you to identify and treat the emotional problems that block you from successfully implementing the lifestyle changes you desire.

Having Sufficient Knowledge and Information

Having sufficient knowledge as to how to lose weight is your first priority. Although most people do know how to lose weight, there is a growing body of research and information that can assist you. There are dozens of diet plans; you can select one or combine parts from several different plans. Once you understand the basic strategies that are involved in dieting, you can design an eating plan that best fits you. If you don't know how to diet, and even if you do, we recommend that you review a few diet programs that can serve as a guide as you develop your plan. *Sugar Busters* (Steward, Bethea, Andrews, et al., 1998) identifies foods that may be fattening, even though they are not generally thought of as such. *Making the Connection: Ten Steps to a Better Body and a Better Life* (Greene and Winfrey 1999) offers an overall approach that involves exercise, eating more fiber and less fat, and drinking more water daily. There are dozens of other books that you might wish to explore.

The more you know, the better equipped you'll be to design an appropriate nutrition program. It takes planning to change your approach to eating and to lose weight. With all the fast-food options available, it will be much harder for you to stick to a healthy diet and achieve your goals if you are not prepared with a plan. Once you understand the basics, you can design a unique eating plan that meets your personal needs.

Changing Your Mind-Set

For most people, losing weight can be challenging. However, if you have a good plan and you put forth the effort, without too much cheating, you will lose weight. However, Americans are bombarded with information about how hard it is to lose weight, which can undermine the desire to even try.

Frustration and Impatience

If you believe that it takes longer to lose weight than it did to gain it, you can become frustrated and/or impatient with the diet process. There is no evidence to support these thoughts or feelings. The fact is, it's just not as much fun to lose weight as it is when you are eating delicious foods and putting on weight. The amount you deviated from your normal food intake to gain weight is exactly what will be required to lose it. This requires a change in your mind-set from one direction (overeating) to another (eating in moderation). You may also have forgotten that you didn't gain all of your weight in two weeks. So don't focus on crash diets and try to lose it all in two weeks. In fact, your body will fight to prevent you from losing weight by slowing your metabolism down (Jibrin 1998). As we all know, however, if you keep overeating, eventually you'll gain those excess pounds.

Think back to all those times that you ate large amounts of fattening foods day after day, engaged in late night eating, or consumed alcohol. Just because it is more enjoyable to put on weight than it is to take it off doesn't change the fact that weight maintenance is still a fair deal. With exercise and a proper change of diet, it is inevitable that you will lose weight.

Effective weight-loss programs require a change in lifestyle. It is not an event that you complete and then abandon in favor of a return to the old habits that created the problem in the first place. Once you view diet and nutrition as a lifestyle process, your plan will change as you learn what foods create problems for you and what is required for you to achieve your goals. We recommend and hope that you will keep this in mind when you determine your timetable to alter your diet so that you can lose weight. The timetable will not determine how long you have been overweight, but rather the time it took for you to gain the excess weight. If you can accept that losing weight is a fair deal, it will help you to minimize the frustration that happens when you don't lose weight as quickly as you may prefer. Once you develop a plan, with the proper foods readily available, you will find it easier to maintain your nutrition program.

Treatment Sequence for Frustration and Impatience

Although these commonsense tips can help you to plan and better maintain your diet, they can't help you to deal with the emotional issues that often undermine your program. This is especially true with frustration and impatience. These two emotions often cause critical problems in losing weight because people give up, thinking that their diet isn't working, "so why bother?" If you find that frustration and impatience are a problem for you, then the following treatment will prove beneficial.

1. Identify the problem with a phrase such as: "I'm not losing weight as fast as I want." Or, "I have cut back on my eating and I still don't lose weight." It is always best to put it in your own words. Think about the problem and rate your level of frustration or impatience on scale of 0 to 10, with 10 meaning that you are completely impatient and frustrated to the point of giving up, and 0 meaning that you experience no impatience and frustration (and you understand that if you stick to your diet, you will lose weight).

2. Treat for the possibility of reversals by tapping repeatedly on the Side of Hand (SH) or rubbing the Sore Spot (SS) while thinking or saying to yourself three times, "I accept myself even though I'm impatient and frustrated about not losing weight as fast as I want." Again, it is always best to say it in your own words. For example, the words "upset" or "distressed" may be preferred to "impatient" or "frustrated." It also may be helpful to tap the SH or rub the SS while saying, "I accept myself with all my problems and limitations."

3. Look at the chart and at diagram 23 to identify the locations for the meridian points for Eyebrow (EB), Under Eye (UE), Under Arm (UA), Under Collarbone (UCB), and Little Finger (LF). While thinking about your feelings of

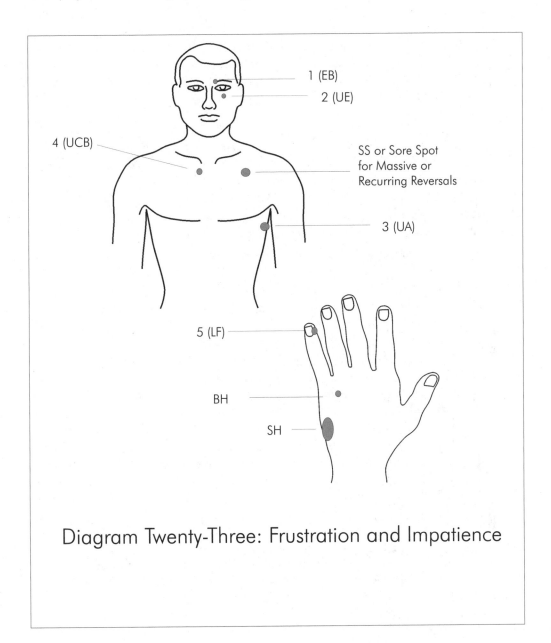

Diagram Twenty-Three: Frustration and Impatience

Treatment Sequence for Frustration and Impatience

Meridian		Location
Eyebrow (EB)	1	Beginning of eyebrow near bridge of nose
Under Eye (UE)	2	Under the center of the eye on tip of bone
Under Arm (UA)	3	Six inches under armpit
Under Collarbone (UCB)	4	Once inch below collarbone near throat
Little Finger (LF)	5	Inside tip of little fingernail on the side

impatience and frustration about dieting, tap five times at each of these meridian points. Tap them in the following order: 1→2→3→4→5→4. **Note:** The UCB is repeated twice in the sequence. Tap only hard enough to feel it. The tapping shouldn't cause any pain.

4. Again, rate your distress on a 0 to 10 scale (a number should just pop into your mind.) If there is no decrease, go back to step 2 and cycle through the sequence again. If there is not a decrease after three attempts, this is probably not an appropriate sequence for this situation, or else there is another sabotaging belief (i.e., reversal) that needs correction. (See step 8.)

5. Next, do the Brain Balancer (BB) by tapping repeatedly on the Back of Hand (BH) while rotating your eyes clockwise, rotating your eyes counterclockwise, then humming a tune, counting to five, and humming again.

6. Repeat the tapping sequence 1→2→3→4→5→4.

7. Again, rate your impatience and frustration from 0 to 10. It should be lower yet. When the distress is within the 0 to 2 range, go to step 9. Sometimes you'll need to repeat the treatment several times while you are imagining your frustration or impatience—or even while you are in the actual situation—before you feel complete relief from the frustrating situation.

8. As long as there is a decrease in your level of frustration or impatience, continue with the treatment sequence until there is very little or no tension remaining. If the treatment stalls at any point, this indicates a mini-reversal. Treat this by tapping on the little finger Side of Hand (SH) while saying three times, "I deeply accept myself, even though I still have some of this problem."

9. When the distress level is 0 to 2, consider doing the Eye Roll (ER) to lower the distress further or to complete the treatment effects. To do this, tap on the Back of Hand (BH), hold your head straight, and, moving only your eyes, look at the floor and then slowly raise your eyes up toward the ceiling.

Although this treatment effectively relieves frustration and impatience, you must be realistic. If you are easily frustrated, it will be necessary to treat this problem regularly before it becomes an occasional occurrence. Although you will still experience moments of impatience and frustration, this approach will significantly reduce this tendency during certain situations in which you would rather feel more patient, such as with your eating plan.

> When trying to lose weight, it is important to consider all potential reversals including massive or deep-level reversals.

Food Cravings

How often have you heard or made the statement, "I need to lose a few pounds." Although this admission is an important step in the process, what you seldom hear is people making and being committed to statements such as, "I'm ready to give up ice cream," "I'm ready to quit drinking beer," or, "I'm ready to give up (name any food)." A difficult part of losing weight is cutting back on consuming foods that are fattening. Unfortunately, fattening foods are often the very foods you crave the most, usually are readily available, and often taste good to you. That doesn't mean that healthy foods cannot be enjoyable as well, and perhaps even more so, but you may need to experiment with different foods and food recipes as you develop an eating plan.

An important step toward successful dieting is to minimize or neutralize your cravings for the foods that are best avoided. We're not suggesting that you will no longer enjoy these foods, but you do need to eliminate cravings that can sabotage your diet. The process is actually quite simple.

1. Identify a food that you crave, such as beer, potato chips, a certain type of candy bar, etc. Think about your desire for this food in a certain situation. For example, imagine you are with friends and they are eating the food for which you wish to eliminate cravings. Alternatively, you might have the food immediately available so that you can see and smell it. Rate your level of craving on a scale of 0 to 10. In this situation, a rating of 6 means you are seriously thinking about giving in to your craving and 8 or more means that you would give in to your cravings.

2. Identify any sabotaging beliefs and treat yourself for potential reversals by thinking about your desire for (name the food) and, while tapping repeatedly on the Side of Hand (SH) or rubbing the Sore Spot (SS) think or say three times, "I deeply accept myself even though I cannot control my craving for (name the food)." If you don't think you can ever get over your cravings, tap under your nose (UN) for a deep-level reversal while saying, "I deeply accept myself even if I never get over my food cravings." It also may be helpful to tap the SH or rub the SS while saying, "I accept myself with all my problems and limitations."

3. Look at the chart and at diagram 24 to identify the locations for the meridian points for Under Eye (UE), Under Collarbone (UCB), Under Arm (UA), and Little Finger (LF). While thinking about your craving, tap five times at each of these meridian points. Tap them in the following order: 1→2→3→ 4→3→2→1. Note that the UE, UCB, and UA are repeated twice in the sequence. Tap only hard enough to feel it. The tapping shouldn't cause any pain.

4. Again, rate your craving on a 0 to 10 scale (a number should just pop into your mind). If there is no decrease, go back to step 2 and cycle through the sequence again. If there is not a decrease after three attempts, this is probably not an appropriate sequence for this situation, or else there is a sabotaging belief (i.e., reversal) that needs correction. (See step 8.)

5. Next, do the Brain Balancer (BB) by tapping repeatedly on the Back of Hand (BH) while rotating your eyes clockwise, rotating your eyes counterclockwise, then humming a tune, counting to five, and humming again.

6. Repeat the tapping sequence 1→2→3→4→3→2→1.

7. Again, rate your craving from 0 to 10. It should be lower yet. When the distress is within the 0 to 2 range, go to step 9. Sometimes you'll need to repeat the treatment several times while you are imagining your craving—or even

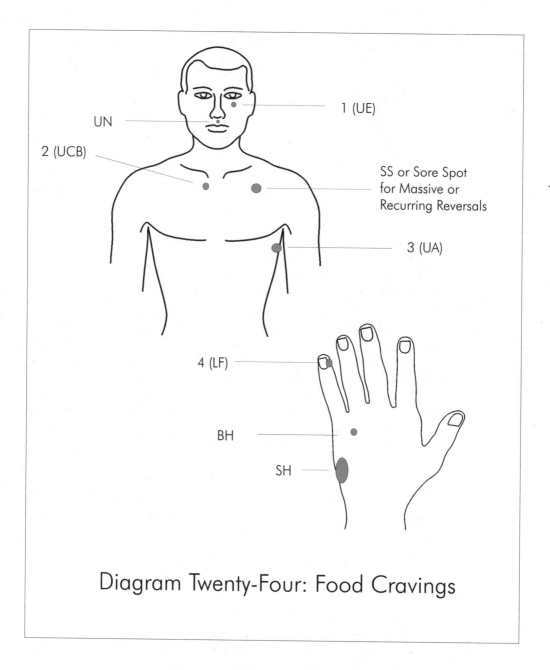

Diagram Twenty-Four: Food Cravings

Treatment Sequence for Food Cravings

Meridian		Location
Under Eye (UE)	1	Under the center of the eye on tip of bone
Under Collarbone (UCB)	2	Once inch below collarbone near throat
Under Arm (UA)	3	Six inches below armpit
Little Finger (LF)	4	Inside tip of little fingernail on the side

while you are in the actual situation—before you feel complete relief from the situation.

8. As long as there is a decrease in your level of cravings, continue with the treatment sequence until there are very little or no cravings remaining. If the treatment stalls at any point, this indicates a mini-reversal. Treat this by tapping on the little finger Side of Hand (SH), while saying three times, "I deeply accept myself, even though I still have some of this problem."

9. When the distress level is 0 to 2, consider doing the Eye Roll (ER) to lower the distress further or to complete the treatment effects. To do this, tap on the Back of Hand (BH), hold your head straight, and, moving only your eyes, look at the floor and then slowly raise your eyes up toward the ceiling.

Alternate Sequence for Food Cravings

If you have treated for any potential reversals and the above sequence was not effective, repeat the treatment and tap on the meridian points using the alternate sequence order of 3→1→2→4→2→1→3.

In most instances this treatment will at least temporarily eliminate your craving for the "forbidden" food. Realistically, however, you may need to repeat this treatment several times before the craving is significantly reduced on an ongoing basis. Also, to substantially alleviate your "addiction," it is important to treat your craving for the targeted food in a variety of situations. For example, you may tend to eat candy bars when you are bored, feeling tired, or watching television. Thinking about each of these situations or contexts while doing the treatment will go a long way toward effectively alleviating your craving for candy bars.

Preparation is an important part of dealing with food cravings. For example, many people want to have a snack in the evening. Although it is best to cut down on late-night eating if you are going to reduce your weight, you may find it hard to eliminate the late-night snack. The problem is that although a bowl of ice cream is very fattening, it is also very easy to prepare. Once the craving starts, you could have ice cream in your mouth in a matter of minutes. What can you substitute that would taste good to you and keep you on your eating plan? It has to be your own choice. The point is that you need to have healthy substitutes to satisfy your cravings.

If you continue to have a problem with the targeted food, read further and work through the problems that are examined in the following personal problems and belief systems sections. Once you eliminate any underlying problems, you will be able to more effectively control your cravings using the treatment sequences provided.

Personal Problems

Throughout previous chapters, we have identified and provided treatments for problems such as anger, rejection, fear, shame, and depression. If you feel that any of those problems still exist in your life, they should be treated as part of your weight-loss program. Most psychologists believe that these underlying problems must be resolved before you can create and implement an effective weight-loss program. We also find that as you treat emotional issues, it becomes easier for you to change your environment and lifestyle. Although we cannot explore every issue related to being overweight, if you honestly examine your life, you can most likely identify the issues that are blocking you from achieving your desired goal. Listed below are some examples:

Sexual Abuse

Some people who were sexually abused as children develop obesity. At a subconscious level they may view their obesity as a shield that protects them by making them less sexually desirable. Of course, not everyone who is obese was sexually abused. If you do have a history of sexual abuse, however, you should utilize the treatments from chapter 10 on resolving painful memories and trauma. Once you have obtained relief from those early traumatic events, you should feel much stronger and better able to deal with other issues in your life, including obesity. You may also have a reversal that deals with feelings of shame. The sequence used to treat shame is in chapter 8.

Rejection

If you live in fear of being rejected or if you have been significantly rejected in the past, you may be inclined to withdraw from social situations and blame yourself or past events for your problems. This only serves to lower your self-esteem and, in many cases, results in you spending more time alone doing sedentary activities, such as watching television. Although television may help to occupy your time, it cannot help you to feel better, and the reduced physical activity can lead to weight gain. Simultaneously, while you are watching TV or are otherwise withdrawing, you may gravitate toward food in an effort to help you feel better. Therefore, you need to treat your feelings and fears of rejection so that you can change your lifestyle and prevent situations that encourage overeating. One approach to alleviating this problem is to use the Midline Energy Technique described in chapter 8.

Depression

Feeling depressed about a situation or an event in your life can radically alter your lifestyle. For instance, you may go to bars and drink to feel better temporarily, which also sabotages your diet plans because alcohol is fattening. Because alcohol also blocks your ability to notice when you are full, it may cause you to overeat as well. Your depression may include feelings of anger and withdrawal from social situations. If you don't treat your feelings of depression, it is unlikely that you will be able to diet effectively. There can be many sources of your depression; chapter 9 will help you to understand the symptoms and employ a treatment.

Shame

If you feel ashamed of yourself for some reason, you may use food as a means of making yourself feel better. Shame can be the result of an event over which you had no control or one that happened when you were very young and lacked the resources to help yourself. To break the emotional cycle that may now revolve around food, the issue you feel ashamed about must first be treated. You can find the treatment sequence for shame in chapter 8.

Anger and Guilt

There is no question that certain foods, due to their pleasurable taste, are used to help soothe a variety of feelings, including anger and guilt. Food often becomes a way of comforting yourself when you have had a bad day. If you are trying to lose weight, however, this approach doesn't support your goal of a slimmer, healthier body. Violating your dietary goals can even produce additional feelings of frustration and guilt, as you realize that you weren't able to stick to your diet. Such emotional reactions can serve to further sabotage your weight-loss efforts. You can find the treatment for anger and guilt in chapter 8.

Frustration, Loneliness, and Weight Loss: A Case Study

At age thirty-six, Sally was attractive yet overweight. She often became angry with herself because she would not lose weight and look her best. Her weak spot was a craving for sweets. When she went on a diet, she would get frustrated and then go on a binge and overeat, usually with very fattening foods like ice cream. It didn't matter if she was hungry. She would keep eating until she ran out of that food or was so stuffed that she became tired and would go to sleep.

A related problem of Sally's was her feelings of loneliness. When she was alone at night, she was more likely to give in to her cravings. The first step for Sally was to use the Midline Energy Treatment described in chapter 8 to help her to cope with her fears about being rejected in social situations. This allowed her to feel better about herself and to be more confident.

After a week of doing energy treatments for her problems, Sally was ready to alter her social life to lose weight. Because she liked to read, she decided to spend more time at her favorite bookstore and coffee shop in the evenings. There she was able to meet friends and socialize. At the same time, Sally was working on her goal to lose twenty-five pounds during a three-month period. She picked a diet plan that worked best for her lifestyle. She chose to drink her breakfast and lunch, using a popular health food powdered supplement that she blended with skim milk and fruit. Although she had to pay more for the better supplements, they were lower in sugar and had more nutrients. She experimented until she found some flavor combinations that satisfied her tastes. She chose a peach-vanilla blended shake in the morning and a banana-chocolate shake for lunch, but she also mixed in other fruits, such as strawberries. This was a great strategy for Sally because lunch historically had been a high fat and calorie disaster for her, often made up of fast foods.

It took Sally the entire three months to lose the twenty-five pounds. During the first month, she used the energy treatments for frustration and impatience to help her deal with not losing weight as quickly as she would have preferred. She also used the treatment for food cravings to reduce her desire for some of her favorite fattening foods. When she went off her weight-loss program, she still drank one meal a day and then identified new lunch and breakfast meals that were not as fattening.

Whenever old habits started to return, however, she treated herself for being reversed and used the appropriate treatments to get her energy balanced again. In this way, she maintained her desired weight.

Belief Systems

There are many beliefs that could block you from successfully making a lifestyle change. These beliefs may fall into the category of deep-level reversals if the belief creates a feeling that you can never lose weight. To treat a deep-level reversal, tap under your nose (UN) while saying three times, "I accept myself even if I never lose weight because I (state your belief)." Following are some of the beliefs that can greatly affect your ability to lose weight.

I'm Too Old

There are some realities—such as advancing age—that must be faced about your physical abilities and the way your body responds to diet and exercise. Age, however, is also a state of mind. If you simply accept the fact that you are growing older, and let go of struggle and upset about this reality, you also will realize that aging has nothing to do with your ability to lose weight. Whatever your situation, once you accept it, you are in a much better mental state to achieve your goals.

Another age-related issue is a tendency to feel that being more shapely shouldn't matter, "because I'm older." Your weight, however, can affect your ability to participate happily in the events of other family members' lives. And, of course, your health always affects the quality of your life. Today, many people are living active lives well into their nineties. As a matter of fact, in some communities a large number of healthy people live to be more than one hundred years old.

I'm Too Fat

When someone believes they are "too fat to lose weight," they usually cannot visualize how they could ever reach their desired weight. They have a short-term focus and think only about what foods they must give up, rather than the wonderful lifestyle they could have if they lost the excess weight. If you fall into this category, you may be massively and deep-level reversed. It is advisable to regularly treat both of these reversals (see chapter 6). After treating the reversals, you can use the visualization exercises in this chapter to realize your thinner, healthier body.

I Can't Change My Diet

Believing that you can't change your diet may indicate a deep-level reversal. Once this reversal is corrected (sometimes this must be done on a regular basis), you should be able to use the other treatments in this book to implement and maintain your new eating plan.

I Have No Time

Believing that you have no time to plan and implement a diet can be a complex problem with multiple issues. Time is always a problem, but there are solutions. The fruit shakes that were referred to in the previous case study are a quick way to have a nutritious meal. Once you treat the time-related, deep-level reversal, other issues may appear that need to be treated as well. For example, although you care about your appearance, it may have become secondary to you, and this may frustrate you. After reviewing any emotional issues that may contribute to the cause of your overeating, treat each one. This may have to be done on a continual basis, as unforeseen situations can regularly create reversals, alter your emotional feelings, and make you more susceptible to food cravings. If you continue to use the energy treatments, however, you will be able to implement and stay with your diet.

It Takes Too Much Effort

If you believe losing weight takes too much effort, you have a deep-level reversal or a motivation-related reversal. To treat this, tap the Side of Hand (SH) while thinking or saying three times, "I accept myself even though I am not motivated to lose weight." By treating the reversal and implementing the sequences for frustration and food cravings (found earlier in this chapter), you should be able to find the energy to lose weight.

I Can't Stop Overeating

If you believe you can't stop overeating, then treat yourself for a deep-level reversal. Another reversal to consider is your resistance to the possibility of losing weight. In this case, tap on Side of Hand (SH) while thinking or saying three times, "I accept myself even though it is not possible for me to stop overeating." Situations or bad habits in your life can also lead to chronic overeating. Once you identify the situations that you feel contribute to your overeating, try to avoid those situations or use the visualizing treatment that follows to help you deal with that problem.

Visualizing Life Situations

You can use visualization to help you determine and become aware of whether you are going to have an eating problem during certain situations, such as birthdays, work-related events, and when you're feeding your children. Visualization will help to minimize the sabotage that occurs at those times. In each case, the object is to visualize a potential problem situation and decide if you need to use energetic treatments to stay on your diet.

Begin with an overall visualization: See yourself at your desired goal weight. If you're having trouble doing this, tap ten times on the Under Arm (UA) and ten times on the Eyebrow (EB) meridian points. You may need to repeat this treatment several times before it works to your satisfaction. It doesn't have to be a clear vision—just an image. Can you visualize yourself at this new weight? How would people respond to you? What other events could happen? These mental visualizations should feel good and help to reinforce your desire to lose weight. If there were any negative feelings or you could only see yourself as overweight, then you are reversed on being able to lose weight. We suggest you use the treatment for a massive reversal (see chapter 6 for details on the Sore Spot (SS) and then use the treatment for frustration and impatience used earlier in this chapter).

Next, identify situations that might cause eating challenges. Once you review a couple of the following examples, you may imagine the situations that would most likely happen to you. In each example, visualize yourself in that situation and then rate your desire or cravings for the foods or beverages. Using the same process, rate yourself on a scale of 0 to 10, with 6 indicating that you are seriously thinking about giving in to your desires and 8 or more indicating that you will give in to your desires. If you feel one of the situations is a particular problem for you, treat yourself for food cravings and repeat the visualization until the feeling is eliminated. Here are some examples:

- You are at work and a colleague brings in several boxes of your favorite doughnuts, more than the staff can eat. The doughnuts are just sitting on the table going to waste. What do you see yourself doing?

- You are at a social club and your friends at the bar are encouraging you to drink. Can you see yourself having only one alcoholic beverage and then ordering low-calorie drinks the rest of the evening?

- You cook large quantities of one your favorite foods. Can you see yourself eating a moderate amount of that food?

- Your children or your mate loves to have tasty, but high-fat, foods in the house. What do you see yourself doing?

- One of the ways you have fun with your children is to eat delicious desserts with them. Can you see yourself having just a bite and then eating a low-calorie food as a substitute?

The goal is to prepare yourself for the life situations that can sabotage your dieting efforts if you aren't prepared for them. Although treating emotional problems is key to losing weight, you may also have created many bad habits that must be eliminated.

Self-Destructive Behavior and Weight Loss: A Case Study

Carlos was a classic example of massive reversal. He had numerous problems, and his gluttony was only one of them. He drank excessively and used other drugs. He generally behaved in a reckless manner. He had trouble keeping his job, but because he was well liked, people protected him. His 300-pound body, however, was becoming a problem. His knees and back were a source of continual pain and he couldn't do any exercise. His eating strategy was to go to happy hour for drinks and a large quantity of high-fat foods, and to eat late at night. He usually went to bed stuffed. His doctor warned him that because he was forty-five years old, his lifestyle could create major health problems, such as a heart attack or diabetes.

Carlos is an example of someone who almost has to literally crash and burn before he is ready to change. Carlos went bankrupt, lost his longtime girlfriend, and had a car accident that put him in the hospital for a week. At that time, he came to see us and we taught him the energy treatments that he needed to balance his system. It was an off-and-on process for two months. He would follow the treatment suggestions, experience some results, and then go back to drinking excessively. This behavior sabotaged the whole process and soon he was overeating again. We encouraged him to join support groups to help him to cope with his many problems. The problem was that his massive reversal would keep coming back and creating the sabotaging and self-defeating thoughts and behaviors. We were finally able to convince Carlos to treat his massive reversal regularly and to apply several other treatments for food cravings, addictions, and anger.

After a few weeks, Carlos finally went to and enjoyed attending an Alcoholics Anonymous meeting. He developed a new group of friends that were not into his old addictive lifestyle. His continual use of the energy treatments and his change in lifestyle helped him to develop the focus to design his diet and to stick to it. Although there were some relapses during the following year, Carlos was able to lose almost one hundred pounds. The key was to stop the drinking and drugs that were sabotaging his life. To do that, he had to change his social life and some of his friends. Carlos is a good example of how changing one part of your life will lead to changes in other areas. Energy treatments that are done on a regular basis can help you to develop the willpower and strength to overcome many limitations in your life.

Toning Your Body

Toning your body is a very important part of the weight-loss process, especially as you become older and are inclined to reduce your physical activity. If you are going to lose a lot of weight, you need to tone your body as part of the process. If you don't, you may not like the flabby way you look after you lose the excess weight. The good news is that if you tone your body, it will start to regain its shape much faster, and you will look better even before you get down to your desired weight. Too often people think that if they aren't doing an extensive exercise program, it won't help. Although it is true that the more calories you burn exercising, the faster and easier it is to lose weight, aerobic exercise isn't a substitute for a toning program.

To tone your body, you should do exercises for your arms, back, and chest by using light dumbbells, and do stomach crunches and leg extensions to firm up the abdomen, hips, and buttocks. There are many good books that discuss how to properly exercise each part of the body. The goal is to do high repetitions for each exercise, without hurting yourself. If you can't do an exercise fifteen to twenty times with a dumbbell, then you are using too much weight. If you have an injury or other health concern, always seek the assistance of a health care professional before beginning an exercise program.

Two common problems that interfere with maintaining any exercise program are time and motivation. As far as time is concerned, the program we recommend should take no more than fifteen to thirty minutes daily to complete, and it can be done while you are watching television. If you are having trouble motivating yourself to do a simple exercise program, do the following treatment to enhance your efforts:

Enhancing Your Motivation to Exercise

1. Imagine a situation when you come home and you have no motivation to exercise, even though it will take just fifteen minutes. Rate your level of motivation on a scale of 0 to 10, with 10 representing that you are highly unmotivated to do the exercises and 0 indicating that you are highly motivated to exercise.

2. Treat for the possibility of reversal by tapping repeatedly on the Side of Hand (SH) or rubbing the Sore Spot (SS) while thinking or saying three times, "I deeply accept myself even though I have little or no motivation to exercise." It also may be helpful to tap the SH or rub the SS while saying, "I accept myself with all my problems and limitations."

3. Now look at the chart and at diagram 25 to identify the locations for the meridians for Under Eye (UE), Under Collarbone (UCB), and Eyebrow (EB). While thinking about your lack of motivation to exercise, tap five times at each of these meridian points. Tap them in the following order: 1→2→3→2. Note: The UCB is listed twice. Tap only hard enough to feel it. The tapping shouldn't cause any pain.

4. Again, rate your motivation on a 0 to 10 scale (a number should just pop into your mind). If there is no decrease, go back to step 2 and cycle through the sequence again. If there is not a decrease after three attempts, this is probably not the appropriate sequence for this situation, or else there is another sabotaging belief (i.e., reversal) that needs correction. (See step 8.)

5. Next, do the Brain Balancer (BB) by tapping repeatedly on the Back of Hand (BH) while rotating your eyes clockwise, rotating your eyes counterclockwise, then humming a tune, counting to five, and humming again.

6. Repeat the tapping sequence 1→2→3→2.

7. Again, rate your level of motivation from 0 to 10. It should be lower yet. When the distress is within the 0 to 2 range, go to step 9. Sometimes you'll need to repeat the treatment several times while you are imagining your lack of motivation—or even while you are in the actual situation—before you feel complete relief from the distressful situation.

8. As long as there is an increase in your level of motivation, continue with the treatment until you feel motivated to exercise. If the treatment stalls at any point, this indicates a mini-reversal. Treat this by tapping on the little finger Side of Hand (SH) while saying three times, "I deeply accept myself, even though I still have some of this problem."

9. When the level of distress is 0 to 2, consider doing the Eye Roll (ER) to lower the distress further or to complete the treatment effects. To do this, tap on the Back of Hand (BH), hold your head straight, and, moving only your eyes, look at the floor and then slowly raise your eyes up toward the ceiling.

Once you complete these treatments, you will feel much more motivated to exercise. You should use this procedure any time you lose your desire to exercise. You can use these same treatments to achieve an average or more ambitious exercise

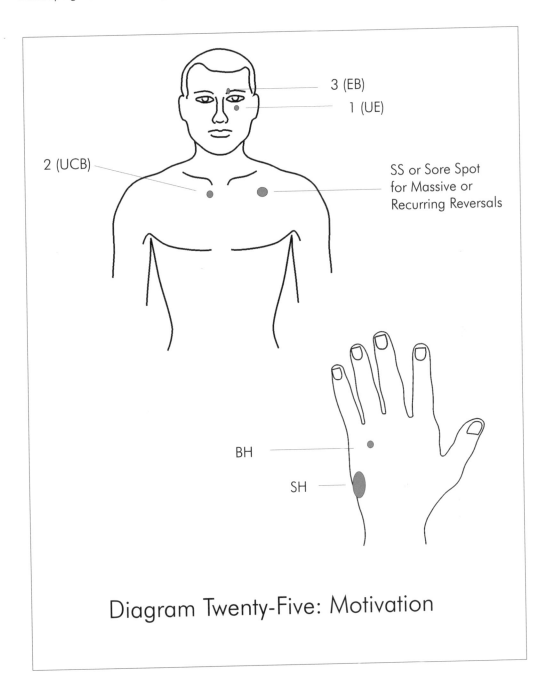

Diagram Twenty-Five: Motivation

Treatment Sequence for Enhancing Your Motivation

Meridian		Location
Under Eye (UE)	1	Under the center of the eye on tip of bone
Under Collarbone (UCB)	2	Once inch below collarbone near throat
Eyebrow (EB)	3	Beginning of eyebrow near bridge of nose

program. Your goal should be to do the toning program on a regular basis, three or four times a week. Any additional exercise you do will help you to lose weight and get in better shape faster.

Summary

Sabotaging thoughts or unhealthy behaviors can destroy the best diet plans by preventing you from staying on your diet. Although knowledge about dieting is important, it is the underlying emotional issues that must be corrected to help you maintain your program. Losing weight is not going to be done for you, but there is no reason for you to believe that you are unable to stick to a diet or an exercise program. You must understand why you are overweight. Yes, a sedentary lifestyle and too many fattening foods in your diet are a problem, but why do you have that lifestyle? Is your appearance really secondary to you or do you have certain beliefs or situations that make it secondary? You need to resolve what causes overeating in your life, and the best way to start is to use the personal profile in chapter 5. Weight loss is a complex and interactive problem, which may require a variety of energy treatments to balance your system and to help you to change your lifestyle to lose weight. If you continue using the energy treatments, you will eventually rid yourself of the sabotaging tendencies that undermine your ability to achieve your goals in life. And, in the end, it is inevitable that you will lose weight.

CHAPTER 13

Eliminating Addictive Behaviors: Smoking, Alcohol, Drugs, and Gambling

It is common knowledge that alcohol, drug, and gambling addictions are a major problem in the United States and throughout the world. They account for untold consequences in terms of money, health, productivity, and happiness. In addition, addiction can wreak havoc in the lives of the addicted person's loved ones. Although tobacco addiction is not as psychologically destructive as alcohol and drugs, it continues to represent a major health problem, as do most addictions.

Addiction is a dependence on a mind-altering substance or activity. When you are addicted, you and your body associate alcohol, drugs, gambling, or tobacco with the alleviation of anxiety and other uncomfortable emotional states. In essence, addiction is dependence upon a "tranquilizer." A fundamental goal of the addiction is the elimination of uncomfortable feelings.

Why do people become addicted in the first place? The fact is that many people use emotion-altering substances and engage in activities without becoming addicted to them. Addiction, however, can become a problem due to hereditary causes (as is the case with alcohol addiction) as well as when an addictive activity or substance is paired with the reduction of discomfort. Some people have a family history or genealogy that sets them up for the development of addiction, due both to genetic and environmental causes. If many people in your extended family have had problems with addiction, this may result in a predisposition to develop addiction. Notice that we said *predisposition*, not *inevitability*. Even if many people in your family and ancestry were or are addicted, this does not mean that you will become addicted too. There's plenty of room for choice. And with energy psychology, there's plenty of room for hope.

From a behavioral perspective, the development of addiction involves *pairing*. That is, if you are stressed, depressed, bored, or in other ways uncomfortable, and you resort to an emotion-altering distraction, such as alcohol, drugs, or gambling to alleviate these feelings, you will increasingly turn to that substance or activity to cope with those emotional states. This is what is referred to as a *stimulus-response bond*. The *stimulus* of emotional discomfort, which may be triggered by all sorts of internal and external cues or triggers, is paired with a substance or activity, which is the *response*. This response is reinforced because it is accompanied by an alleviation of the uncomfortable feelings. In time, you may develop an addiction. Keep in mind, however, that the development of addiction is more involved than the simple stimulus-response.

If we back up somewhat, it becomes obvious that the addiction itself is not the primary problem. True enough, once you are addicted, all sorts of problems enter your life, and these need to be dealt with too. But the most fundamental problem is the way you cope with those original and continuing uncomfortable feelings of stress, anxiety, depression, and so forth. To a large extent, these feelings are the result of what may be referred to as *perturbed thought*, which causes a disruption in your body's energy system. For example, you may have the thought that your life is stagnant. To simply hold this thought in mind without believing that it is true cannot cause a disturbance in and of itself. However, if for whatever reasons you believe that the thought is valid, it may result in a feeling of anxiety or despair. Those feelings, of course, can significantly add to your difficulties, possibly making it even more unlikely that your life will be productive.

Chronic uncomfortable feelings generally do not help you to move your life in a positive direction. Most often, such feelings interfere with your ability to get in touch with your resources, such as your hope and courage, and affect your ability to plan an effective course of action. As noted, perturbed thoughts result in a disruption in your body's energy system that, in turn, causes chemical, neurological, and behavioral challenges that further contribute to the problem. Removing the disruption from these core thoughts that trigger the addiction process is a primary key to recovery. This is where energy psychology techniques can help you to overcome your addiction.

Comprehensive Treatment

Although energy treatments are helpful to recovery, chronic addictions require a comprehensive treatment approach. Besides involvement in intensive individual and family therapy, we highly recommend twelve-step programs such as Alcoholics Anonymous, Narcotics Anonymous, and Gamblers Anonymous. These programs provide a wonderful support system, a fellowship that assists the addicted person in many steps to recovery, including recognizing their need for abstinence, making amends for past wrongdoing, developing a relapse prevention plan, contributing to the welfare and sobriety of others, and focusing on spiritual development. For those who have a difficult time with the spiritual component of programs such as Alcoholics Anonymous, perhaps seeing it as a religious denomination of sorts, there is Secular Organizations for Sobriety (SOS), which enlists many principles similar to the above organizations, but also focuses on scientific approaches to overcoming addiction.

It is imperative that the addicted person practice abstinence. There is no good scientific evidence that a person can become a social drinker or drug user once they have experienced extreme alcohol or drug dependence. In fact, there is considerable clinical evidence to the contrary. This also seems to hold true for people who have been addicted to gambling and even tobacco. Therefore, we highly recommend that if you have had a problem with addiction, you not become seduced by any claims that it is possible to occasionally drink, use drugs, gamble, or smoke. If you start to believe that you can occasionally engage in these activities, remember that this is an aspect of addiction that leads to relapse. In Alcoholics Anonymous and Narcotics Anonymous they talk about "Slick," who is the addictive part of the addict's personality. Slick is very good at deceiving you into believing that you can *have just one*, that you *deserve to drink or use*, that *no one will ever know*, and other similar manipulations. This is all an aspect of addictive thinking and relapse. It is also consistent with what energy psychology refers to as psychological reversal.

Additionally, it is crucial for the addicted person to use the personal profile (see chapter 5) to identify and treat beliefs and behaviors that may be the source of their energy imbalance. This process, used in combination with the urge reduction treatments and psychological reversal treatments that follow, will help to break up the addictive pattern.

In this chapter, we provide energy psychology and related techniques that can be used to augment other therapeutic approaches. These techniques will help you to eliminate addictive urges and support your recovery process. If you start to have relapse-related thoughts, it is important that you repeat the treatment process that is in this chapter.

Psychological Reversals

As we have noted throughout this book, psychological reversals are frequently the primary obstacles to getting over any problem. When you are psychologically reversed, regardless of the substance or activity—smoking, alcohol, drugs, or gambling—you continue to use at an addictive level even though you know that what you are doing is bad for you. In a sense, when you are reversed, you treat something that is bad as though it is good or as though it were helping you. This type of faulty thought process draws you back to addictive use even after you have abstained for a period of time. Being psychologically reversed prevents otherwise effective treatments from working. It is important to avoid becoming psychologically reversed if you are going to remain on the road to recovery from addiction. To achieve this, it is important to treat yourself for reversals on a regular basis. During the initial phase of recovery, it is important to correct reversals frequently throughout the day, even as often as once an hour. This can easily be prompted by setting a wrist alarm to sound every hour, or by whatever other means you might prefer.

The importance of regularly treating psychological reversal is highlighted by the experience of one woman who was addicted to pain medication. This patient did not have a pain problem, but narcotics were her drug of choice. After she went through the energy treatment described below, this woman's urges could be reliably alleviated both in sessions and independently on her own. Unfortunately, this woman had a psychological reversal that caused her to refuse to use the treatment every time an urge occurred. When she was asked why she chose to take pain pills rather than implement the urge reduction treatment, she said, "I don't use that all the time. It works!" Obviously, when this woman was in a state of psychological reversal, she preferred doing what was bad for her (the drugs) to something that could support recovery (the treatment). As she became aware of this tendency to be psychologically reversed, she was able to consistently correct for the reversal and then be well on her way to recovery.

There are certain types of reversals that appear most frequently with addiction. In addition to the reversals covered in chapter 6, the reversals below commonly affect addicted individuals.

Deprivation Reversal

With deprivation reversal, you feel terribly deprived when you are not engaged in your addiction. It's as though your unconscious is whining. To treat this reversal, tap on the Side of Hand (SH) or rub the Sore Spot (SS) while saying or thinking three times, "I deeply accept myself even though I'll feel deprived if I get over my addiction to (name your addiction, e.g., alcohol, drugs, gambling, etc.)."

Identity Reversal

With identity reversal, the addiction has become a part of your personality. To treat this reversal, tap on the Side of Hand (SH) or rub on the Sore Spot (SS) while saying or thinking three times, "I deeply accept myself even though this addiction is a part of my identity."

Self-Acceptance

When doing these corrections, some people have a difficult time making the statement, "I deeply accept myself," because they realize that they really don't accept themselves. This is all the more reason why this phrase should be used. In time, it helps to instill a deeper sense of self-acceptance, which is an important aspect of being able to get over any problem.

Developing Emotional Commitment

Some time ago, one of the authors of *Energy Tapping* was highly addicted to nicotine. He smoked two to three packs of cigarettes daily. Every time he would muster up enough disgust to enable him to quit the repulsive habit of smoking, he would eventually relapse. Immediately preceding relapse, all of the reasons for quitting smoking became less significant, more foggy, and even forgotten. Only after he was again smoking at an addictive level did the original reasons for quitting become, once again, all too apparent. To paraphrase Mark Twain, "It ain't hard to quit smoking; I've done it a hundred times."

Certainly, it isn't easy to remain substance-free with any addiction. The author eventually realized that he started smoking again because he continually forgot the reasons he quit in the first place. Just before his next attempt at quitting, he wrote down a list of his reasons, which included the following: clothing smelling like cigarettes, bad taste in his mouth every morning, fear of a heart attack, wasted money, considerable tension at the end of the day after smoking excessively, being controlled by cigarettes, family complaints and concerns, tending to plan his day around when he can have his next cigarette, and so on. Upon quitting smoking, he carried this list with him at all times, realizing that at some point his motivation would fade and reviewing these reasons would help him reactivate his emotional commitment to not smoke. The emotional commitment is what allowed him to be successful. To simply consider it to be a fairly good idea to quit smoking or to alleviate any other addiction in your life is one thing, but to have a strong emotional commitment about it is quite another.

Ongoing emotional commitment truly yields results. In this way, the author was able to maintain his course anytime he found his resolve beginning to waver. His last attempt to quit smoking was more than seventeen years ago, and he has remained a comfortable nonsmoker ever since. If energy psychology had been around at that time, it would have been a much easier task for him to quit. Now, he uses the energy treatments for those very rare periods when thoughts and urges to smoke return. These techniques are described in detail below.

Urge Reduction Treatments

The urge reduction treatments described below can be used to treat any addictive urge, including urges for tobacco, alcohol, drugs, gambling, and so on. The treatment will generally eliminate the urge, sometimes briefly and sometimes for extended periods. Once the urge is eliminated and you find that you cannot resurrect it, it is time to focus on developing new and more positive directions in your life. This is a very important part of the treatment process, and if you cannot do it on your own, you should seek the assistance of qualified professionals and support groups. As you use the treatment sequences on a regular basis, the period of time that you remain urge-free will continue to increase.

Complex Urge Reduction Treatment

1. If you are currently experiencing an addictive urge/craving, rate it on a 0 to 10 scale, 10 representing the highest level of urge and 0 indicating no urge. Otherwise, think about a situation that tends to trigger urges for you and rate the level of that urge.

2. Treat for the possibility of reversal by tapping repeatedly on the Side of Hand (SH) or rubbing the Sore Spot (SS) while saying or thinking three times, "I deeply accept myself even though I have this urge." It also may be helpful to tap the SH or rub the SS while saying, "I accept myself with all my problems and limitations."

3. Look at the chart and at diagram 26 to identify the locations for the meridian points Under Eye (UE), Under Collarbone (UCB), Under Arm (UA), and Little Finger (LF). While thinking about the urge, tap five times at each of these meridian points. Tap them in the following order: 1→2→3→4→3→2→1.

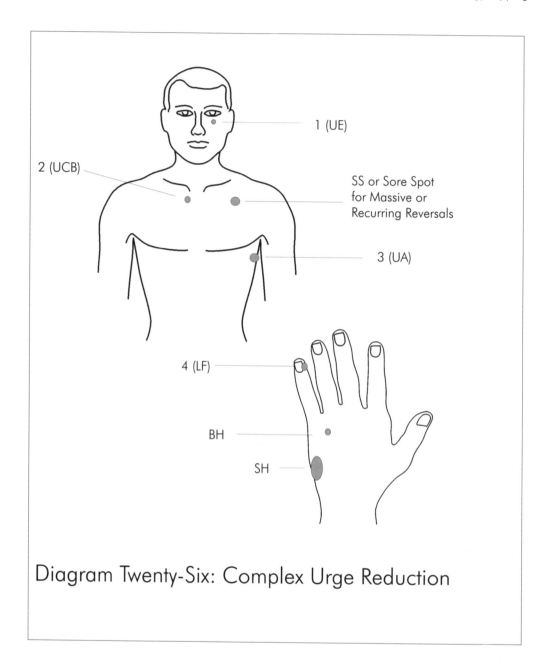

Diagram Twenty-Six: Complex Urge Reduction

Treatment Sequence for Complex Urge Reduction

Meridian		Location
Under Eye (UE)	1	Under center of eye on tip of bone
Under Collarbone (UCB)	2	One inch under collarbone near throat
Under Arm (UA)	3	Six inches under armpit
Little Finger (LF)	4	Inside tip of little fingernail on the side

Note: The UE, UCB, and UA are repeated twice in the sequence. Tap only hard enough to feel it. The tapping shouldn't cause any pain.

4. Again, rate your addictive urge on a 0 to 10 scale (a number should just pop into your mind). If there is no decrease, go back to step 2 and cycle through the sequence again. If there is not a decrease after three attempts, which is rare, go on to the Highly Complex Urge Reduction Treatment.

5. Next, do the Brain Balancer (BB) by tapping repeatedly at the Back of Hand (BH) while rotating your eyes clockwise, rotating your eyes counterclockwise, then humming a tune, counting to five, and then humming again.

6. Repeat the tapping sequence 1→2→3→4→3→2→1.

7. Again, rate your urge from 0 to 10. If there is a decrease, continue with the treatment sequence until there is very little or no addictive urge remaining. (See step 9.)

8. If at any point the urge stops decreasing, this indicates a mini-reversal. Treat this by tapping on the little finger Side of Hand (SH) while saying three times, "I deeply accept myself even though I still have this urge." Then repeat the treatment until there is very little or no urge left.

9. When the urge level is 0 to 2, do the Eye Roll (ER) to decrease the urge further or to complete the treatment effects. To do this, tap on the Back of Hand (BH), hold your head straight, and, moving only your eyes, look at the floor and then slowly raise your eyes up toward the ceiling.

If the urge should return at a later time, repeat these treatments. In time, the recurrence of addictive urges will become less and less frequent. When you are unable to resurrect the urge after doing this overall treatment, it is best to avoid thinking about your addiction. Once you are urge-free, become involved in activities that are far removed from the addiction.

Although the Complex Urge Reduction Treatment effectively reduces most addictive urges, at times it proves to be insufficient. In this case, a more comprehensive treatment is needed, such as the one that follows.

Highly Complex Urge Reduction Treatment

1. If you are currently experiencing an addictive urge/craving, rate it on a scale of 0 to 10, with 10 representing the highest level of urge and 0 indicating no urge. Otherwise, think about a situation that tends to trigger urges for you, *really think about it*, and rate the level of that urge.

2. Treat for the possibility of reversal by tapping repeatedly on the Side of Hand (SH) or rubbing the Sore Spot (SS) while thinking or saying three times, "I deeply accept myself even though I have this urge." It also may be helpful to tap the SH or rub the SS while saying, "I accept myself with all my problems and limitations."

3. Look at the chart and at diagram 27 to identify the locations of the meridian points for Eyebrow (EB), Side of Eye (SE), Under Eye (UE), Under Nose (UN), Under Bottom Lip (UBL), Under Collarbone (UCB), Under Arm (UA), Under

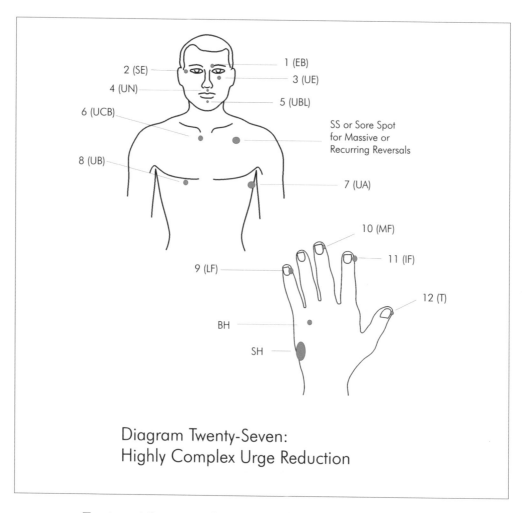

Diagram Twenty-Seven:
Highly Complex Urge Reduction

Treatment Sequence for Highly Complex Urge Reduction

Meridian		Location
Eyebrow (EB)	1	Beginning of eyebrow near bridge of nose
Side of Eye (SE)	2	Side of eye on bony orbit near temple
Under Eye (UE)	3	Under the center of eye on tip of bone
Under Nose (UN)	4	Under nose and above upper lip
Under Bottom Lip (UBL)	5	Under bottom lip in cleft of chin
Under Collarbone (UCB)	6	Under collarbone next to chest bone
Under Arm (UA)	7	Six inches under armpit
Under Breast (UB)	8	Directly under breast on rib
Little Finger (LF)	9	Inside tip of little fingernail on the side
Middle Finger (MF)	10	Inside tip of middle fingernail
Index Finger (IF)	11	Tip of index fingernial on the side nearest the thumb
Thumb (T)	12	Outside tip of thumbnail

Breast (UB), Little Finger (LF), Middle Finger (MF), Index Finger (IF), and Thumb (T). While thinking about your urge/craving, tap five times at each of these meridian points. Tap them in the following order: 1→2→3→4→5→6→7→8→9→10→11→12. Tap only hard enough to feel it. The tapping shouldn't cause any pain.

4. Again, rate your urge or craving on a 0 to 10 scale (a number should just pop into your mind). If there is no decrease, go back to step 2 and cycle through the sequence again. If three rounds of this treatment do not alleviate the addictive urge, you should consider other possible reversals, i.e., the Midline Energy Treatment in chapter 8 and the Over-energy Correction in chapter 2.

5. If there is a decrease of two or more points, do the Brain Balancer (BB) by tapping repeatedly at the Back of Hand (BH) while rotating your eyes clockwise, rotating your eyes counterclockwise, then humming a tune, counting to five, and humming again.

6. Repeat the tapping sequence 1→2→3→4→5→6→7→8→9→10→11→12.

7. Again, rate your urge/craving from 0 to 10. It should be lower by at least two points? If it is lower, continue with this treatment until there are very little or no signs of urge remaining.

8. If progress of urge reduction stalls at any time, this indicates a mini-reversal. Treat this by tapping on the little finger Side of Hand (SH) while saying three times, "I deeply accept myself, even though I still have some of this urge." Then resume the treatment sequence, alternating with the Brain Balancer (BB), until the urge is gone.

9. When the urge/craving is 0 to 2, consider doing the Eye Roll (ER) to lower the urge/craving further or to complete the treatment effects. To do this, tap on the Back of Hand (BH), hold your head straight, and, moving only your eyes, look at the floor and then slowly raise your eyes up toward the ceiling. Then rate your urge level again. This technique generally results in a feeling of calm and relaxation, eliminating any remaining urge.

As noted earlier, when you are unable to resurrect the urge after doing this treatment, it is best to avoid thinking about your addiction. Now is the time to become involved in positive activities far removed from the addiction.

The two treatment sequences above are methods of alleviating addictive urges. These techniques can be used whenever an urge arises, for whatever reasons. However, there are numerous internal and environmental triggers for these urges and to be thorough, as many triggers as possible need to be neutralized with this method. Internal triggers may include feeling stressed, tired, hungry, nervous, lonely, angry, depressed, etc. Environmental triggers, depending on the addiction, may include a cup of coffee, passing a bar, being at a specific location in your city, encountering certain people, etc. Anytime these triggers occur, using an addictive urge reduction treatment will help to neutralize the impact of the trigger. Urge reduction treatments, however, may not prove sufficient to alleviate depression, guilt, and anger. In this regard, other treatment sequences in this book will be useful to help you stay on the road to recovery. When necessary, freely refer to those sections of the book.

For example, one patient was having excellent results relieving the desire for alcohol by using the urge reduction treatment. At times, however, he experienced a deep feeling of "emptiness" that would cause him to consider drinking to make the "pain go away." He said that although he knew that drinking would settle the feeling, he also knew that the feeling would return once he was sober again. Although this man's feeling certainly had much to do with the events of his life, his first step involved implementing the energy treatments for depression, which worked rapidly to eliminate his "emptiness" feeling. Then, he began to fill his life with positive elements, such as becoming involved in Alcoholics Anonymous, satisfying work, and healthy, loving relationships. Of course, this took some time. With dedication and the help of energy psychology, however, his life improved dramatically.

Summary

In this chapter, we have covered treatment for addictive urges and psychological reversals that interfere with recovery commitment. Using these treatments on a regular basis can go a long way toward eliminating addictive urges. Addiction, however, is often related to other emotional issues, such as social anxiety, depression, anger, trauma, guilt feelings, and energy toxins. These areas are covered in other chapters of this book. If you have an addiction problem, we recommend that you address it in a comprehensive way. Besides utilizing the techniques covered in this book, make other positive, healthy life decisions. Your life and happiness, as well as the lives and happiness of those you love, are at stake.

CHAPTER 14

A Satisfying Relationship

The titles of books written about male-female relationships are very revealing as to how most Americans approach and deal with the dynamics of their primary connections. Consider titles such as: *Intimate Enemies, Men Who Hate Women and the Women Who Love Them, Men Are from Mars and Women Are from Venus, Perfect Husbands and Other Fairy Tales, Why You Can't or Won't Make Your Partner Happy,* and *How To Make Anyone Fall in Love with You.* Based on titles such as these, it would seem our relationships occur on a battlefield, where the people we love hate us and are from different planets. We fantasize about perfect partners, but we refuse to make the partners in our relationships happy even though, in the end, we still want to be loved by them. If you are having problems in your relationship, these ideas may not be foreign to you. Most of us, however, still want to be in a successful relationship.

There are many best-selling books on the topic of relationships that offer good ideas and strategies. In the end, however, your ability to rise above negative emotions and self-sabotaging thoughts is the primary key to your relationship success. This will help you to choose the right person and to develop behaviors that will keep your relationship strong and growing in the right direction. Your relationship is not a "thing" that is separate from you. Instead, it is an ongoing activity in which you are responsible for your actions and your responses to the actions of your partner.

> Relationships—good, bad, or nonexistent—are the most important and complex aspects of your life.

It could easily be argued that families are the core of all relationships and represent the foundation of our society. Yet, in many ways, that foundation is falling apart.

Each year more than a million couples get divorced, and their children are separated from at least one of their parents. To some degree, every divorce or breakup of a long-term relationship is a traumatic event. It is never an easy decision. The termination of a relationship is often decided over a long period of time and is commonly accompanied by anger, frustration, and loss. Each person involved in the breakup must relinquish an important part of their life, and certainly raising children as a single parent is much harder and more emotionally draining than it is with a loving partner.

On the other side of the relationship coin are the growing number of people in their thirties and forties who have not found their partner in life. They also struggle with their frustration and doubt about why they are not in a relationship. They wonder if they are doing something wrong or what is wrong with them. Although people continue to strive for and seek relationships, they often behave in ways that sabotage themselves.

It would take an entire book devoted exclusively to relationships to thoroughly cover this complex subject and important issue. Although there are specific treatments for fixing bad relationships and creating good ones, this is not a simple task. The quality of your relationships is a reflection of how you feel about yourself and, from that, how you relate to those around you. Therefore, many of the treatments that will help to improve your relationships have already been examined in previous chapters. In this chapter, however, common relationship issues are addressed and treatment sequences are provided that have proven especially useful to relationships.

When we think of "healthy relationships," words such as love, caring, tolerance, forgiveness, and giving come to mind. When relationships are not healthy, however, the words are quite different, including hatred, misunderstanding, intolerance, conflict, anger, resentment, sadness, frustration, and vindictive behavior. What happens?

One common situation is that long-term or marital relationships often degenerate into an endless battle about controlling what you and your partner have to do in the relationship. The strategies and behaviors used to gain that control, even temporarily, will determine the success or failure of your relationships. As is true of all the issues discussed in this book, relationship problems can come partly from a lack of knowledge. It may behoove you and those you love for you to read a few of the popular books on the market. Unfortunately, the numerous best-sellers written about relationships have not truly affected the divorce rate. This obviously indicates that there is another problem.

In energy psychology, we believe that energy imbalances and psychological reversals prevent people from behaving in ways that can benefit their relationships. Self-sabotaging thoughts and behaviors may temporarily reinforce poor judgment as well as allow people to behave in a manner that angers and creates an energy imbalance in their partner, which complicates the problem even further.

The selected topics that are examined in this chapter include choosing the wrong person, plunging too quickly into a relationship, loneliness, rage, blame, relationship obsessions, and abusive relationship dynamics. In addition, some common relationship feelings and behaviors are explored, including nagging, anger, frustration, rejection, and vindictive behavior. Effective treatment sequences are provided for each.

Developing Relationships

Anyone can pick the wrong person with whom to be in relationship, especially if that person has a quality you immediately find attractive. This is only a problem if you choose one wrong person after another, over a number of years. In effect, you keep choosing people who are not appropriate partners for you, while simultaneously rejecting the right type of people. In these situations, the "right type of person" has a quality that you do not find immediately attractive, or they lack a trait that is especially appealing to you, so you push them away before you get to know them and their other attractive qualities. Although the problem of choosing the wrong person can be true for someone in their twenties, it is usually more of an issue for people who are over thirty years of age. In the end, you must decide what is true about you and your relationship behaviors. Your friends and family can be a source of valuable information about what you do in this area in your life.

The problem can be in the form of an endless string of short-term relationships or becoming involved in long-term relationships that you know are ultimately not going to work. Of course, if you are psychologically reversed on this problem, it can blind you to what is really going on in this part of your life. If you repeatedly fall in love and end up brokenhearted, you are most likely sabotaging the relationship part of your life.

The first step in treating relationship issues with energy psychology is to deal with any possible reversals and to complete the energy treatments for other problem areas. To do this in a thorough manner, review chapters 5 and 6 to identify any problems you believe are blocking your success or creating sabotaging beliefs. The next step is to identify the relationship situation that needs to change. Some examples include:

- I rarely get involved in long-term relationships.

- I often seek relationships with men/women who use me.

- I tend to choose partners based on looks/money/power and not on how they make me feel.

- I find it very difficult to find anyone I love.

- I get bored easily and give up on relationships.

- I am very picky and chase many good partners away.

- I am often involved with men/women who make me feel that I'm not good enough.

The list can be endless. It is up to you to figure out, in your own words, what is happening to you in the relationship category. Once you select the situation, then you need to identify possible reversals (i.e., underlying beliefs) such as:

- I don't deserve to be married or to have a mate.

- I don't deserve to be in a relationship with men/women who treat me right.

- I'll never be in a relationship that works.

- I won't do what it takes to be in a good relationship.

- It's impossible for me to find anyone who I love romantically.

- I don't feel I am good enough to have a long-term relationship.

- It would be unsafe for me to have a secure relationship.

- I would be deprived in other ways if I got married.

- It's not possible for me to commit to one person.

- I seek relationships with people who intimidate me.

- I become easily bored with people who don't intimidate me.

Psychological Reversals

There are four reversals or sabotaging situations that you should consider for treatment before you use the energy sequences to deal with a specific problem. If you have multiple problems and your relationship is only one of them, then use the treatment for a massive reversal (briskly rub the Sore Spot (SS) on the left side of the chest while thinking or saying three times, "I deeply and profoundly accept myself with all my problems and limitations"). If you have given up and believe that you will never find the right person, or that you will never resolve a specific relationship problem, then use the treatment for a deep-level reversal. You can apply this strategy to the relationship as a whole by tapping on the Under Nose (UN) and yhinking or saying the following statement three times, "I deeply accept myself if I never have a success-ful, happy, loving relationship." Another concern is that, at an unconscious level, you have come to believe that you don't deserve to have a good relationship. For this, tap directly under your bottom lip (UBL) while thinking or saying three times, "I deeply accept myself even if I don't deserve to have a successful, happy, loving relation-ship."

Most problems can be resolved by using the treatment sequence for a specific reversal (tap on the SH). This type of reversal may be important in treating your rela-tionship problem as a whole or any specific aspects of the problem, such as having a tendency to become angry toward your partner or having a desire to cheat. Remem-ber that reversal corrections are not necessarily permanent. Repeated corrections may be—and usually are—necessary. There are many problems that can negatively affect the vibrancy and longevity of relationships, including painful relationship memories, loneliness, rejection, and more.

Painful Relationship Memories

When you have a memory of a past relationship where you were hurt very badly, you may unconsciously prevent yourself from being hurt again by sabotaging current relationships. This can be the case even if you feel no pain now, but still have an uncomfortable memory and, at times, wish the previous relationship could have turned out differently. In these situations, you should refer to chapter 8, which addresses painful memories, and treat that problem.

Loneliness

Feeling lonely or feeling that you are unable to be alone and be comfortable with yourself can affect potential relationships. To correct this, think about a situation that would distress you and treat yourself for specific reversal. First, tap on the Side of Hand (SH) while thinking or saying three times, "I deeply accept myself even though I am unable to be alone." Then, tap twenty to thirty times on the Back of Hand (BH) while thinking about being alone. Then, tap five times on the Under Collarbone (UCB). This may need to be followed by the Brain Balancer (BB). Repeat this process until you feel comfortable and secure with the idea of being alone. (See chapter 8 for more details.)

Rejection

If you feel unable to deal with any rejection and have given up even trying to get involved in a relationship, treat yourself for specific reversal. First, tap on the Side of Hand (SH) while thinking or saying three times, "I deeply accept myself even though I have this fear of rejection." Then, tap five times at each point in the following sequence: Eyebrow (EB), Under Eye (UE), Under Arm (UA) and Under Collarbone (UCB). This may need to be followed by the Brain Balancer (BB). Repeat this process until you feel comfortable that you can cope with rejection. (See chapter 8 for more details.)

Other Issues

There may be additional issues that indicate that you don't feel good enough about yourself to be in a successful relationship. In this situation, you must identify the exact problem, such as not feeling attractive or not feeling successful. Treat yourself for specific reversal. First, tap on the Side of Hand (SH) while thinking or saying three times, "I deeply accept myself even though I have this problem."

If you search through the previous chapters, you will find treatment sequences for most of the problems that may be blocking you from developing and maintaining a positive relationship. You are encouraged, however, to treat yourself daily for relevant reversals, as they often block the development of healthy relationships.

Choosing the Wrong Partner

In this section, we will present two case studies and appropriate treatment sequences. As noted, relationship treatments are much more complex than most other issues. The following scenarios provide many examples, but you can substitute other treatments if there are additional problems that need correction.

The Story of Tara: A Case Study

Tara was a bright, attractive, successful woman who had never been married, liked to socialize, and periodically had short-term relationships. Tara was attracted to men in power positions. The ones she chose to be with, however, misled or cheated on her. The problem was that her relationships with those men didn't work, and she continually made the same type of mistakes. She also used a lot of her energy trying to make those relationships work. In the end, she felt disappointed and hurt when the men stopped calling or broke off the relationship.

Although there could be a number of reasons for this situation, in this case, Tara was choosing the wrong type of man for her. She was a very thoughtful woman who was interested in how people think and feel about situations in life. She also needed a man who would give her the attention that she needed to feel happy. One problem was that when she met men who showed a lot of interest in her, but were not the power types that she preferred, she would shut down and become bored. She often rejected them without getting to know them, because she assumed that they weren't exciting enough. Interestingly, in her own life, Tara is very much like the average person. What she didn't do is give men in less powerful positions a chance. Instead, by seeking the wrong type of man for her, she maintained a low self-image that reinforced her belief that only by being with someone very powerful or successful could she feel good about herself. The treatments for problems of this nature are complex, and people do not instantly change. There are numerous steps, but they can be done quickly. Once the treatments began, it started to create a new awareness for Tara about men.

Choosing the Wrong Person: Treatment Option 1

1. Define the problem in a sentence or two. It always is best to define it in your own words. Rate the problem on a scale of 0 to 10, with 10 being the worst situation and 0 meaning you feel clear about the type of person for you.

2. Treat for the specific reversals that interfere with your ability to develop a good relationship by tapping repeatedly on the Side of Hand (SH) or rubbing the Sore Spot (SS) while thinking or saying the problem three times. In Tara's case, for example, it would be, "I deeply accept myself even though I need to be with men who I consider powerful and exciting." Another related reversal to correct may be, "I deeply accept myself even though I prefer men/women who don't love me and who lower my self-image." Although this may appear to be at odds with what you are trying to achieve, you must first accept your behavior before you can change it.

3. Next, balance your energy system to help you stop seeking or being attracted to the men/women who are not good for you. Think about a person that you think was/is not good for you, but with whom you sought (or still seek) a relationship. Use the addiction treatments covered in chapter 13 to deal with this problem.

4. Again, rate your attraction to men/women who are not good for you on a 0 to 10 scale. If there is no decrease, go back to step 2 and cycle through this sequence again. If there is not a decrease after three attempts, then this is either not an appropriate treatment sequence for you, or else there is another sabotaging belief (i.e., reversal) that needs correction. (See step 8.)

5. Next, do the Brain Balancer (BB) by tapping repeatedly on the Back of Hand (BH) while rotating your eyes clockwise, rotating your eyes counterclockwise, then humming a tune, counting to five, and humming again.

6. Repeat step 3.

7. Again, rate your level of distress from 0 to 10. It should be lower yet. When the distress is within the 0 to 2 range, go to step 9. Sometimes you'll need to repeat the treatment several times while you are imagining your concern—or even while you are in the actual situation—before you feel complete relief from this problem.

8. As long as there is a decrease in your level of distress, continue with the treatments until there is very little or no distress remaining. If the treatment stalls at any point, this indicates a mini-reversal. Treat this by tapping on the Side of Hand (SH) while saying three times, "I deeply accept myself, even though I still have some of this problem."

9. When the distress is 0 to 2, consider doing the Eye Roll (ER) to lower the distress further and to complete the treatment effects. To do this, tap on the Back of Hand (BH), hold your head straight, and, moving only your eyes, look at the floor and then slowly raise your eyes up toward the ceiling.

10. This is a complex problem that requires additional treatments. The next step is to treat the "lack of interest" that you feel about men/women that would be best for you (unconsciously, you know who they are). In this case, think about a person whom you like, but for whom you don't feel an interest. Don't worry, you don't have to date that specific person, what you are doing is tuning in that feeling. To treat this problem, use the Midline Energy Treatment (MET) found in chapter 8.

11. Next, you should treat for a better sense of self or a positive belief about yourself. To do this, use the MET treatment while thinking or saying to yourself, "I am an attractive and intelligent person and I deserve to meet a man/woman who cares for me." This treatment should be repeated until you feel the validity of this statement. To determine this, rate from 0 to 5 the level of your belief about this statement, with five indicating that you absolutely believe it. Once you get to a five, you have completed this task. At times, it will be necessary to repeat this treatment so that the positive belief becomes an ongoing and active part of how you feel about yourself.

12. Lastly, you must develop more patience when you meet a new person who doesn't fit your exact criteria. Use the treatment for impatience in chapter 12, while thinking about how you feel about this new person.

The primary goal of this treatment is to stop wasting your energy on men/women who don't really care about you. These situations create reversals, lower your sense of self, and keep you stuck in negative, unproductive behaviors. Once you eliminate the problem, you will be more open to meeting the right type of person for you and, equally important, stop the emotional damage that occurs from continually chasing the wrong people.

The Story of Kyle: A Case Study

When Kyle came to see us, he was forty-two years old and had never been married. He had a good job and enjoyed many hobbies that kept him active and involved. He had a fear that if he were to get married, his wife would never be satisfied or that she would be an emotional wreck. He imagined that he would spend all of his time catering to her needs and, in effect, lose his own lifestyle, one that he really enjoyed. He had been involved with several women in the past who exhibited such behaviors, and that caused him to end those relationships. In two of those relationships, he really cared for the person, and he wanted to avoid going through the pain of separation again. Kyle felt confused and, in part, believed that the next woman would have the same problems. Perhaps unconsciously, Kyle behaved in a manner that attracted needy women, or even sought them out to perpetuate his sabotaging beliefs.

Choosing the Wrong Person: Treatment Option 2

1. Identify the problem in a statement such as, "I was traumatized by two prior relationships that did not work out." You also believe that all men/women are only going to create problems in your life. Rate your level of distress from your past relationships on a scale of 0 to 10, with 10 being the worst situation and 0 meaning that trauma from past relationships does not currently cause problems in your life.

2. Treat for the possibility of the reversal that all men/women are the same by tapping on the Side of Hand (SH) or rubbing the Sore Spot (SS) while thinking or saying three times to yourself, "I deeply accept myself even if I believe that all men/women will only create problems in my life." To treat the reversal that you can never attract emotionally healthy people, tap the Under Nose (UN) three times while saying, "I deeply accept myself even if I can never attract men/women who are emotionally healthy."

3. Think about a situation in your past relationships that traumatized you. To treat this problem, use a treatment for trauma in chapter 10.

4. Again, rate your distress about past traumatic relationships on a 0 to 10 scale (a number should just pop into your mind). If there is no decrease, go back to step 2 and cycle through this sequence again. If there is not a decrease after three attempts, then this is either not an appropriate sequence for you, or else there is another sabotaging belief (i.e., reversal) that needs correction. (See step 8.)

5. Next, do the Brain Balancer (BB) by tapping repeatedly on the Back of Hand (BH) while rotating your eyes clockwise, rotating your eyes counterclockwise, then humming a tune, counting to five, and humming again.

6. Repeat step 3.

7. Again, rate your level of distress from 0 to 10. It should be lower yet. When the distress is within the 0 to 2 range, go to step 9. Sometimes you'll need to repeat the treatment several times while you are imagining your concern—or

even while you are in the actual situation—before you feel complete relief from this problem.

8. As long as there is a decrease in your level of distress, continue with the treatments until there is very little or no distress remaining. If the treatment stalls at any point, this indicates a mini-reversal. Treat this by tapping on the little finger Side of Hand (SH) while saying three times, "I deeply accept myself, even though I still have some of this problem."

9. When the distress level is 0 to 2, consider doing the Eye Roll (ER) to lower the distress further and to complete the treatment effects. To do this, tap on the Back of Hand (BH), hold your head straight, and, moving only your eyes, look at the floor and then slowly raise your eyes up toward the ceiling.

Kyle used these treatments to get over his trauma about bad relationships and his beliefs that all women are the same and will ruin his lifestyle. The first behavior change he noticed after treatment was that he no longer sought women who were needy and, when needy women did approach him, he was able to see the problem and not become involved. He also started to view women differently. Although he has not yet found his mate in life, he feels much clearer about who he wants to date and he believes that he can become involved in a relationship again.

Relationship Obsessions

Relationships, or the lack thereof, always have the potential to create obsessive behaviors. Sometimes, people lose all rational perspective when they feel attracted to another person, even if the interest is not mutual. They feel compelled to continually phone the person and, in the extreme, to stalk them. This loss of control blocks people from moving on with their lives and from being attracted to others. In the extreme, obsession is a complex problem that requires outside therapeutic help. But energy psychology can address many obsessive behaviors that can undermine your ability to have a relationship. Although the case study below deals with marital obsession, the treatment could easily apply to those who are casually dating, for example, men who continually call women who show no reciprocal interest.

The Story of Kim: A Case Study

Kim is thirty-six years old and has never been married. Even when she is not dating someone, Kim's favorite topic to talk about is her wedding. She talked about all the ugly dresses she was forced to wear as a bridesmaid and what she would do differently. The details she provided about this nonexistent event, (her fantasized wedding) revealed her obsession with getting married. Instead of simply enjoying dating, she was obsessively focused on finding the perfect husband. She also felt ashamed and embarrassed that she was not married, and this feeling worsened with every wedding invitation she received. These negative feelings made Kim extremely picky about whom she would date. If they did not fit her fantasy, then she would think, "Why waste my time?"

Treatment for Obsession

1. Identify the obsessive behavior in a statement such as, "I must get married." Also, identify any beliefs, such as, "I should only date men/women who clearly meet all my requirements for marriage." Think about a specific situation and rate your feelings of obsession on a scale of 0 to 10, with 10 being completely obsessed and 0 indicating that you have no obsessive thoughts at all.

2. Treat each sabotaging belief with the appropriate treatment. If there are multiple problems, treat yourself for a massive reversal. Otherwise, for example, tap on the little finger Side of Hand (SH) or rub the Sore Spot (SS) while thinking or saying three times, "I deeply accept myself even though I am obsessed about getting married." The next reversal may involve finding the perfect husband/wife. To do this, tap the Side of Hand (SH) or rub the Sore Spot (SS) while thinking or saying three times, "I deeply accept myself even if I am looking for the perfect husband/wife."

3. Look at the chart and at diagram 28 to identify the locations for the meridian points for Under Eye (UE) and Under Collarbone (UCB). While thinking about the obsessive feeling, tap each of the meridian points five times. Tap them in the following order 1→2→1. Note: The UE is repeated twice in the sequence. Tap only hard enough to feel it. The tapping shouldn't cause any pain.

4. Again, rate your feelings of obsession on a 0 to 10 scale (a number should just pop into your mind). If there is no decrease, go back to step 2 and cycle through the sequence again. If there is not a decrease after three attempts, this is probably not an appropriate sequence for you, or else there is another sabotaging belief (i.e., reversal) that needs correction. (See step 8.)

5. Next, do the Brain Balancer (BB) by tapping repeatedly on the Back of Hand (BH) while rotating your eyes clockwise, rotating your eyes counterclockwise, then humming a tune, counting to five, and humming again.

6. Repeat tapping sequence 1→2→1.

7. Again, rate your level of distress on a 0 to 10 scale. It should be lower yet. When the distress is in the 0 to 2 range, go to step 9. Sometimes you'll need to repeat the treatment several times while you are imagining your concern—or even while you are in the actual situation—before you feel complete relief from this problem.

8. As long as there is a decrease in your level of obsession, continue with the sequence until there is very little or no obsession remaining. If the treatment stalls at any point, this indicates a mini-reversal. Treat this by tapping on the little finger Side of Hand (SH) while saying three times, "I deeply accept myself, even though I still have some of this problem."

9. When the distress level is 0 to 2, consider doing the Eye Roll (ER) to lower the distress further or to complete the treatment effects. To do this, tap on the Back of Hand (BH), hold your head straight, and, moving only your eyes, look at the floor and then slowly raise your eyes up toward the ceiling.

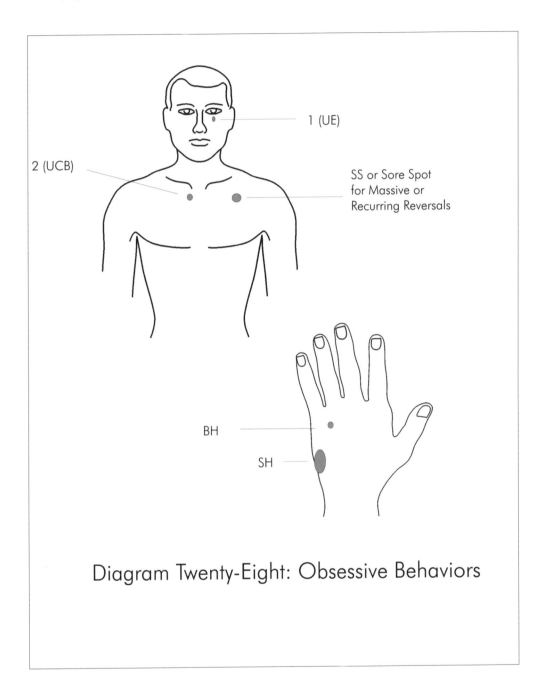

1 (UE)

2 (UCB)

SS or Sore Spot
for Massive or
Recurring Reversals

BH

SH

Diagram Twenty-Eight: Obsessive Behaviors

Treatment Sequence for Obsession

Meridian Point		Location
Under Eye (UE)	1	Under the center of the eye on tip of bone
Under Collarbone (UCB)	2	One inch under collarbone near throat

Because Kim was obsessed with getting married, she was reversed and her behaviors and beliefs sabotaged her chances of finding the right person for herself. Kim used the above treatments and eventually eliminated her obsession with marriage. She no longer feels any need to talk about her future wedding. She has not found her marriage partner yet, but she feels more comfortable dating. She believes that she has started to look at men differently and has had fun dating men whom she previously would have defined as "less than perfect."

Identifying Sabotaging Beliefs

The goal of this exercise is for you to specifically identify any beliefs that may block your ability to have a good relationship. All you have to do is use paper and pencil and start writing down your beliefs. They could be the list of traits you require your future partner to have or your beliefs about men or women in general. You are looking for the beliefs that block you from having the relationship that you desire, i.e., one that will be truly successful. Here are a few examples:

- Men always cheat.
- Women are only after money.
- Women are never satisfied.
- Men are only interested in a woman's looks.
- All men care about is sex.
- He/she will want to control me.

Next, identify the set of beliefs that are more specifically about yourself. For example:

- I will never settle for less than exactly what I want.
- I am not good enough to have a great relationship.
- I do not deserve to have a great relationship.
- I am too old to have a satisfying relationship.
- It is too hard to find a relationship that works.
- I'm afraid of commitments.
- I can't make a relationship work.

Although there are many beliefs that can interfere with having a positive relationship, the essential goal is to identify them, target them, and then alleviate them by using the energy treatments. It may not be sufficient to simply try to talk yourself out of the belief with rational disputing and positive thinking. For example, if you think you are too old to get married, remembering that more than 10 percent of all marriages in the United States involve people over the age of forty (National Center for Health Statistics 1997) probably will not affect your beliefs.

You need to treat the self-sabotaging belief that you are too old to have a successful, loving relationship by addressing the following reversals:

1. Tapping on the Side of Hand (SH) while thinking or saying three times, "I deeply accept myself even though I believe I'm too old to have a successful, loving relationship."

2. Tapping the Under Nose (UN) while thinking or saying three times, "I deeply accept myself even though I believe I'm too old to ever have a successful, loving relationship."

3. Tapping on the Under Bottom Lip (UBL) while thinking or saying three times, "I deeply accept myself even though I believe I'm too old to deserve to have a successful, loving relationship."

Sometimes these beliefs work in combination with each other. Those who are unable to find a suitable partner often believe (unconsciously) that they are not deserving of a good relationship, that it's impossible for them to have a successful relationship, and that relationships are unsafe. These underlying beliefs and concerns sabotage their relationships.

Often people will meet someone who treats them well and has interests and many characteristics that please them, yet they don't follow through in developing a relationship with that person. The surface rationale or excuse might be that the person doesn't look good enough, doesn't make enough money, or isn't exciting enough. Deep inside, however, they push away because they don't feel that they deserve to be treated that well. What often happens is that these people spend their time and energy seeking partners who have the looks, money, and excitement, along with a knack for making them feel second-best. They do this because being made to feel second-best matches the feeling and belief that they have inside, an unconscious belief that drives them to fail. To correct the beliefs and reversals that are blocking you, you must identify them in a sentence. Don't worry about being exact—you know what you feel and believe. Once you treat these reversals—and you may have to do this on a daily basis for a while—it will free up your thinking and feelings, and you will spend less time chasing the wrong people.

The Relationship Plunge

Another type of relationship problem might be referred to as the *relationship plunge*, which is the tendency to rush into a relationship before you really get to know the person. In this case, you immediately are attracted to the person for various reasons such as their looks, style, mannerisms, achievements, or interests. You fall deeply in love right away, and then later you come to realize that you and this person are simply not compatible. At this point, some people leave the relationship, only to repeat the same mistake with someone else. Others make the error of sticking it out, living in a state of boredom or unhappiness.

If you have an obvious desire to take the relationship plunge, you may scare away the other person. Such behavior comes across as needy, and the reason you desire to spend time with your potential partner is not clear. The following treatment sequence will address your tendency to plunge into relationships too quickly.

Treatment for the Relationship Plunge

1. Identify the problem in a statement such as, "I try to make relationships happen too quickly or I always chase men/women away." Think about an appropriate situation and rate your feelings of your need to rush into things about a specific situation on a scale of 0 to 10 scale, with 10 indicating the highest obsession and 0 indicating no obsessive feelings at all.

2. Treat for the possibility of reversal by tapping on the Side of Hand (SH) or rubbing the Sore Spot (SS) while thinking or saying three times, "I deeply accept myself even though I rush into relationships." You can be more specific and use your own words. It also may be helpful to tap the SH or rub the SS while saying, "I deeply accept myself with all my problems and limitations."

3. Look at the chart and at diagram 29 to identify the locations for the meridian points for Forehead (F), Under Nose (UN), Under Bottom Lip (UBL), and Chest (CH). While thinking or saying aloud to yourself, "I rush into relationships," tap five times on each of these meridian points. Tap them in the following order: 1→2→3→4. Tap only hard enough to feel it. The tapping shouldn't cause any pain.

4. Again, rate your feeling about the situation on a 0 to 10 scale (a number should just pop into your mind). If there is no decrease, go back to step 2 and cycle through sequence again. If there is not a decrease after three attempts, this is probably not an appropriate sequence for you, or else there is another sabotaging belief (i.e., reversal) that needs correction. (See step 8.)

5. Next, do the Brain Balancer (BB) by tapping repeatedly on the Back of Hand (BH) while rotating your eyes clockwise, rotating your eyes counterclockwise, then humming a tune, counting to five, and humming again.

6. Repeat the tapping sequence 1→2→3→4.

7. Again, rate your level of distress from 0 to 10. It should be lower yet. When the distress is in the 0 to 2 range, go to step 9. Sometimes you'll need to repeat the treatment several times while you are imagining your concern—or even while you are in the actual situation—before you feel complete relief from this problem.

8. As long as there is a decrease in your level of distress, continue with the treatments until there is very little or no distress remaining. If the treatment stalls at any point, this indicates a mini-reversal. Treat this by tapping on the little finger Side of Hand (SH) while saying three times, "I deeply accept myself, even though I still have some of this problem."

9. When the distress level is 0 to 2, consider doing the Eye Roll (ER) to lower the distress further and to complete the treatment effects. To do this, tap on the Back of Hand (BH), hold your head straight, and, moving only your eyes, look at the floor and then slowly raise your eyes up toward the ceiling.

The tendency to plunge into relationships often comes from a belief that you are not good enough or that you'll never find someone to love. A sense of desperation may strongly influence your approach to relating. When this is the case, that inner

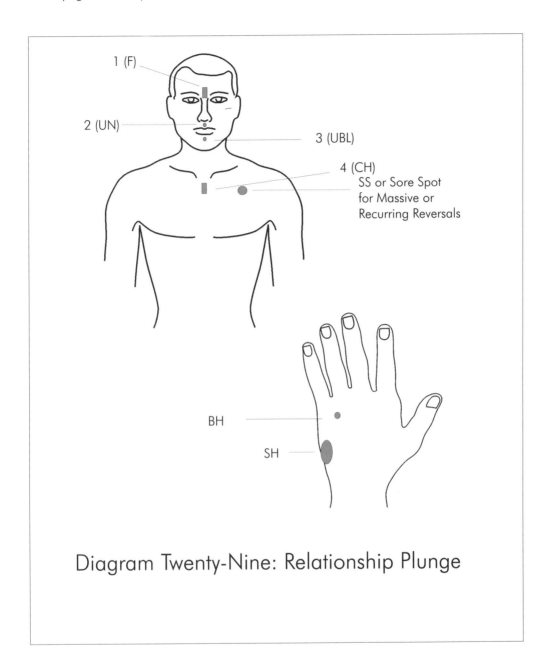

Diagram Twenty-Nine: Relationship Plunge

Treatment Sequence for Relationship Plunge

Meridian Point		Location
Forehead (F)	1	One inch above and between eyebrows
Under Nose (UN)	2	Above upper lip and below center of nose
Under Bottom Lip (UBL)	3	In depression between your lip and chin
Chest (CH)	4	Two inches below and between collarbones

sense of urgency and low sense of self-worth should also be targeted by using the following reversal correction:

1. Tapping on the Under Bottom Lip (UBL) while thinking or saying three times, "I deeply accept myself even though I believe that time is running out and I'm not good enough to have a loving relationship."

2. Then again tap the points five times that are illustrated on diagram 29: Forehead (F), Under Nose (UN), Under Bottom Lip (UBL), and Chest (CH), while saying aloud or to yourself, "Rushing into relationships."

Besides using this treatment before you even begin a relationship, you should also use it whenever you find yourself beginning to take the plunge. By doing this, you can help yourself to remain secure while getting to know the person. You need to accumulate enough experience with the other person before falling "hopelessly in love." In this way, love truly becomes a choice.

Understanding and Accepting Differences

In 1992, John Gray wrote the best-seller *Men Are from Mars, Women Are from Venus*. In his book, Gray attempts to help men and women understand their differences and to better communicate with one another. Gray offers insightful advice about how men and women typically respond to situations and how each can learn to react differently to improve their relations. Although he provides readers with numerous scenarios, two recurring themes throughout the book are:

1. Women should stop blaming or acting in a disapproving manner when their mates make mistakes or are in difficult situations. Supporting your partner in these situations can eliminate many problems.

2. Men need to be more attentive through affectionate gestures, such as flowers, touches, and hugs. And they must also show more interest in their mate's daily life. Showing your partner that you care also can eliminate many problems.

Although we do not wish to oversimplify Gray's book, these two simple behaviors are difficult to maintain on a regular basis, and may be the cause of many problems in relationships. We encourage you to read books of this nature to increase your knowledge and further stimulate your thinking about relationships. We also recommend *Divorce Is Not the Answer: A Change of Heart Will Save Your Marriage* by George Pransky (1992) and *Why Marriages Succeed or Fail: and How You Can Make Yours Last* by John Gottman (1995). These books offer common sense and research-based information about various sources of relationship problems and how to correct them.

To create the relationship you desire, however, you must invest your time in the self-examination that is required to determine what beliefs or behaviors are creating problems and blocking you from achieving success. Once you have done this, you can use the energy treatments in this book to eliminate or minimize these tendencies. Simply stated, insight and knowledge are often not enough to create healthy relationships. You need to target unwanted thoughts, feelings, and behaviors and then balance your energy around these issues with the treatment sequences in this book.

Relationship Issues

The following section deals primarily with the negative emotions and behaviors that may be hurting or ruining your relationships. Although we have selected a few examples here, no doubt you know which feelings and behaviors are having the greatest affect on your relationships. Be sure to review previous chapters to treat those problems.

Accepting Your Partner and Eliminating the Urge to Nag

One reason you nag your mate is because they behave in a manner you refuse to accept. For example, in the waiting room in a doctor's office an elderly man walked toward the exit door, pulled a cigar from his coat, put it in his mouth, and pulled out his lighter. His wife, who was following closely behind him, exclaimed to everyone sitting nearby, "Look at him! Look at him! He hasn't even left the doctor's office and he's trying to smoke that stinking cigar!" To which the man replied, "I'm ninety-two years old. Sixty years she has nagged me about this cigar, sixty years." As the man proceeded out the door trying to light his cigar, his wife followed him, shaking her head.

In almost every marriage or long-term relationship, there is some behavior or belief that one partner has that drives the other partner crazy. These behaviors sometimes are referred to as *pet peeves*, and they often lead to one of the most common complaints in relationships—a nagging partner. This type of partner believes that by continually nagging and often berating their mate, they will change (control) their partner's behavior. What usually happens, however, is that the person being nagged withdraws emotionally from their nagging partner. This doesn't mean that the nagging mate doesn't have a legitimate concern; it's just that the strategy of excessive nagging rarely works to produce the desired result. Nagging is a combination of anger and frustration. If the nagging is incessant and ineffective, you can be sure that a psychological reversal lies at the heart of it.

1. Think about a situation where you nag or do not accept a behavior of your partner. Try to be as specific as possible. Rate your level of frustration and/or anger on a scale of 0 to 10, with 10 representing the most distress and 0 indicating no distress.

2. Treat for the possibility of reversal by tapping repeatedly on the Side of Hand (SH) or rubbing the Sore Spot (SS) while thinking or saying three times, "I deeply accept myself even though I nag my partner when (name the situation)." It also may be helpful to tap the SH or rub the SS while saying, "I deeply accept myself with all my problems and limitations."

3. Look at the chart and at diagram 30 to identify the locations for the meridian points for Eyebrow (EB), Under Eye (UE), Under Arm (UA), Under Collarbone (UCB), and Little Finger (LF). While thinking about the situation (don't get into it so much that you experience any major discomfort during the process), tap five times at each of these meridian points. Tap them in the following order: 1→2→3→4→5. Tap only hard enough to feel it. The tapping shouldn't cause any pain.

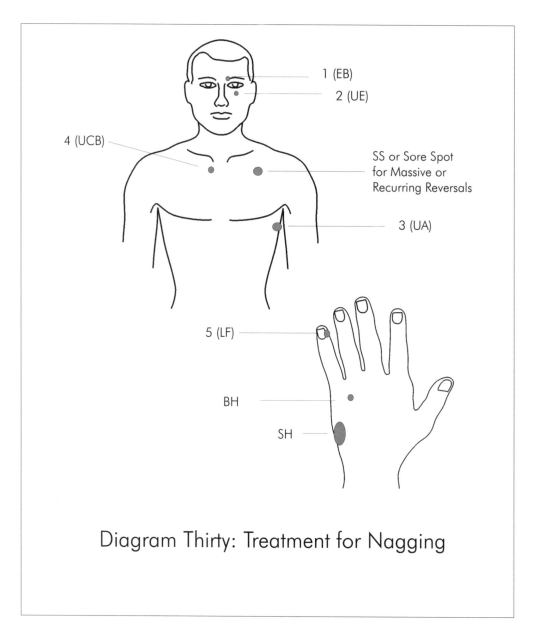

Diagram Thirty: Treatment for Nagging

Treatment Sequence for Accepting Your Partner
and Eliminating the Urge to Nag

Meridian		Location
Eyebrow (EB)	1	Beginning of eyebrow near bridge of nose
Under Eye (UE)	2	Under the center of the eye on tip of bone
Under Arm (UA)	3	Six inches below and under the armpit
Under Collarbone (UCB)	4	One inch under collarbone near throat
Little Finger (LF)	5	Inside tip of little fingernail on the side

4. Again, rate your feeling about this situation on a 0 to 10 scale (a number should just pop into your mind). If there is no decrease, go back to step 2 and cycle through the sequence again. If there is not a decrease after three attempts, this is probably not an appropriate treatment sequence for this event, or else there is another sabotaging belief (i.e., reversal) that needs correction. (See step 8.)

5. Next, do the Brain Balancer (BB) by tapping repeatedly on the Back of Hand (BH) while rotating your eyes clockwise, rotating your eyes counterclockwise, then humming a tune, counting to five, and humming again.

6. Repeat the tapping sequence 1→2→3→4→5.

7. Again, rate your level of distress from 0 to 10. It should be lower yet. When the distress is within the 0 to 2 range, go to step 9. Sometimes you'll need to repeat the sequence several times while you are imagining the distress—or even while you are in the actual situation—before you feel complete relief from the distressful situation.

8. As long as there is a decrease in your level of distress, continue with the treatments until there is very little or no distress remaining. If the treatment stalls at any point, this indicates a mini-reversal. Treat this by tapping on the little finger Side of Hand (SH) while saying three times, "I deeply accept myself, even though I still have some of this problem."

9. When the distress level is 0 to 2, consider doing the Eye Roll (ER) to lower the distress further and to complete the treatment effects. To do this, tap on the Back of Hand (BH), hold your head straight, and, moving only your eyes, look at the floor and then slowly raise your eyes up toward the ceiling.

In addition to nagging, there are a number of behaviors that can stem from anger or frustration. These can include low or no sexual desire for your partner, cruel remarks, and a general lack of caring about your partner. You need to treat any associated negative beliefs and reversals, and then treat your feelings of anger and frustration. To do this, refer to the various chapters in this book that provide treatment sequences for the emotions you are experiencing.

Vindictive Behavior

When you are feeling vindictive, your behavior is blinded by anger, resentment, and an unwillingness or inability to forgive and forget. If you have children, vindictive behavior can be very destructive because often your negative emotions can lead you to use your child as a vehicle to hurt your partner. Everyone loses in a vindictive situation. If you are reversed on this issue, however, you will not see yourself as vindictive.

To treat vindictive behavior, you need to identify, examine, and address any painful memories that are causing it (see chapter 10 on trauma and painful memories). Next, determine and treat the emotions that are driving your feelings (see chapter 8). Do you need to eliminate your feelings of anger? Do you need to forgive your partner? If you feel stuck in your vindictive behavior, reversals are often at the source, as you are no longer thinking rationally about your partner when you are wishing to hurt them (see chapter 6 on reversals and self-sabotage).

Battered Partners, Rage, and Blame

We would be remiss if we did not mention how energy psychology can affect the complex and dangerous issues of abusive relationships. On the surface, these types of relationships are a mystery. Why would someone stay in a relationship with a person who continually blames them for their problems and takes out their rage by beating them? For both the person who is battered as well as the one who batters, massive reversals are generally the driving force. Our hope is that if either partner repeatedly treats their massive reversal (see chapter 6), they will see the problem for what it is and use the other treatments in this book to treat the painful memories, rage, and addictions that are often at the core of abuse issues. However, because abusive relationships are dangerous, outside therapeutic help is a necessity in most instances.

Treatment for the Battered

If you are involved with a partner who has hit you or who abuses you verbally, the following treatment sequence may be helpful. These treatments need to be repeated regularly.

1. Think about a situation when you were abused and rub the Sore Spot (SS) on the left side of your chest while thinking or saying three times, "I deeply and unconditionally accept myself with all my problems and limitations." Then tap on the Side of Hand (SH) while saying three times, "I deeply and unconditionally accept myself even though I allow myself to be in this unfulfilling and abusive relationship, and even if I unconsciously believe that I deserve to be abused."

2. Now define your problem in a statement and use the treatment for trauma provided in chapter 10.

3. If you have any related problems, such as a drinking problem, fear of being alone, or trouble dealing with rejection, these issues must also be treated.

Although these treatments can prove to be helpful, in view of the significance of this problem, we again strongly recommend that you seek the assistance of a qualified therapist.

Treatment for the Batterer

If you find that you are unable to control your insecurity and anger, resulting in your hitting or being cruel and abusive toward your partner or other people, regularly use the following treatment:

1. Think about a time when you were abusive to your partner and rub the Sore Spot (SS) on the left side of your chest while thinking or saying three times, "I deeply and unconditionally accept myself with all my problems and limitations." Then tap on the Side of Hand (SH) while saying three times, "I deeply and unconditionally accept myself even though I'm abusive."

2. Now define your problem in a statement such as, "When I am drunk, I let my anger go out of control, I beat my partner, and I blame him or her for my problems." Now use the treatments for anger and rage provided in chapter 8.

3. If you have any related problems, such as a heavy drinking, shame, jealousy, or dealing with rejection, they must also be treated.

We strongly recommend that you seek the assistance of a qualified therapist to help you resolve this damaging behavior as safely and expediently as possible.

It is important that both the batterer and battered recognize that serious problems exist in their relationship. One way to do this is to treat any sabotaging beliefs and related problems, such as alcoholism. The more clarity you attain on this issue, the more likely you will seek the outside assistance that is needed. Clarity may also help the battered individual to recognize that their safety is at risk and to take the proper steps to deal this problem.

Summary

It is impossible in one chapter to do justice to the complex issue of relationships. The issues that exist in relationships are endless. You cannot change your partner. They will change only if they are willing to participate in self-examination and apply treatment applications. Therefore, you must focus on how you can help *yourself* to cope with these problems and to develop strategies to resolve them. You can also examine how your behaviors create or maintain problems in your relationship.

Emotionally charged issues, such as infidelity, may require multiple treatments, but you must first treat any reversals that are blocking your ability to deal with the problem. Your self-sabotaging behaviors may be helping to maintain the problem and/or may be preventing you from finding a strategy to stop it. Always treat any related emotional feelings, such as anger or jealousy (even when you believe they are justified), and painful memories or trauma. For some people, the problems in their relationships are chronic, meaning that they experience them in most or all of their relationships.

Our advice is: Don't give up even if repeated and ongoing energy treatments are required. Relationship problems often have a long history attached to them and, generally, no one can push your buttons better than a family member, especially your mate.

Consider whether your mate or the people with whom you are in a relationship are energetically imbalanced or if their behavior sabotages your relationship. If your treatments are effective, then you should be able to feel or recognize your relationship issue and be able to respond in an appropriate manner. This certainly doesn't mean that every situation will work out in an ideal way, but it may allow you to avoid spending much of your time upset about your relationships.

In closing, relationships are ongoing activities. You are responsible for your actions and your response to the actions of your partner. If your relationships are not working well, then there is some behavior or belief that is helping to sabotage them. Relationships are far too complex an issue to present specific case studies that cover all relationship issues. If you use the personal profile in chapter 5, however, and list all of your problems and treat them, you will eliminate the underlying issues and should have less difficulty using energy psychology to treat the specific issues in your relationships.

CHAPTER 15

Tools for a Lifetime

Be the change you want to see in the world.

—Mahatma Gandhi

Energy Tapping has introduced a new approach to therapy and self-help, based on harnessing the powers of your body's own energy system to overcome psychological and emotional problems. Many people consider energy psychology to be a far-reaching approach. We have provided a number of therapeutic sequences that can be used to rapidly eliminate or significantly reduce a variety of problems, including traumas and painful memories, depression and low moods, anxiety and phobias, other uncomfortable emotions, and limiting beliefs. Energy psychology even makes it possible for you to efficiently enhance your golf swing, or batting average, and realize improvement in other areas of your life. And it's simple. All that's required is for you to identify the problem by thinking about it, and then tap in sequence on specific meridian points to treat the problem.

Although we find this approach to be highly effective, in reality nothing works all the time, at least not in our business. There is always room for improvement, as there should be. However, of all the methods we have had the opportunity to study and practice so far, energy psychology is heads above the rest. We believe that it is *the therapy* for the new millennium. You're going to see and hear a lot more about it in the years to come. As a self-help approach, it offers you wonderfully effective tools for a lifetime. It's the psychological equivalent of the Heimlich maneuver.

In this final chapter, we would like to explore some ideas about the current and future practice of energy psychology. We hope that this will spur interest and innovation in the application of this approach to areas we haven't even considered.

Into the Mainstream

As increasing numbers of therapists are trained in the application of energy psychology, they are applying this efficient method to assist their patients and clients in resolving many long-standing problems, such as those described in *Energy Tapping*. This approach is applicable to many other areas, such as chronic pain, allergies, and many other physical and psychological conditions. Although we did not specifically address these areas in the present volume of this book, we encourage you to attempt some of these sequences, especially the Midline Energy Treatment (MET), to treat and resolve anything you'd like. Feel free to try it on anything.

Energy psychology is entering the mainstream not only due to its efficiency, but also due to the great need that exists throughout society. Most traditional therapies do not yield quick results and, with some concerns, they aren't effective at all. Although using energy psychology to treat certain problems sometimes necessarily takes a longer period of time, there are many problems that can and should be resolved rapidly. The sooner a psychological problem is resolved, the less likely it is that it will become a chronic, debilitating problem. We believe that it is sometimes the form of therapy itself that actually causes certain conditions to become chronic. For example, if you experience a severe trauma and the therapy you choose involves extensive reviewing of the trauma, even dredging up all varieties of forgotten traumas, then the therapy may not only prove to be emotionally upsetting, but it can also cause the traumas to become more deeply ingrained. This process, referred to as *retraumatization*, is very unlikely to happen with effective use of energy psychology techniques. The same consideration applies to a wide array of problems that people seek to resolve in therapy.

There are many conditions that people tolerate because they believe that therapy is invariably a long-term, arduous process. Because this is generally not the case with energy psychology, people are more inclined to pursue the brief, highly effective therapy that this approach can afford. We believe that the healthier your energy system, the healthier you will be overall, physically, emotionally, and psychologically.

Energy Psychology and the Future

Energy psychology is so efficient and effective that in time it will be applied extensively in the areas of therapy, medicine, education, vocational guidance, business, sports, various performance areas, and so on. The applications appear to be limitless.

In the area of education, we believe that energy psychology is readily applicable to the needs of inner-city children who suffer many barriers to their success, such as violence in the neighborhoods and in the schools. Energy psychology offers opportunities for students to alleviate obstacles to motivation, overcome test anxiety, and surmount learning blocks. Equipping school psychologists and counselors with these methods will lead to improvement in these and related areas for students. Extensive use of these methods may also help to reduce the incidence of problems in the larger community.

Energy psychology also complements traditional medical approaches. The impact of stress on physical health, for example, is well documented. Excessive and continual stress can limit the healing process, slow down recover from surgery, and lead to many other illnesses and problems, such as heart disease and hypertension. Energy psychology provides a tool that you can use to gain more personal control over your health.

Using energy work to enhance sports performance is a relatively new area. This easily applied technique can help athletes to reduce anxiety and alleviate sabotaging beliefs that produce many mental errors. It provides a means of regaining focus in crucial situations and helps athletes to separate their natural ability from their mental mistakes.

In the areas of business and vocational pursuits, energy psychology offers efficient means of coping with job stress, enhancing creativity, alleviating relationship problems, improving morale, etc. Managers who are trained in these methods can help to establish an energy balance that will result in a positive trickle-down effect that benefits the whole organization.

Insight

Maybe you believe that simply treating a psychological problem by tapping is not enough. You may also prefer to have some insight into the cause of your problem, which might lead you to seek talk therapy. Many discussion-focused therapists use energy psychology techniques during client sessions. These techniques are applied at strategic points during the session to quickly resolve areas in which the client feels stuck. This still leaves plenty of room for insight.

Having insight into your issues may be important to you even if you aren't working with a professional therapist. In this case, after you treat your specific issue—trauma, depression, anger, etc.—take some time to think about the problem that you used to have. Frequently, relevant insights will emerge. Generally, you will find that you think quite differently about the problem once the emotional charge is gone. Insightful thoughts can go a long way toward preventing the original problem from returning and can produce a sense of satisfaction in your newfound understanding.

Beyond Tapping

Once your energy system becomes balanced through energy tapping, you can identify the interconnection between your thoughts and feelings. Notice that after treating a problem with energy psychology, thoughts about the problem no longer have a negative emotional charge. You now feel calm and centered about the issue. This experience allows you to truly realize that your thoughts cannot have a negative effect on you unless you allow them to. You are now in a position of choice. This is an important lesson to take with you throughout life. Each time you balance your energy around an emotionally charged issue, it becomes easier to simply dismiss such negative thoughts in the future, even without having to tap on meridian points. Essentially, you are training your brain and your energy system to remain more consistently in balance.

Feelings

Our lives are filled with the wonderfully diverse positive emotions of curiosity, anticipation, surprise, joy, gratitude, love, respect, appreciation, and so on. We cherish these feelings, but we also have the capacity for negative emotions, such as fear, irritation, anger, rage, jealousy, guilt, sorrow, grief, shame, etc. Here the term *negative* should not be interpreted as meaning *bad*. In reality, there is no such thing as a bad emotion. All emotions are essentially a part of you; they were present even before your infancy. Emotions are forms of information and communication. For example, fear or anxiety alerts us to danger; anger tells us that we strongly disapprove of something; guilt lets us know that we ourselves have violated a value or a moral; with jealousy we see someone trying to "rob" us of something that is ours; and the list goes on. Just as we benefit from the emotions of joy and love, the so-called "negative" emotions listed above also serve an admirable purpose.

Energy Tapping is about getting to the point where we can experience the full spectrum of emotions, even the negative ones, without them dominating our entire existence. In the words of the Sufi poet, Rumi, "Welcome and entertain them all! Because each has been sent as a guide from beyond." Negative feelings become a problem only when we predominantly reside in their landscape, that is, when we spend most our time living there. We never want to get to the point, however, where we lose the capacity to make the differentiation that our negative emotional responses afford us. It's not about creating a Stepford society, but about properly utilizing this approach to eliminate emotional responses that have become problems in our lives.

In closing, we would like to express our gratitude to you for taking the time to explore and apply these effective tools in your life. We believe that energy has a resonating effect, both positive and negative. As more and more people come to apply this approach to enhance their energy and positively improve their lives, the lives of others will benefit and, in time, possibly the whole of society will be better for it. Changing yourself is truly the place to begin if you wish to help others. As Mahatma Gandhi wisely advised, "Be the change you want to see in the world."

Bibliography

Beck, A.T., and G. Emery. 1985. *Anxiety Disorders and Phobias*. New York: Basic Books.

Becker, R.O. 1990. *Cross Currents*. New York: G. Putnam and Sons.

Becker, R.O., and G. Selden. 1985. *The Body Electric*. New York: Morrow.

Bohm, D. 1980. *Wholeness and the Implicate Order*. Boston: Routledge and Kegan Paul.

Burr, H.S. 1972. *Blueprint for Immortality: The Electric Patterns of Life*. Essex, England: Saffron Walden.

Burton Goldberg Group. 1993. *Alternative Medicine: The Definitive Guide*. Puyallup, Washington: Future Medicine Publishing.

Callahan, R.J., and J. Callahan. 1996. *Thought Field Therapy and Trauma: Treatment and Theory*. Indian Wells, CA: Self-Published.

Callahan, R.J. 1985. *Five Minute Phobia Cure*. Wilmington, DE: Enterprise.

Chopra, D. 1993. *Ageless Mind Timeless Body: The Quantum Alternative to Growing Old*. New York: Three Rivers Press.

Craig, G., and A. Fowlie. 1995. *Emotional Freedom Techniques: The Manual*. The Sea Ranch, CA: Author.

de Shazier, S. 1988. *Clues: Investigating Solutions in Brief Therapy*. New York: Norton & Company.

de Vernejoul, P., P. Albarède, and J. C. Darras. 1985. Study of the acupuncture meridians with radioactive tracers. *Bulletin of the Academy of National Medicine (Paris)* 169:1071-1075.

Diamond, J. 1985. *Life Energy*. New York: Dodd, Meade, and Co.

Diepold, J. (1999). Touch and Breathe. Paper presented at the Energy Psychology Conference: Exploring the Creative Edge, 16 October, in Toronto, Canada.

Durlacher, J. 1994. *Freedom From Fear Forever*. Mesa, AZ: Van Ness.

Ellis, A., and R. A. Harper. 1975. *A New Guide to Rational Living*. Englewood Cliffs, NJ: Prentice-Hall.

Ellis, A. 1995. *Better, Deeper and More Enduring Brief Therapy: The Rational Emotive Behavior Therapy Approach*. New York: Brunner/Mazel.

Figley, C.R., and J. Carbonell. 1995. The Active Ingredient Project: The Systematic Clinical Demonstration of the Most Efficient Treatments of PTSD, a Research Plan. Tallahassee: Florida State University Psychosocial Stress Research and Clinical Laboratory.

Gallo, F. 1996. Therapy by energy. *Anchor Point*. Salt Lake City, UT. June, 46-51.

Gallo, F. 1996. Reflections on active ingredients in efficient treatments of PTSD, Part 1. *Electronic Journal of Traumatology*, 2(1). Available at http://www.fsu.edu/~trauma/.

Gallo, F. 1996. Reflections on active ingredients in efficient treatments of PTSD, Part 2. *Electronic Journal of Traumatology*, 2(2). Available at http://www.fsu.edu/~trauma/.

Gallo, F. 1998. *Energy Psychology: Explorations at the Interface of Energy, Cognition, Behavior and Health*, New York: CRC Press.

Gallo, F. 1999. A no-talk cure for trauma. In *The Art of Psychotherapy: Case Studies from the Family Therapy Networker*, edited by R. Simon, L. Markowitz, C. Barrilleaux, and B. Topping. Pages 244-255. New York: John Wiley & Sons.

Gallo, F. 2000. *Energy Diagnostic and Treatment Methods*. New York: W. W. Norton & Company.

Gerber, R. 1988. *Vibrational Medicine*. Sante Fe, NM: Bear and Company.

Gottman, J. 1995. *Why Marriages Succeed or Fail: And How You Can Make Yours Last*. Great Falls, MT: Fireside Books.

Gray, J. 1992. *Men Are from Mars, Women Are from Venus*. New York: Harper Collins.

Greene, B., and O. Winfrey. 1999. *Making the Connection: Ten Steps to a Better Body and a Better Life*. New York: Hyperion.

Haley, J. 1963. *Strategies of Psychotherapy*. New York: Grune and Stratton.

Hawkins, D. 1985. *Power versus Force: The Hidden Determinants of Human Behavior*. Sedona, AZ: Veritas Press.

Jeffers, S. 1987. *Feel the Fear and Do it Anyway*. New York: Ballentine Books.

Jibrin, J. 1998. *The Unofficial Guide to Dieting Safety*. New York: MacMillan.

Johnson, E. H. 1990. *The Deadly Emotions: The Role of Anger, Hostility, and Aggression in Health and Emotional Well-Being*. New York: Praeger Publishers.

Kendler, K. S., E. E. Walters, K. R. Truett, A. C. Heath, M. C. Neale, N. G. Martin, and L. J. Eaves. 1994. Sources of individual differences in depressive symptoms: analysis of two samples of twins and their families. *American Journal of Psychiatry* 151:1605-1614.

Koestler, A. 1967. *The Ghost in the Machine*. London: Hutchinson & Company.

Langman, L. 1972. The implications of the electro-metric test in cancer of the female genital tract. In *Blueprint for Immortality: The Electric Patterns of Life*, edited by H. S. Burr. Pages 137-154. Essex, England: Saffron Walden.

Linde, K., and G. Ramirez. 1996. St. John's Wort for depression—an overview and meta-analysis of randomized clinical trials. *British Medical Journal* 313:253-258.

Lockie, A., and N. Geddes. 1995. *The Complete Guide to Homeopathy*. New York: Dorling Kindersley.

McDougall, W. 1938. Fourth report on a Lamarkian experiment. *British Journal of Psychology* 28, 321-345.

Myss, C. 1997. *Why People Don't Heal and How They Can*. New York: Three Rivers Press.

National Center for Health Statistics. 1997. Latest final mortality rates. Vol. 47. No. 19. Washington, DC.

National Heart, Lung, and Blood Institute. 1998. Clinical guidelines for overweight and obesity. Washington, DC.

Olds, J., R. Schwartz, and H. Webster. 1996. *Overcoming Loneliness in Everyday Life*. Secaucus, NJ: Birch Lane Press.

Peale, N.V. 1996 (Re-issued Edition). *The Power of Positive Thinking*. New York: Ballentine Books.

Pransky, G. S. 1992. *Divorce Is Not the Answer: A Change of Heart Will Save Your Marriage*. (Also published as *The Relationship Handbook*.) Blue Ridge Summit, PA: HSI and TAB Books.

Pulos, L. 1999. Personal communication.

Rapp, D. 1991. *Is This Your Child?: Discovering and Treating Unrecognized Allergies in Children and Adults*. New York: William Morrow.

Sears, B., and B. Lawren. 1995. *Enter the Zone: A Dietary Road Map to Lose Weight Permanently*. New York: Harper Collins.

Shain, M. 1983. *Hearts That We Broke Long Ago*. New York: Bantam Books.

Sheldrake, R. 1988. *The Presence of the Past*. New York: Times Books.

Steward, H., M. Bethea, S. Andrews, and L. Balart. 1998. *Sugar Busters: Cut Sugar to Trim Fat*. New York: Ballentine Books.

Unestahl, L. 1988. Evolution of Psychology Conference.

Vincenzi, H. 1994. *Changes: A Self-Help Book for Adolescents*. Philadelphia: Future Press.

Wall Street Journal. 1999. Nearly half of all employees are a little angry at work, 7 September. Section C, p. 31.

Weil, A. 1995. *Health and Healing*. Boston: Houghton Mifflin.

Weil. A. 1996. *Spontaneous Healing*. New York: Ballentine Books.

Wolpe, J. 1958. *Psychotherapy by Reciprocal Inhibition*. Stanford, CA: Stanford University Press.

More Applications of Energy Psychology

The treatments provided throughout this book can be utilized in a variety of settings such as when training clinical staff, or to improve performance in the workplace. Gallo and Vincenzi, both licensed psychologists, are available for individual consultation, seminars, and professional development workshops. Although they are able to travel, Gallo is located near Pittsburgh and Cleveland, and Vincenzi is located near Philadelphia and New York.

If you would like more information about the application of energy psychology, contact:

Fred P. Gallo, Ph.D.
Psychological Services
40 Snyder Road
Hermitage, PA 16148
TEL: 724-346-3838
FAX: 724-346-4339
fgallo@energypsych.com
www.energypsych.com

Harry Vincenzi, Ed.D.
P.O. Box 2569
Bala Cynwyd, PA 19004
215-701-7077
tapenergy@aol.com

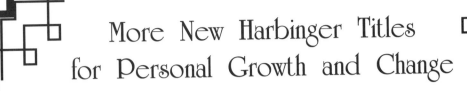

More New Harbinger Titles
for Personal Growth and Change

FROM SABOTAGE TO SUCCESS

Helps you zero in on self-defeating behaviors and learn skills that will break down the barriers that keep you from reaching your life's true potential.
Item SBTG $14.95

MAKING HOPE HAPPEN

A powerful program shows you how to break old habits, overcome roadblocks, and find new routes to your goals.
Item HOPE $14.95

YOU CAN FREE YOURSELF FROM ALCOHOL & DRUGS

A balanced, ten-goal recovery program helps readers make needed lifestyle changes without forcing them to embrace unwelcome religious concepts or beliefs.
Item YFDA Paperback, $14.95

THE SELF-FORGIVENESS HANDBOOK

Guided exercises, refined over the years in Thom Rutledge's practice and motivating workshops, take you on an empowering journey from self-criticism to self-compassion and inner strength.
Item FORG $12.95

SIX KEYS TO CREATING THE LIFE YOU DESIRE

Psychotherapists and authors Mitch Meyerson and Laurie Ashner help you break through your barriers to true fulfillment and personal achievement.
Item KEY6 Paperback $19.95

WANTING WHAT YOU HAVE

Shows how proven cognitive therapy techniques can help make it possible to achieve contentment and meet the challenges of modern life with balance and serenity.
Item WANT $18.95

Call toll-free 1-800-748-6273 to order. Have your Visa or Mastercard number ready. Or send a check for the titles you want to New Harbinger Publications, 5674 Shattuck Avenue, Oakland, CA 94609. Include $3.80 for the first book and 75¢ for each additional book to cover shipping and handling. (California residents please include appropriate sales tax.) Allow four to six weeks for delivery.

Prices subject to change without notice.

Some Other
New Harbinger Titles

Depressed and Anxious, Item 3635 $19.95

Angry All the Time, Item 3929 $13.95

Handbook of Clinical Psychopharmacology for Therapists, 4th edition, Item 3996 $55.95

Writing For Emotional Balance, Item 3821 $14.95

Surviving Your Borderline Parent, Item 3287 $14.95

When Anger Hurts, 2nd edition, Item 3449 $16.95

Calming Your Anxious Mind, Item 3384 $12.95

Ending the Depression Cycle, Item 3333 $17.95

Your Surviving Spirit, Item 3570 $18.95

Coping with Anxiety, Item 3201 $10.95

The Agoraphobia Workbook, Item 3236 $19.95

Loving the Self-Absorbed, Item 3546 $14.95

Transforming Anger, Item 352X $10.95

Don't Let Your Emotions Run Your Life, Item 3090 $17.95

Why Can't I Ever Be Good Enough, Item 3147 $13.95

Your Depression Map, Item 3007 $19.95

Successful Problem Solving, Item 3023 $17.95

Working with the Self-Absorbed, Item 2922 $14.95

The Procrastination Workbook, Item 2957 $17.95

Coping with Uncertainty, Item 2965 $11.95

The BDD Workbook, Item 2930 $18.95

You, Your Relationship, and Your ADD, Item 299X $17.95

The Stop Walking on Eggshells Workbook, Item 2760 $18.95

Conquer Your Critical Inner Voice, Item 2876 $15.95

The PTSD Workbook, Item 2825 $17.95

Hypnotize Yourself Out of Pain Now!, Item 2809 $14.95

The Depression Workbook, 2nd edition, Item 268X $19.95

Beating the Senior Blues, Item 2728 $17.95

Call **toll free, 1-800-748-6273,** or log on to our online bookstore at **www.newharbinger.com** to order. Have your Visa or Mastercard number ready. Or send a check for the titles you want to New Harbinger Publications, Inc., 5674 Shattuck Ave., Oakland, CA 94609. Include $4.50 for the first book and 75¢ for each additional book, to cover shipping and handling. (California residents please include appropriate sales tax.) Allow two to five weeks for delivery.

Prices subject to change without notice.